STAR RHYTHMS

Readings in a Living Astrology

edited by

William Lonsdale

North Atlantic Books

Star Rhythms: Readings in a Living Astrology (revised edition)

Copyright © 1979, 1982 by William Lonsdale

ISBN 0-938190-00-8

Publisher's Address:
North Atlantic Books
635 Amador Street
Richmond, California 94805

Cover Design: Paula Morrison

Grateful acknowledgements to the "Mercury Star Journal" for the articles by Willie Sucher, Dan Lloyd, Adam Bittleston, and John Meeks, and to "Dell Horoscope Magazine" for the articles by Dane Rudhyar. And a special note of thanks to Cathy Rose.

Star Rhythms is sponsored by the Society for the Study of Native Arts and Sciences, a nonprofit educational corporation whose goals are to develop an ecological and crosscultural perspective linking various scientific, social, and artistic fields; to nurture a holistic view of arts, sciences, humanities, and healing; and to publish and distribute literature on the relationship of mind, body, and nature.

Library of Congress Cataloging in Publication Data
Main entry undr title:

Star rhythms.

   Includes bibliographical references.
   1. Astrology—Addresses, essays, lectures.
I. Lonsdale, William, 1947—   . II. Title.
III. Series: Io ; no. 27.
[BF1708.1.S69 1982]   133.5   82—14454
ISBN 0-938190-00-8 (pbk.)

CONTENTS

INTRODUCTION

Three astrological streams are featured in this anthology. Each of these shows us a way beyond the maze of much of contemporary astrology. The cosmic rhythms call us to a greater and truer life that is in tune with the whole out of which we arise and to which we return. These three streams evoke the language of the cosmic star rhythms as these indwell every phase of our life on earth.

The only one of these greater streams that has become widely known began to be uncovered in the early strivings of Marc Edmund Jones for a more sophistocated modern approach to astrology. Jones was blessed with the kind of pioneering mind that could venture further and combine a greater range of elements than anyone else had yet managed. He gathered an incisive interpretive astrology from the far reaches of cabalism, the Western esoteric tradition, Platonic philosophy, American New Thought, the Gospel of St. Matthew, modern science, and practical life-experience. The distinctive element throughout his 65 years of astrological work has always been a psychological realism that regards the whole human being against the backdrop of the starry heavens. Marc Edmund Jones stands as by far the greatest interpretive astrologer of modern times. His systematic ordering of the chaos of traditional astrology into a workable synthesis has been an invaluable contribution toward eventually making astrology respectable in a contemporary perspective.

Unfortunately, Jones in the process borrowed somewhat too freely from traditional astrology, respected its archaic formulas excessively. Thereby, he weighed down his Sabian system with an overload of medieval concepts dressed-up in modern guise. This is most evident in the formulas and keywords he has resorted to in each of his books. It is most significantly retrogressive in his casting aside of karma and reincarnation as fundamentally irrelevant side issues distracting from a streamlining of astrology for modern usage. Only a direct awareness of the pervasively subtle and deep workings of karma and reincarnation can open up the astrological world-view to admit more light.

Dane Rudhyar came across the works of Marc Edmund Jones at a point in the 1930's when Jones' diligent efforts were beginning to bear abundant fruit. Rudhyar already had come into his own as an artist/philosopher with a prophetic vision of the coming crises in humanity and a stark eloquence in speaking forth out of this vision. Particularly notable in his background was an involvement with depth psychology a la Jung and Kunkel, as well as being steeped in the Theosophy of Blavatsky. He recognized the value of Jones' work, and proceeded to infuse it with his own brooding intensity and then to reformulate it for a broader public, as he has done now for some 45 years. Rudhyar's feeling for the challenges ahead in humanity's evolution has wiped away many traces of medievalism and promoted in their place a "humanistic" or now "transpersonal" astrology that at its best is vivid, alive, and deeply moving. Rudhyar knows how to stir the imagination by highlighting the newly unfolding dimensions of human potentiality. Included in this anthology are four articles by Rudhyar that go much further into his approach toward individual life cycles than any of his previously published works have done. These articles speak for themselves.

Because of Rudhyar's particular way of viewing life, the pivotal importance of karma and reincarnation is no more evident in his writings than in those of Jones. This one glaring gap is filled in the second of our three star-streams.

In ancient times, astrologer-priests of Egypt and Chaldea were the bearers of a cosmic wisdom stream that everyone instinctively recognized as pointing towards the very core of their life-striving. When these elders spoke out of their initiatory clairvoyance, they wove together the vast cosmic reaches with physical-material earth experience. They knew whereof they spoke.

As mankind lost touch with its cosmic origins, individuals recurrently appeared who could "read the stars." No longer was it entirely clear what sources stood behind their communications. It even got to the point that many sensed "demons" behind the veiled warnings and prognostications of an astrologer. As time went on, fewer and fewer of the advance guard of thinkers and spiritual seekers took seriously what the astrologers had to say.

Although modern astrologers have attempted to throw off this history and to formulate a more scientific and in some cases ethical theory and practice, until the hidden roots of a deeper wisdom are again tapped into, they will never advance very far from the inherited medieval approach. Elaborate techniques and pragmatic common sense cannot be the road to a renewal of the ancient star wisdom.

Rudolf Steiner understood at the turn of the 20th century that citizens of the new world that was beginning to dawn could never again turn their gazes back to atavistic sources of inspiration, that the forerunners of a new humanity must now look forward and think as well as act out of a wakeful, living form of cognition. Steiner investigated every major area of human knowledge and concern, with his own inner faculties awakened and alive in the modern sense. What he brought back for the spiritual searcher was a new cosmological impulse, one so radical and advanced that it has yet to be fully taken up by anyone, much less carried further. This cosmology of human freedom, as I call it, restores the mystery teachings that give meaning and substance to astrology, but brings these forward in a new way, one that requires special inner development. However, the essential message of this new cosmology is open to everyone who is willing to work earnestly toward the overthrow of old concepts and the embrace of new ones.

The tragedy of Steiner is that these crucially important discoveries of his have become obscured by the smokescreen produced by many of those who have tried to follow after him. It is my impression that a veritable army of grim guardians have attempted since Steiner's death in 1925 to protect, guide, and hold back much of his vision and contribution to modern evolution. Their rigidity has scared off adventuresome contemporary seekers and thinkers and has so well succeeded in keeping Steiner's message to humanity under wraps that it is exceedingly difficult to get at where Steiner's impulse really lies.

There have been a few who have tried to penetrate this "occult" barrier in order to break through to the vital legacy of Rudolf Steiner. Elizabeth

8

Vreede, who Steiner said knew him best of those around him, was one of these, and she researched new approaches to astronomy, astrology, and the most direct expression of this renewed cosmology, which became known as astrosophy or star wisdom. Willi Sucher then carried on the work much further, studying for the past 50 years the historical, biographical, therapeutic, and spiritual ramifications of astrosophy, as well as astrology and astronomy. In recent years, young Americans have begun to recognize the value of his painstaking researches. This anthology contains the first broad public circulation of any substantial segment of his writings, a narrative of the mythologies associated with the fixed-star constellations and their deeper significance. As Sucher has laid the foundations for applying Steiner's cosmology of human freedom in a particular respect, so also have others taken up Steiner's initiative in this area. Some of their efforts are now available in the British "Mercury Star Journal" and the American "Astrosophical Studies". We present here a few select articles from "Mercury Star Journal" to indicate something of the variety of work already being done in this stream. The smokescreen that guards Steiner still hovers a bit around these articles as well, but the first rays of dawn peek through at certain points, suggesting the possibilities that lie ahead.

Our third astrological stream is the least well-known and the most unusual of all. Amidst the current clamor of methods and approaches to interpreting the astrological chart, very few in our age can actually read the cosmic script as did the star-seers of old. Ann Ree Colton is one who can and does. She stands alone among those I have come across in being able to see into the etheric chart and to decipher its meaning for the individual in a wakeful, non-trance state. She was trained in etheric astrology and astronomy for two years in the 1920's, on the inner planes. (It is interesting that all three star-streams crossed in the 1920's, with Steiner doing much of his most important work then, and Jones also being intensively guided.) A spiritual teacher using higher clairvoyant powers for almost 50 years now, she nurtures the growth of a relatively small group of students and writes occasional books such as her recent masterpiece, *Kundalini West*. In her person and her teachings she revives the tradition of those few throughout the ages who have seen the outward physical chart as a transparent portal to the real person within. Astrology is merely one of many areas she has mastered, but her ability to decode the cosmic script as a result of the preparatory training she received has been quite an inspiration to me.

As with the other streams, there are obstacles and drawbacks here too. The form, approach, and language in which Ann Ree Colton speaks and writes are most helpful only to those who within themselves are developing a similar perspective and capacity. Her imaginative, inspirational, intuitive version of esoteric astrology is definitely not for everyone. She inwardly clothes her perceptions in an old-fashioned style. Her direct clear guidance can throughout be readily sensed by whoever is receptive, but it is equally obvious that to do what she does requires both a rare gift and intensive inner preparation. This type of approach remains reserved for the few who are ready to take the steps necessary to make themselves worthy vehicles for a new astrology.

9

The one representation in this anthology of this third stream is my own lengthy essay on the planetary aspects. My way of working attempts to encompass and bring together the Jones-Rudhyar psychological holism, the Steiner-Sucher cosmological depths of understanding, and the Ann Ree Colton inspirational inwardness, in a way that reflects the experiences of the post-World-War-II generation. I should add that this is of course a somewhat distant goal. I spent several years working intensively with the Jones and Rudhyar published and specialized writings as my primary foundation in astrology, along the way reading as well absolutely anything else that seemed worthwhile. I then took up the Anthroposophy of Steiner and Sucher, and have recently been working regularly with Willi Sucher. My path through astrology has been marked throughout by an undeviating inner guidance, somewhat reminiscent of Ann Ree Colton's experience, pointing ever onward toward a fresh approach to astrology. Permeating all of this astrological and spiritual work has been my life in the American stew of the '60's and '70's. Jones, Rudhyar, Steiner and Colton all were born in the 19th Century, and Willi Sucher at the beginning of the 20th. I was born in 1947. I participated with great fervor in the folk music revival, the radical political protests, the psychedelic explosion, the retreat to communes and cults, the searching for spiritual answers, and the return to individual and family experience that have progressively set the stage for the Aching '80's. All of this is in my astrology. Several books I'm working on for the future should be able to carry this impulse a great deal further.

I have tried to put together in this anthology a sampling of some of the directions that we will need to be moving into if astrology is ever to emerge from its idiosyncratic quaintness of the past and its self-conscious trendiness of the present. Here's to the future, may we meet it with open eyes and a clear heart.

William Lonsdale

Book One

THE MEANING AND USE OF PROGRESSIONS
by Dane Rudhyar

One of the many astrological topics which needs clarification and a more revealing and significant approach is what is usually called "progressions"—or secondary progressions. According to textbooks being studied today, it is possible, by considering the positions of the planets each *day* after birth, to foretell at least some of the basic events that can be expected each corresponding *year* after birth. The basic principle is that there is some sort of correspondence between the daily cycle of the earth's rotation around its axis and the yearly cycle of our planet's revolution around the Sun.

The moment of the "first breath" of the human organism establishes, as it were, the person's permanent individual character underneath all subsequent changes; this is the birth-chart. But changes are incessant after birth. The earth rotates; the Sun, Moon, and planets move on in their orbits—and the astrologer claims that what happens in the solar system during the 24 hours after birth *somehow* gives us basic clues to changes occurring in the human being during the whole first year of his life, each hour corresponding to a fortnight of actual existence.

Thus, if a person is born on January 1, 1965, at noon Greenwich Time, the positions of the planets at noon January 2—called the "progressed planets"—will refer to the person's development and the basic events of his life on January 1, 1966, and so on. If one wants to know what the person will face around his 20th birthday (1985), one will write down the progressed positions of the Sun, the Moon, and the planets for January 21. On that day, some of the aspects between the planets are different from those on January 1; the new aspects will be referred to as "progressed-to-progressed" aspects. But the new positions of January 21 can also be related to the positions in the January 1 birth-chart—for instance, the "progressed Moon" during the morning of January 21 is at 23° 57' Virgo, making a conjunction with the position Mars had at birth on January 1, 1965. Such a conjunction will be called a "progressed-to-radical" (or natal) aspect.

My purpose here is not to state in greater detail the technique for the calculation of such progressions, but rather to try to understand *why* they should have any validity at all and to what area of predictability they most logically refer. Obviously, the positions of the Sun, Moon, and planets for January 21, 1965, do not refer to celestial *facts* noticeable at the time of the 20th birthday (January 1, 1985) of the person born on January 1, 1965.

The factual positions of the planets on that January 1, 1985, when referred to the positions of the planets in the January 1, 1965 birthday constitute what are called "transits." Transiting positions are existential facts; progressed positions are not. If they are to be considered as facts, it can be so only if they are integrated into a picture of the entire life process which began even earlier than birth—that is, at the moment of impregnation of the female ovum by the male spermatozoon.

The Doctrine of Correspondences

To say that the progressions have validity because somehow the day cycle "corresponds" to the year cycle can only mean that they constitute a purely *symbolic* factor. The "doctrine of correspondences," as it is called, has been made responsible for almost anything along so-called occult lines. On the basis of such an assumed correspondence between celestial cycles, a system of "tertiary progressions" has been taught in which a cycle of the Moon after birth is made to correspond to a year of the life after birth; and any cycle could be made to correspond to any other.

We could just as well say that if you want to know how your child will be at the age of 30 days, you should look at the planets' positions 30 years after his birth. Who knows, this might "work"—but it involves practical difficulties until our electronic computers have been made to figure out exactly all planetary positions for every 4 minutes 10,000 years ahead as well as back. It is indeed rather fascinating to think that a baby might have died at the time of his first birthday in 1599 A.D. because there is this year a conjunction of Mars, Uranus, and Pluto in opposition to Saturn affecting what was his natal Sun. Why, theoretically, stop at the equivalence of year and day? One could use the same concept and relate a precessional cycle of around 26,000 years to a solar year or a day; a degree of precession (about 72 years) could be related to a whole precessional cycle, etc.

All such correspondences can be theoretically valid, just as it may be true to say that there is a structural correspondence between a man, as microcosm, and the universe, or macrocosm. Such concepts belong to the field of pure symbolism, and astrology as it is practiced today is a symbolic type of knowledge. Symbols are very powerful, and we deal with them constantly. Words are symbols, as are all slogans and catch phrases, all rituals. A national flag and anthem are symbols. The English Queen is a symbol; so is the White House. The whole sky has been for man, struggling out of the chaos of the jungle (and there is a psychological jungle very much in evidence today), the great symbol of "order"—which means periodicity and predictability.

We must, of course, use symbols, but we should try to use them while realizing vividly *the kind of life processes* to which they refer. We should try to understand and to feel the concrete processes of which the abstract symbols reveal the essential structure. Thus, if I say that a day after birth "corresponds" to a year of actual living for an individual person, it should not be enough to take intellectual refuge in the concept of the symbolic equivalence of the earth's daily rotation and the earth's yearly revolution. What we must try to realize is what it is that *actually happens* in a human being during the days after his birth—i.e., what *process* is at work within him or her. It must be a basic and far-reaching process if it is true that what occurs *in that process* ten days after birth actually has a direct repercussion upon the bio-psychic state of that person at the age of ten.

We should be able to know what the process is, for if we do not, we are likely to misunderstand the symbol—i.e., the character of the progressions, the field of experience to which they should be referred—and to use it wrongly or apply it to the wrong level of existence. We may believe, for instance, that the symbolical techniques which we call "progressions" refer to actual physical-plane events, while actually they may have meaning in terms of some psychological factor behind the events, a factor which *may or may not exteriorize itself as events.*

What then is happening within the total psychosomatic organism of the baby during the days following birth? Can we know? I believe that we can get an idea of the deeper process going on after birth if we think of the relation between conception and birth, also between the prenatal and the postnatal forms of existence, which I will discuss next.

The Prenatal and Postnatal Development of Man

It has been shown that in the earliest stages of development from the fecundated ovum, the human embryo repeats very briefly the successive stages of the evolution of life on earth. This evolution has occurred in what we call the "biosphere"—the very narrow area on either side of the planet's surface. The biosphere is the realm of life on earth; it includes the seas, the surface of continents and the atmosphere only to a very few miles up. It is the planetary womb within which all earthly life is given *form and substance* and finds itself dominated by the power of gravitation.

When the embryo reaches a certain stage of development, it becomes entirely "human;" sexual differentiation begins to take place. It begins to move and kick; finally, it is "delivered" into the realm of air. It gasps for air, and in that act, the pattern of blood circulation is changed, dividing itself into its arterial and venous circuits; the breathing rhythm is established. It would also seem that thereafter another kind of rhythm is built up which refers to the cerebrospinal nervous system and pulsations in the cerebrospinal fluid in which that system is bathed; unfortunately, modern biology does not seem to be as yet very aware of what takes place in this nervous system of the baby or has not yet interpreted what it knows within an overall concept of a well-defined process.

There are nine months of prenatal life. But the cycle of the year encompasses twelve months, and our zodiac—which is a symbolical expression of this yearly cycle and of the earth's orbit—has twelve signs. If we really understand what a cycle means, we should ask ourselves the obvious question (but obvious questions are very often *not* asked): What happens during the three months *after* birth?

This is the key. Something happens during these 90 to 92 days which is so basic that it affects the entire life of the person—a life which may well last some 90 years. It is something as basic as the change which took place in the embryo during the three months *before* birth.

We can well say that after six months of growth, the embryo is sufficiently *humanized* to be born as a viable organism in the world of humanity. Before that, the embryo was not yet quite human; it belonged to the earth's biosphere together with all other living things. But at or near the beginning of the seventh month, it enters the field of the human kingdom; it belongs to a certain race and ancestral lineage as an *actual* and viable organism; and it develops its human-ancestral potential during three months more in a particular mother's womb—or, in cases of premature birth, in an incubator and hospital which are the products of human civilization throughout the ages.

Then, normally, the baby is born. His tiny body will grow more or less rapidly, still so closely bound to his mother that he seems hardly separate from her. But he breathes; gradually, his eyes focus, his senses become alert. A prodigious process is at work correlating and adjusting to the myriad of impacts upon the brain. It will take three more months for the Sun to return to the position it occupied at the moment of impregnation of the mother's ovum. What happens during these ninety days within the baby? Simply this: on the basis of his first act of independent existence (the first breath), the child is building the foundations for the gradual actualization of the essential characteristics of his human status—i.e., individual selfhood—through the development of *individualized potentialities of intelligence*.

But what do I mean by this word "intelligence?"

Intelligence, Power of the Spirit in Man

Perhaps I can express this meaning quite clearly by using the Christian symbol of the Trinity and saying that God, the Father, refers to the basic genetic structure of the human organism; God, the Son, to the potentiality of individual selfhood represented by the birth-chart—i.e., to the fact that this particular human organism came out of the mother potentially able to fulfill his destiny as an individual person. The Holy Spirit represents that power which will enable this person *actually* to become an active, essentially free and responsible "individual"—and this power is what I mean by intelligence.

The birth-chart, as I see it, constitutes the formula of our true individual selfhood. It persents us with the picture of that particular being which the universe, or God, is creating at that particular time and place which sees the start of our independent existence. As we undergo birth, we have a *past*— which is our prenatal condition as an embryo, end of a long series of ancestors, human and pre-human. We are *now* our birth-chart, our "signature of destiny," our essential individuality as a potential individual; but let us not fail to see that the birth-chart, at birth, is only the pattern of the *possibility* of becoming in actual fact an integrated and fulfilled person from whom the principle of divine Sonship (the Christ within) would radiate forth in love and creativity.

Why is that possibility not always realized? It is fundamentally because we have to actualize this possibility in the collective environment of a family, a culture, a society, a race, a planet—all of which exert upon the growing child and adolescent constant and powerful pressures, many of which tend to obscure, stifle, or distort and adulterate this individual birth potential (i.e., what Zen calls our "fundamental nature"). *Every* birth-chart could lead to the manifestation of "divine Sonship" in one form or another; but this process of actualization of our potential of individual selfhood (i.e., the God within) requires the development of the conscious mind through a multitude of impacts and relationships, for it must be a *conscious* process.

Our family, our religion and culture, our society and all interpersonal relationships derived from its patterns of behavior provide us with raw

16

materials for the growth of our conscious mind and the necessary development of an ego. But this very process produces all sorts of tensions, fears, withdrawals, unnatural desires, ambitions, etc., which nearly always tend to make us what we are *not* essentially—i.e., other than what our birth-chart should reveal we *are*, potentially.

Transits vs. Progressions

It is to all these impacts, pressures, and influences of the environment (psychic and mental as well as geographical, cultural, and social) that the *transits* refer in astrology. These transits constantly exert a pressure upon our permanent and essential identity, symbolized by our birth-chart. The pressures may cause pleasure, happiness, exaltation—or pain, misery, and depression. Some may strengthen basic factors in our nature; others may tend to disintegrate our personality. But, generally speaking, they are that which every day and year after year challenges us. What is it in us which will accept these challenges and make of them opportunities for becoming more and more that which we potentially are? This is our "intelligence."

This power of intelligence is, I repeat, the Holy Spirit within us. It alone can transmute all that we find in our outer and inner (i.e., psychic-mental) environment into *food for our growth as an individual person* conscious of being that which it was originally as a particular birth potential. The birth potential remains what it is; this is the permanent factor in us, the seed form the "fundamental tone" of our individual being and destiny. But nearly everything that surrounds us will tend to change its vibration, even with the very best intention, even through parental love and all kinds of love.

Thus, astrological transits forever tend to change the form of our essential birth potential; and it is in the progressions that we can witness the Holy Spirit—the power of intelligence—at work within us. It is during the days and weeks after birth that this power of intelligence primarily develops, for it is then that, confronted with the family environment—and with all that is back of its ways of life, its biases, and its beliefs—the Holy Spirit continues the process of formation of the necessary means and capacities by using which the human being can intelligently handle the everyday challenges of the rest of his life and thereby follow the *path of personality integration.*

From conception to about the end of the sixth month of embryonic existence, earth materials are being structured by the planet's life to become organized into a human being. For three months afterward, this human being is developing the specific capacities that belong to his family, his race, his society so that he may be able to emerge out of the mother as a *potential* individual person. Three months remain in the year's cycle which followed conception; during these months, the nervous system begins to react to the impact of the external environment. In this process, the seeds of intelligent responses to life are sown within the infant by the Spirit.

These seeds, these interior directives of the Spirit, "program" what the growing individual person will gradually release throughout the years of his life as conscious or unconscious decisions and choices. What we call progressions in astrology today refer to this "programming." The infant's nascent intelligence is being directed along a definite path of exteriorization of his birth potential. We can see this path traced by the motions of the Sun, Moon, and planets each moment after birth.

Three months of this programming refer to 90 years—which means also a little over three entire revolutions of Saturn and three returns of Saturn by transit to its natal position. The first two returns during the 30th and the 59th years are basic turning points in the structural development of the personality and its approach to basic factors in its environment. Relatively few people today experience a third Saturn return and not many more reach beyond the return of Uranus to its natal place at the age of 84—a return indicating a basic change of relationship to the environment.

What all this indicates is that what unfolds *within* the cerebrospinal nervous system of the infant during the first three months of life fundamentally determines the way he or she will later respond to life's challenges—that is, the type of intelligence (in the sense I use this word here) he or she will display year after year, 7-year cycle after 7-year cycle, 30-year cycle after 30-year cycle. This intelligence manifests in various ways; *it has to manifest in various ways* to meet the challenges symbolically represented by the day-by-day transits. As we observe the changing positions of the planets after birth and the aspects they make day after day after birth, we can get a bird's-eye view of how these life challenges are being or will be met through the life. What the progressions picture, as it were "algebraically," is *not* the challenges, but the type of intelligence available to meet them. The actual events result from the meeting.

It should be obvious, however, that a knowledge of what will be needed to meet certain types of challenges will tell us also that a certain category of events is expectable at that time. During a particular phase of my life, my progressed Sun opposed my progressed Moon (i.e., a progressed Full Moon), in conjunction with my natal and progressed Uranus in Scorpio and the eleventh house, while transiting Uranus was beginning to cross back and forth over my descendant (the cusp of my house of marriage). This was a highly critical and "cathartic" period which produced divorce and soon after, re-marriage.

The events were most predictable, in view of the general Uranus emphasis and of this planet's transit over the natal descendant. But what the progressions of the Sun and the Moon indicated were not so much the events as such—they could have been different and nearly were, in fact—as the inevitable stimulation of the type of intelligence ingrained in my nervous system which would be capable of facing the need for change and for radically altering a situation which had begun rather soon after the conjunction of the progressed Sun and progressed Moon (i.e., progressed New Moon) some 14 to 15 years before, but which had by then (the time of the progressed Full Moon) proven empty and meaningless.

Likewise, a progression of Mars to natal Saturn may correlate with an accident or illness, but what the progression reveals is not the accident *in itself,* but the mobilization of a basic energy for survival or recuperation. One should never speak of an unfortunate or essentially adverse progression, for such a kind of progression refers rather to the actualization of a latent capacity to assert the basic power of individual selfhood against the painful or tragedy-producing pressures of one's environment; and let me stress here again that there is also an inner psychic environment which is just as important as the outer one — and often more so!

The Progressed Planets

In the ninety-day period following the birth moment, the positions of the planets beyond Mars do not change very much, although at times even a very few degrees of progression may most significantly bring to exactness a natal aspect between, say, Jupiter or Saturn and other planets. The Sun progresses only some 90 degrees, but its passage from one sign to the next usually marks a very noticeable modification in a person's basic responses to life. As Mercury and Venus remain always fairly close to the Sun, they cannot move around the whole zodiac by progression in a lifetime. Only the Moon can do so, and the progressed Moon returns to the Moon's natal place every 27 to 28 years, thus usually making at least two complete circuits around the birth-chart and, in the process, passing over all natal planets and house cusps twice.

As in astrology nothing is totally and individually significant which does not make a complete cycle of motion, the most significant factor in the progression technique is the Moon. More significant still, however, is the cyclic change in the soli-lunar relationship — that is, the lunation cycle of some 30 days. In terms of progressions, this means a 30-year cycle, the "progressed lunation cycle."*

From the way I see and analyze it, the progressed lunation cycle (from one progressed New Moon to the next) provides us with an over-all moving picture within which all other progressions find their place and acquire a broader meaning in terms of the total development of the personality. Essentially it is the progressed Sun which marks the successive steps in the actualization of the Spirit-imparted intelligence which enables a human being to become fulfilled as a conscious and creative individual person. Progressions depend primarily upon a *solar* cycle; it is the 12-month solar cycle of the year which controls the 9-month gestation period and the three-month post-natal process of building in the patterns of intelligent and effectual responses to life in the cerebrospinal nervous system — thus, the formation of a potentially complete human person.

For this reason, the progressed sun's motion year after year is the basic factor, and the Sabian Symbol of the degree on which the progressed Sun is located during each 12-month period is often quite revealing.** For instance, at the time of the above-mentioned highly Uranian progressed Full Moon in my life, the progressed Sun was on a degree symbolized by "a new continent rising out of the ocean." *Something* had to emerge within me — a new approach, a new mode of intelligence. Yet there can be emergence, in such a case, at two or three levels — and it is the level which conditions *the actual events,* not vice versa.

If the progressed Sun symbolizes intelligence in action, the progressed Moon represents the energy being distributed to sustain the application of this intelligent power of integration — thus, also the focus of the individual person's attention upon one field of experience or another. The natal house through which the progressed Moon is passing at any time indicates what this field of experience is, and the passage of the progressed Moon over the four angles of the natal chart is particularly significant. The progressed Mercury has much to do with the character and effectiveness of the mental apparatus through which the person's attention is being focused. The years of life which correspond to a change in the direction of Mercury's motion (from direct to retrograde, or vice versa) are seen to be in most cases periods of change in relation to the environment or to the collective mentality of one's community.

The progressed Venus should give indications concerning the sense of value and the feeling responses of the individual, as these are being modified by experience and age. The progressed Mars may move far enough from Mars' natal position to indicate changes in the relationship between the desires and life ambition of a person and the external objects which draw him out and help him to mobilize his energies. In any case, it is the angular relationship (aspects) of the progressed planets to the Sun and the Moon (natal and progressed) which is the most basic factor in progressions, plus the entrance of these planets into new signs and houses.

---

* cf. Dane Rudhyar, *The Lunation Cycle* (Shambhala Publications, Boulder, Colorado: 1967). The progressed lunation cycle refers to the cycle of aspects formed between the progressed Sun and progressed Moon from one conjunction, i.e., New Moon, to the next. —Ed.

** cf. Dane Rudhyar, *An Astrological Mandala:* The Cycle of Transformations and its 360 Symbolic Phases (Random House, New York: 1973)

CONVERSE PROGRESSIONS AND THE NEW MOON BEFORE BIRTH
by Dane Rudhyar

As I have shown in the previous article, "The Meaning and Use of Progressions," the real and existential meaning of what astrologers call progressions (or, at times, secondary progressions) derives from the fact that the normal period of gestation of a human organism is nine months, while the cycle of the year lasts twelve months. The year in the ordinary type of geocentric astrology is a "solar" factor, and the Sun is the source of all the basic energies that circulate throughout the solar system and which make possible life on earth. A child is a living organism. This organism originates in the union of male and female reproductive cells within the mother's womb. The fecundated ovum multiplies itself through a process of successive division. Each resulting new cell—and there are many billions of them in the newborn child—carries at its core what has been called a "genetic code" which directs its particular function in the child's body.

Each human embryo as it develops within the womb is said to *recapitulate* very briefly the series of biological evolutionary developments of life forms in the "biosphere"—i.e., within the very narrow space extending above and below the planet's surface. Once the embryo has become truly "human," it can be assumed that in a less obvious and perhaps unrecognizable manner it passes through the stages which led human races to the level of a biological development characterizing at this present day the racial group of mankind to which the parents belong.

A human embryo is not "viable" until it reaches about the beginning of the seventh month of gestation. Then the embryo is completely "human," and there are many cases of premature births at such a time. If the prematurely born baby survives, it is thanks to extreme and in a sense artificial care—that is, he or she survives because human beings have *collectively* developed a culture and especially a science which enables them to complete what "life" (in the biological and planetary sense) has left incomplete and condemned to extinction.

If the embryo reaching its seventh month of gestation has become *potentially "human"* it normally takes three months more for it to complete the expected stages of a development which will make it *potentially an "individual"* —that is, a human organism ready to perform its role in a human society as a would-be individual person endowed with intelligence and with the capacity to make at least relatively free choices in answer to the challenges of his or her environment.

This capacity to operate among one's fellow human beings as an individual person is only potential at birth; and I have shown how the development of this power which I define as intelligence is, as it were, "programmed" (or set in its basic pattern of operation) during the three months *following* birth. Three months represent 90 to 92 days; in the astrological technique of the "progressions," each of these days is made to correspond to one year of the actual life of the individual. Progressions, thus, refer to the development of this "intelligence" which I have defined as the power enabling a person to act as a free and responsible individual as he faces the infinitely complex relationships, challenges, and oportunities of everyday life.

If this be true, what then could be said actually to happen to the human child-to-be during the three months *preceding* birth—the seventh, eighth, and ninth months of gestation? If we know the basic meaning of these three last months of intrauterine existence, can we deduce from this an applicable type of astrological knowledge?

Converse Progressions

The idea occured to astrologers that one might find it significant to "progress backward" a birth-chart. Just as in the usual type of progressions one day *after* birth gives basic clues to the development of the individual person one year after his birth, so in "converse progressions," one day *before* birth is said to give valid indications to what will happen to the person also when one year old. The two procedures are symmetrical; and whether one moves ahead, let us say, ten days in the ephemeris or one moves backward ten days in the ephemeris, one obtains in both cases some basic information relating to the person's life when he is ten years old.

The people who use both methods unfortunately do not differentiate clearly—or at all—between the two types of information obtained, on the one hand, by direct progressions (based on the actual motions of the planets after birth) and, on the other, by "converse" progressions. Yet, obviously, if ordinary progressions are already symbolical in character, the converse progressions are even far more so. What could be *actual* in the correlation between the positions of planets ten days before you are born and what you will experience at the age of ten? If converse progressions "work"—and they often do—they work as symbols; but as symbols of what? If astrology has any logical foundation, these converse progressions obtained by reading the ephemeris backward from the birth moment cannot refer to the same type of conditions, experiences, or phases of personal development as the ordinary progressions based on the forward movement of the planets.

Many people have had the experience that what they were living through was actually, though in some undefinable manner, the consequence of antecedent causes—i.e., of events of long ago. One may interpret such a strange feeling by accepting the hypothesis of "reincarnation." This concept of reincarnation can be understood in several ways; but, in any case, we can well say that our present is at least partially conditioned by the past—by the past of our parents, by the ancestral traditions and prejudices which have been stamped upon our receptive mind in early childhood, and by the evolutionary past of mankind.

Most devout Christians believe that man is born with an innately perverted nature as a result of the "original sin" in Eden. Is this not an instance of the manner in which an immensely distant event can condition a man's psychic development? I have personally known several persons for whom the realization of the assumed fact that his or her nature had been inherently perverted by the sin of Adam and Eve brought out a real psychological crisis in adoles-

22

cence or midlife—and, in one instance, a passionate conversion to Catholicism of the most rigid type. Of course, our whole Christian culture—especially during the Middle Ages, but also later on in the case of great minds like the French scientist-philosopher Pascal—has been conditioned by this poignant belief in what was considered to have been a fact of past history.

I also knew a wonderful female painter whose life had been tragically overshadowed by a scandal in the life of a revered and famous grandfather she had hardly ever met. We *are* indeed affected most directly and internally by basic occurrences antedating our birth as an individual person. Carl Jung refers to this when he speaks of the great power of "Archetypes of the Collective Unconscious." The famous French philosopher of the early-19th century, Auguste Comte, made the statement that, "Humanity includes as effective presences many more of the dead than of the living."

In the light of such observations, let us now consider what occurs during the last three months of the normal gestation period. The child-to-be prepares him- or herself for a life as an individual person in direct relation—i.e., without a maternal intermediary—with other people and with the universe as a whole. This process has to operate, as it were, *through* the past of humanity, of a particular race, culture, and family. I might say that we reach a new condition of individual existence only by passing through and overcoming our ancestors—and especially our parents. Moreover, if we believe in the cyclic re-embodiment of a spiritual Principle (or "Soul"), then we will have to realize that we inherit the *karma* of those persons who were our predecessors, somewhat as a U.S. president inherits the consequences of the successes or failures of the preceding administrations.

If a man born in 1921 had to face a crisis in his life at the age of 20 after Pearl Harbor, was it not largely because a small group of senators, even before he was born, defeated Wilson's attempts at building a strong and effective League of Nations? So the young man engaged in the Pacific War and was maimed, and his whole life was altered. Perhaps the event would show up astrologically as a "converse progression" for the 21st year of his life. There was nothing much he could do about it, most probably. It was truly "fate." He had to bear the *collective karma* of his nation—and possibly a more individual *karma* referring to the lives of past personalities of whom he was the spiritual heir.*

As I see it—and I cannot find any other logical and significant justification for "converse progressions"—going backward in the ephemeris from the day and hour of birth means to uncover ever deeper strata of the collective unconscious which has *preconditioned* our personality and its innate tendencies. It is like digging a deep well and bringing back to the light of consciousness the fossilized remains of a past antedating our birth. It reveals what we had to pierce through in our ascent toward a new potentiality of individual existence —i.e., toward the birth of our present personality. We had to do it within the dark unconsciousness of the prenatal state during the last 90 days (more or less) of the gestation process which ended with the *victory* of birth.

Freud and his disciples relished the idea of a "birth trauma;" but since the brilliant insights of the great pioneer, Jacob Moreno, founder of Psychodrama, repolarized the concept of birth some 40 years ago, we should realize that birth *is* a victory over the pressure of the ghosts of the human past. Our birth-chart reveals the pattern of this victory. But no victory is won only once and for all time. As we grow stronger, year after year, we also are faced by ever deeper layers of the past. Symbolically speaking, as the tree rises toward the sun, it also sends its tap root ever deeper down.

As we grow older, our "intelligence" (as I have defined the term) should develop and enable us to meet—or, shall I say, to "redeem"—ever deeper layers of our ancient ancestral past. The life movement of personal growth to which all progressions refer is, therefore, operating *at the same time in two opposite directions*—in the direction represented by the actual motions of the planets during the days after our birth (the usual progressions) and the other complementary and regressive motion toward the past represented by the converse progressions.

I believe it is wise to consider only the most important of the converse progressions—particularly perhaps the times at which planets, especially Mercury, may change the direction of their motion (i.e., from direct to retrograde, or vice versa), the times at which New and Full Moons occurred during these three months preceding birth. The last New Moon preceding birth is particularly significant; but before I speak of it, let me state that, as with direct progressions, one can consider "progressed-to-progressed" aspects (the New Moon before birth is the most important of those) and also "progressed-to-natal" aspects. In the latter case, one relates the position of a planet some days before birth to the position of another planet in the birth-chart. If one looks for *events*, progressed-to-natal aspects are the more likely indications of actual occurrences; but, usually, they should be backed by other normal progressions and/or transits to refer to actual occurrences.

The main point, when dealing with converse progressions, is that events which they may indicate are far more "fated" than those which the ordinary forward-in-time type of progressions represent. Every astrological technique referring to a motion *backward* in the zodiac implies the element of fate; by "fate" I mean that power which compels us to deal with some "unfinished business," something done inadequately or wrongly, or something left undone —thus, what theologians call sins of omission as well as of commission.

This general principle applies even to the retrograde periods of planets, especially of the planets close to the earth—Mars, Venus, and Mercury. During such retrograde periods, we are, as it were, given the opportunity of reconsidering the value and meaning of what we have done, felt, and thought in the past; and this means, positively speaking, the opportunity of becoming stronger, more careful, and wiser as we meet our future challenges. Of course, very often we do not use such an opportunity constructively; and, when the planet "turns direct" at the end of its retrograde period, we return to our old habits, often with even worse results.

The New Moon before Birth

At New Moon, symbolically speaking, the power of the Sun fecundates the feminine and receptive Moon. The Moon is closely related to the biosphere of our planet—that is, to the surface of the earth where living entities are born, grow, and decay. It is the "Great Mother" of all that lives on our planet. Each New Moon represents a *new life impulse;* and this impulse or surge of life energies has a particular quality or rhythm somewhat different from other life impulses. Its character is symbolized by the degree and sign of the zodiac on which the New Moon occurs.

Unless a person is born precisely at the moment of a New Moon, one takes one's first breath a certain number of days after a New Moon—that is, one is born within a "lunation cycle," the duration of which is about 30 days. A person may have been born while the Moon appeared in the sky as a thin crescent, near a Full Moon, or some time between the last Quarter and the next New Moon. The angular aspect between the Moon and the Sun in one's birth-chart determines the *phase of the soli-lunar relationship* at which one was born—what I have called the "lunation birthday"—provided one differentiates waxing from waning aspects (for instance, a First Quarter from a Last Quarter aspect, both phases constituting square aspects of the Moon to the Sun).

The point with which we have to deal here is, however, simply that because a person is born within a lunation cycle and because the New Moon beginning this cycle stamped, as it were, the entire cycle with its astrological character, the New Moon before birth is of great significance for the person; it indicates in some manner the particular nature and quality of the basic life force vitalizing his or her entire organism. Every human being could be said to drink of the stream of life of which the New Moon before birth was the source. The quality of this "water" circulating through and sustaining the body (and, as well, the psyche) has much to do with the nature of the human being's growth, especially during the formative years of his or her life. It is therefore quite valuable indeed for anyone to study the pattern of the solar system at the time of the New Moon before birth and to relate it to the birth-chart. It is particularly important to see whether the New Moon before birth occurred in the same sign as the natal Sun or in the preceding one.

In the case of the famous astrologer Evangeline Adams (February 8, 1868), birth occurred just past Full Moon, with the Sun at 19°7' Aquarius. The New Moon before her birth took place on January 24 at 4°8' Aquarius, in conjunction with Mercury and in close sextile to Saturn in Sagittarius and in her natal ninth house. This New Moon before birth refers to the background of this eminent woman and to the excellent mental capacities she inherited, either from her ancestors or from a "previous existence." It represents the *root forces* at work in her personality. The emphasis on Aquarius was very strong in her life and character.

Abraham Lincoln also had his natal Sun in Aquarius, on the 24th degree; but as his natal Moon was close behind at 28° Capricorn—making of him what I call a "Balsamic Moon Type," his New Moon before birth occurred at 25°35' Capricorn, just past a conjunction with Mercury. This might suggest that in some past, "he" had already been concerned with political issues.

The well-known writer and indefatigable critic of social evils, Upton Sinclair, was born with the Sun at 27°27' Virgo and four more planets in Virgo. His natal Moon was in Cancer; but the New Moon before his birth occurred at

4°47′ Virgo, past a conjunction with Uranus and going toward a conjunction with Mars and Mercury. The natal Virgo emphasis was, thus, completely sustained by his past.

In my case, while my natal Sun is at 2° Aries and my natal Moon on the 25th degree of Aquarius, my New Moon before birth occurred at 5°51′ Pisces, very close to a retrograde Mercury and in sextile to Saturn retrograde. It occurred, according to the converse progressions technique, when I was about 26, at a most important turning point in my life—among other things, just at the time I began to study astrology in Hollywood. The conjunction of converse Mercury and converse Sun had occurred a year or so before, when I reached California. Conjunctions of the progressed Mercury and Sun are always important (whether "direct" or "converse"), for at those times Mercury changes from being morning star to being evening star, or vice versa. My 26th and 27th years established the foundations for the development of my mature mind; until then, I had been only gradually emerging from the background of my European culture and my French ancestors.

As a lunation cycle lasts about 30 days, a "progressed lunation cycle" lasts 30 years. *Going backward* in the ephemeris, I find that the preceding New Moon occurred at 5°43′ Aquarius, square an opposition of Saturn to Mars. This *second* New Moon before birth corresponded to age 56, another significant turning point in the midst of serious financial problems. It fell in the second house of my natal chart. The exact square of converse Sun to converse Saturn had occurred less than two years before and had begun the process which took a more decisive turn at the converse New Moon. Not too much occurred in terms of direct progressions at the time, but some transits were rather strenuous. As it turned out, the life process then had a strong *karmic* significance, in at least a superficially negative sense.

On the other hand, the first New Moon before my birth occurred at a time when my normally progressed Sun was making the best possible aspects of my lifespan: a sextile to natal Venus, a trine to natal Jupiter, a trine to progressed Mars conjunct my natal Jupiter. The progressed Moon was vitalizing the entire configuration from Aquarius. *Karma* was then operating in the most positive sense of the term—as the fruition of "past" service and spiritual endeavors.

I need hardly add that this converse progressions technique should be used with great care and with wise understanding. Its results have to be carefully balanced with the other type of progressions and with the transits. A person's individual existence is a very complex process. The achievements-yet-to-be draw us, the past pulls us to what has been. The present is the ever-shifting balance sheet. The tree as it grows reaches both upward with its trunk and downward with its roots—a great symbol of the life of an individual in whom faith and aspiration ever blend with fearlessness and the quiet will to fulfill human destiny.

---

*For an in-depth explanation of Rudhyar's approach to reincarnation and karma, *cf. The Planetarization of Consciousness* (A.S.I. Publications, New York: 1977) Part II, Chapter 7, "Soul-Field, Mind and Reincarnation." —Ed.

THE CYCLE OF THE PROGRESSED MOON:
THE WAY TO MATURITY
by Dane Rudhyar

One of the most valuable tools the astrologer has in his study of the development of a human being into a mature person is the cycle of the "progressed Moon". This cycle lasts twenty-seven and one-third years, as it is an astrological interpretation of the period which the Moon actually takes to return to a point of departure in the zodiac, a period of 27.3217 days.

The equivalence of one day of planetary motion after birth to one year of actual living is the basis of what the astrologer usually calls secondary progressions or simply progressions. Back of such an idea of equivalence is the concept according to which a birth-chart is like a seed. The seed contains in potentiality the entire future development of the plant growing from it. The full-grown oak is latent and condensed in the germinating acorn.

From the very moment the germinating process begins—which, in a human life, is the first moment of independent existence, the first breath—certain changes occur in rapid succession within the incipient germ. These changes are basic, and they control the later processes of development of the tree. We might find summed up in them the whole of the structural unfoldment of the oak.

By structural unfoldment, I simply mean the successive operations which are required for the tree to grow to maturity: (1) the emergence of the germ from the seed as the latter breaks in two; (2) the struggle of the germ against the crust of the soil; (3) the adaption of the tender sprout to the sunlight (its becoming green, for instance—i.e., the growth of the chlorophyll); (4) the adjustment of this sprout to climate and atmosphere, the growth of its roots, drawing from the soil new chemicals; (5) the production of leaves from the stem; (6) the development of hard fiber and of protective bark; (7) the flowering; (8) the process of fertilization, often through the intermediary of insects; (9) the development of the fertilized cell, the seed-to-be; (10) the growth of the fruit; (11) the maturation of the seed and the simultaneous changes in the plant (in yearly plants, the drying up of the stem); (12) the release of the seed and its fall into the soil.

These twelve phases of the life of a plant are very basic. If we take them in their broader and symbolical (or archetypal) sense, we can find their equivalents in all living organisms. They assuredly have their parallel in the gradual unfoldment of a human person, at the psychological as well as at the biological levels—indeed, a mature individual person is the result of interaction between these two.

Beyond these interactions, and intervening in the processes of personality growth at critical turning points, there is, moreover, a factor of purposeful guidance, a power of transformation and transcendence which seeks to make of man *more* than a biological organism and an animal. This, therefore, draws him in the direction of a further process of integration. This process leads to the integration of the animal-human personality with a purpose and a special

27

quality of existence in which should be expressed in time the at first latent divine character of the individual.

The first process, with its twelve basic phases, refers to the field of life and personality. It is, symbolically speaking, a lunar process. The second process of integration is traditionally related to the Sun, origin of light and heat. It is a solar process. The former refers to the development of biological and psychological functions; the latter, to the gradual realization in a human individual of his deeper "truth of being", purpose and destiny and of the source of power which alone makes it possible for this individual truth and purpose to become actualized and, to some extent at least, fulfilled.

What we call maturity is primarily understood as a condition of biological and psychological fulfillment; but there is also a spiritual kind of maturity which is produced by the illumination of the personality by the solar aspect of man. The Sun, or divine self, shines through the personality.

Here I am dealing with the lunar process of unfoldment of the personality. The following article will focus upon the solar process of growth. The process is complex; and the progressions of the Moon do not entirely cover its many aspects, needless to say. But the nearly-28-year cycle, measured by these lunar progressions is a very valuable "frame of reference". It enables us to orient ourselves significantly when we try to discover at any time through what phase of this whole process of biopsychological unfoldment we are living.

The Progressed Moon in the Houses

A particular phase of the whole process of bio-psychological unfoldment is revealed by the position of the progressed Moon in the houses of the chart, calculated, at least approximately, for the exact moment of birth. The character of the natal house in which the progressed Moon is located at any time defines the basic meaning of the opportunities for personal growth which are then inherent in the individual's pattern of life. Where your progressed Moon is, there you should seek to focus your attention, insofar as your personal development is concerned. There also life will tend to bring the most significant and valuable type of experiences for you—that is, those you primarily need for your growth toward a condition of personal maturity.

What you need is by no means necessarily what you want to happen! We all have a tendency to shrink from many experiences and confrontations which are of vital importance. Our laziness or self-indulgence seeks to ignore or evade experiences which we, as a total personality, should have at any special time in order to mature rightly and, as it were, on schedule. We procrastinate. We wear blinders so as not to see the clearly indicated path. When the direction changes according to the schedule of our growth—the schedule stamped, as it were, into the original seed of our individual nature—we prefer to keep on enjoying the types of activities with which we have become pleasantly familiar. Then we miss the new opportunities.

We may, of course, not miss them entirely. We may let them happen, as it were, sideways or remotely. We do not focus upon them in clear, conscious endeavor. But we really grow only through that upon which our whole

28

attention is focused. We must engage ourselves fully in what we are doing. A gear, half-engaged, shrieks and snaps easily. In our kind of personality transmission, we may not break down; but at least we lose momentum, the clutch slips, and power is wasted in the race of life.

When I say the race of life, I am not speaking of hectic haste and competitive excitement; what I refer to is the plain fact that our growth is, whether we like it or not, a measured process—also an irreversible one. An opportunity, lost through inattention or because of blurred focus, may repeat itself years later; but your ability to meet it will have been altered in the meantime. Your organism may have lost some of its resilience and capacity for focused self-mobilization. In any case, what the full acceptance of this opportunity would have eventually led to may be frustrated by the delay.

The essence of evil is waste and procrastination. It is particularly so at a time of crisis, of change of gears in one's dynamic movement toward fulfillment. Yet, of course, undue haste, nervous agitation and a hectic pulling at the gear shift can produce even worse results. But we become agitated and hectic in our motion mostly when we have previously wasted time and opportunity when we feel frustrated—and we clamor to regain the lost time.

We never can quite regain lost time, unfortunately! We can only assimilate thoroughly the lesson our loss has brought to us. Then, by incorporating what we have learned with the experience of the new field ahead, we may enrich these new experiences with a depth of wisdom such as often does not come except through sorrow and through the quiet assimilation of our relative failure.

The Age Factor

At the moment of birth, the Moon is located in one of the natal houses, below or above the birth horizon and east or west of the meridian of the birth place. It is also in one of the twelve signs of the zodiac. The cycle of the progressed Moon starts from this natal position (in one house and in one sign). The progressed Moon moves through the whole natal chart—which I consider as a fixed, unchanging factor, a kind of blueprint of the whole life—in twenty-seven years and about four months. It moves in counter-clockwise motion, in the order of the houses—that is, from the third house to the fourth house, then the fifth, etc.

As the Moon moves with varying speed through the zodiacal signs—and also the number of zodiacal degrees in a house varies greatly, depending on the latitude and the sign rising at birth—it follows that the progressed Moon may stay much longer in one house than in another. In temperate climates, the difference easily varies between one year or one year and a half, and four or five years, the average being two years and some months. This means that the schedule of growth of our personality allows for more or less time to concentrate upon any one of the twelve basic phases of this growth.

As people, in most cases, live more than twenty-seven years, the lunar cycle is normally repeated two, three or even four times. Theoretically, each new time should see the personal unfoldment taking place at a higher level of operation and, above all, of consciousness, understanding and purpose. But many people do not reach much higher than the biological, ancestral and traditional level of personality which characterizes the first twenty-seven or twenty-eight years of a normal life. The second level (up to about fifty-five) should refer to the unfoldment of the truly individual potentialities—to that which singles a person out of the average and the collective type and makes of him or her a relatively unique individual with and character and a purpose strictly his or her own.

The third and fourth levels give the possibility of further growth in consciousness and wisdom in effective service to the community and to humanity as a whole, or, if the human being has never been truly "individualized" and has drifted along with the collective tide, he or she settles into old age, as the biological energies of the body wane.

We should also realize that the meaning of the passage of the progressed Moon through any of the natal houses is deeply influenced by the age factor. If a person is born with the Moon in the sixth house, it is evident that the accent on human relationship, indicated as the progressed Moon reaches the seventh house, must have a different meaning than it would have if the natal Moon were in the twelfth house. The seventh-house passage in the first case would correspond with infancy; and whatever relationships would be implied would have to be mainly those of the infant to the objects of his immediate environment. On the other hand, in the second instance, the seventh house passage would come around the age of fourteen or fifteen and the element of intimate relationship would carry the flavor of adolescent longings or bravado.

The age of the person must be the first thing to consider when one studies a birth-chart with a view toward helping that person better to understand his or her temperament and opportunities for growth. The study must include progressions because, when talking to a person, the astrologer must address himself or herself to that person's need as it is then—and age is very basic in ascertaining the character and level of operation of that need.

First-House Passage

When the progressed Moon crosses the ascendant and as it passes through the first house, one should watch for the opportunity to take a new breath, symbolically speaking, and to make a new beginning. The ascendant crossing can often be effectively used as a means to rectify a chart, to discover the exact moment of birth or of the first breath. However, as one grows older, the inertia of the past often does delay the new move, the change of residence or the creative awareness of a new rhythm of existence and a new tone of selfhood. Whether or not an outer event occurs, the challenge is to realise oneself consciously in a new way. If this takes place in infancy, the result may not be too obvious; yet a change of residence, a new quality of relationship between the parents, altering the tone of the psychic substance of the child's growth and, above all, an inner contact with soul energies may mark the start of a new rhythm of existence.

As the person grows up, the passage of the progressed Moon over the natal ascendant may indicate an effort at individualization, at becoming one's true self. Usually, such an effort is polarized by some outer change but this is not essential. Often the progressed Moon over the natal ascendant of a woman or man occurs at marriage time, but not always. The house position of the progressed Moon when one first marries significantly characterizes the place the marriage occurs in the overall pattern of the life, thus revealing the way one should meet the experience so as to extract from it the most meaningful harvest.

Second-House Passage

This house stands for all that one owns and for the quality of one's sense of ownership—i.e., the characteristic attitude toward, and the use one makes of possessions, whether they be money and things of value or innate faculties and abilities. What has been started during the first-house period should thus be substantiated, made concrete, usable, applicable during the Moon's progression through the second house. The demand of life during this period is to learn how to use significantly what is available: vitality, wealth, mental powers, etc.

Third-House Passage

As the progressed Moon reaches the natal third house, one should concentrate upon the development of a more sensitive and responsive nervous system— through various contacts, experiments and communications—and of a more active intellect, enabling one to correlate many things and various kinds of sensations. One should organize what one owns into a thoroughly effectual instrumentality for carrying out one's interests, and sense of purpose.

At the first level of bio-psychological activity, this means the discovery, by the child, of the world around him in all of its queer facets; by the adolescent, of the realm of thought, culture, science, philosophy and of human behavior. The focus of attention then is not the field of real intimate relationship, but rather the effort to test how people "tick" and to trick them into revealing their character and the limits of their powers.

Fourth-House Passage

During such a period, life requires the focusing of attention and energies upon gaining stability or increased security. For the child, stability comes from his or her experience with parents, particularly the mother. He seeks to define himself to himself. Such a process of self-defining can be done at several levels—in the home and family; later, in the community life in which one participates; still later, in terms of some wider or more transcendent group or field of work, acting as a matrix for higher-level unfoldment. The basic challenge and opportunity life presents then is that one should solidly establish oneself in terms of some basic and focalized allegiance. Then only can power be made available, for then you stand; one is rooted; one has become part of the great power-alignment integrating the Sun above and the soil below—or the whole globe.

Fifth-House Passage

Now comes the challenge of self-expression or, more precisely, of how to release excess vital and personal energy so that (1) one grows from the release; (2) no one (oneself included) is hurt by it; and (3) one uses one's powers according to their intrinsic nature, with purity, without adulterating elements or chaotic and unrhythmic haste. During such a period, more than at any other time, it is important to give of oneself unstintingly and warmly, but also to focus one's attention upon the *how,* the *why* and the *to whom.* By meeting these issues one will grow.

Sixth-House Passage

The keynote of such a period is self-improvement and self-reorientation. It tends to be a period of readjustment, perhaps crisis, because our fifth-house performances are rarely adequate or spontaneous and harmonious enough; then they lead to difficulties or ill health. It is necessary during this period to focus one's attention on learning new techniques, on self-analysis, on improving one's responses to the challenges of life.

At times, the trend seems to be in some other direction. Marriage may occur with the progressed Moon in the sixth house, for instance; in this case, one can see that the basic purpose of this marriage is to teach one something vital about oneself and how to improve or deepen one's approach to people. One's mate is revealed as one's teacher, not perhaps by what he or she says, but by the problems and perhaps the crisis which the marriage brings, sooner or later.

Seventh-House Passage

This house is the field of all experiences through which one learns to meet one or more individuals as equals and partners. Here is the opportunity to surrender egocentric attitudes and transform them by love and cooperation. One should learn how to share with others, particularly to share ideals and motives for action. Obviously, the kind of experiences and opportunities one will meet at such a time will depend greatly upon one's age. But at any age, we may grow through cooperation and sharing; and the love of a child playmate may be as vital in our development as the passion of the mature lover, seeking to lose himself or herself in the beloved.

Eighth-House Passage

The purpose of the eighth-house experience in the over-all pattern of personal unfoldment is twofold: the very substance of the egocentric consciousness (and its frame of reference) should be renewed, and the cooperative sharing learned during the preceding period should become productive. The two things are, of course, related. Because the new life experienced during the seventh-house phase of the lunar cycle is productive of valuable fruits, ego can be made to give up its old pattern of feeling, thinking and behavior. Conversely, as egocentric attitudes fade out, the fruition of love and partnership becomes richer and more satisfying.

However, it may also be that the partner has proven deceiving, unworthy or binding (subtly or obviously), in which case conflict may occur. This can also take place if the ego refuses to surrender its privileges and biases and the love experiences have been lacking the strength or meaningfulness required to make this surrender attractive or seemingly valid.

Ninth-House Passage

This is the time when one should seek understanding. Through these months (or years) one ought to focus his or her attention upon learning the "laws of life", as well as those of human nature and of society. It can be a time of outer expansion and travel to distant places. But the basic purpose remains to understand more and, through understanding, to grow wiser—and perhaps to assume responsibility as one who teaches the way of understanding. In some cases, the process may be hard and exacting. Neither the individual ego nor the love nature may want to understand. Indeed, we often fear understanding! The law may defeat one; one may be judged. Yet that, too, means growth and is necessary for real maturity.

Tenth-House Passage

When the progressed Moon crosses the zenith of the birth-chart, a time for achievement—professionally or in any other more personal ways—is often experienced. Achievement means literally coming to a head. Life and its processes can, or at least should, come to a head then in one's own personal nature. Again the age factor will give various meanings to such a culmination of efforts or energies. An infant could not achieve much if his progressed Moon would reach his natal midheaven at the age of two or four! Yet, conceivably, even the infant's success in meeting early challenges may affect his whole life. Besides, at this level of organic growth, the tenth house refers mostly to one of the parents. Babies can concentrate very effectively on achieving some definite results with their parents.

Eleventh-House Passage

This section of the birth-chart has been called the house of friends, hopes and wishes. More basically, it refers to what follows after achievement—or, at least, after having established oneself in society as a member of a class, a profession, an occupational group. Such a tenth-house establishment allows one, in many cases, to fulfill some hopes and wishes and to make social contacts or friendships. But, in a deeper sense, one may then also be confronted with the realization that social position, success or fame are not ends in themselves. One may feel a peculiar sense of inner emptiness, a need to go further, to transform the social patterns along which one grew up.

As the progressed Moon passes through the eleventh house, one may relax and enjoy the fruits of one's achievements. But the deeper drive of the life and the spirit within is toward a new beginning. In the symbolical illustration of the yearly cycle of vegetation which I mentioned at the beginning of this article, this is the time when the seed is forming, maturing within the fruit.

Thus, the challenge is: "Look for the seed within!" It is the God within—the urge to begin again, but at a higher level.

Twelfth-House Passage

This is the last phase of the cycle: a transition. It can mean a preparation for rebirth or rebeginning, or it can be a weary letting go. The challenge is not to become weary, not to feel oppressed and weighed down by the ghosts of the past years, but to gain the courage of wielding the sword of severance—the sword which Christ said He brought to the world—and to make a clean place on which one may build anew, fearlessly, joyously, purely, as a newborn baby waiting to greet the future.

Then the cycle of experience begins again. One is summoned to start on a new (or relatively new) rhythm of being at a new level. Once more, the progressed Moon crosses over the ascendant. A new set of experiences opens up. Maturity takes on a new meaning, lunar cycle after lunar cycle.

SOLAR GROWTH THROUGH THE ZODIAC:
THE PROGRESSED SUN
by Dane Rudhyar

The Sun is the source of light and heat for the whole solar system and for our planet in particular. Solar energy, according to the symbolism of astrology, is distributed for day-by-day use to the living organisms on the Earth's surface by the rhythmic to-and-fro motions of the Moon. Solar *light* is thus transformed into *life* within the "sublunar sphere"—that is, within the space bounded by the Moon's orbit around our globe.

The planets also contribute to the transformation of the basic and original Sun-force. They reflect and symbolically differentiate it into various types of energies, which are absorbed by all entities on the Earth. These planetary energies are also focused and distributed by the Moon as it rapidly revolves around our globe. Half of the time the Moon is *inside* of the Earth's orbit where it focuses the energies of the inner planets, Mercury and Venus. Half of the time the Moon is *outside* of our planet's orbit, focusing the energies of the outer planets, from Mars to Pluto and beyond, and perhaps also the emanations of the distant stars linked with our Sun.

As we saw in a preceding article, the biological and psychological processes of growth within a living organism can be clocked, as it were, mainly by the rhythm of what are called "progressions" of the Moon. On the theoretical basis that "one day after birth equals one year of actual living" the motion of the Moon after the moment of birth gives us an insight into the basic phases of the "structural unfoldment" of a living organism, and particularly of a human personality.

Such a lunar pattern of unfoldment establishes important turning points and outlines basic phases in the gradual development of a man or woman on the way to "maturity"—and, later, on the incline that leads to eventual disintegration and death. I have already analyzed these basic phases in terms of the passage of the progressed Moon through each of the twelve natal houses of the birthchart.

However, this twelve-fold path to maturity is not the only indication we should consider when studying the progressive growth of a human person. There are solar progressions as well as lunar ones; only as the Sun actually moves only about one degree of the zodiac in one day, the progressed Sun advances only by this same measure each year of life. This slow motion means that the progressed Sun can only cover two or three signs (60° to 90°) of the zodiac during the span of a person's life.

This being the case, it is logical to assume that the times when the Sun by "progression" passes from the sign in which it was located at birth to the next sign, then, some thirty years later, to the following sign, etc. should indicate important changes—changes, that is, in whatever the progressed Sun represents in a human life.

The Meaning of the Progressed Sun

The Sun in astrology stands for that basic type of life-energy used by the total organism of personality, body and psyche. It is the "fuel" on which the "engine of personality" operates. The presence of the Sun at birth in one of the twelve signs of the zodiac indicates which of the twelve basic types of "fuel" is primarily consumed by the human being in the business of living.

Obviously this analogy cannot be carried too far or taken too literally; but it shows that the type of fuel used (whether it is wood, coal, oil, electricity or atomic power) determines the general kind of structure and mode of operation of an engine, and the *quality* of the power made available for work. More than this, it also indicates—if this is an ordered and purposeful universe—the general type of purpose for which the engine (that is, the personality) has been produced. What is revealed, however, is not the precise, strictly individual purpose, but the fundamental type of activity and work which "God", or destiny, "expects" the person to produce, and which therefore the person is essentially *fit* to produce. Astrology defines, through the twelvefold zodiac, twelve such types. When we speak of an Aries or Gemini person we mean a person whose basic type of life-energy fits him best to perform the kind of activity and work characterized by the zodiacal signs Aries or Gemini.

Such a type of life-energy remains fundamental throughout the life-time. Yet age obviously changes much in a person. It affects the character and rhythm as well as the intensity of the life-energy and vitality. Some basic factors remain the same, but the *point of application* of the vital forces is normally transferred from one level to another, from the purely organic-bodily to the psychological-social, and perhaps eventually, to the spiritual spheres. At the same time the life-purpose tends to clarify itself; the instinctual consciousness is shifted to the emotional-intellectual, and the social or spiritual levels. Such a gradual shifting of the focus of a person's ability to perform useful and significant work has a definite tidal rhythm. This rhythm may be so overlaid by superficial or secondary waves and eddies that it cannot be clearly noticed; yet it is there. It can be made clearer by studying solar progressions.

The Three Phases of Life

Let us take the familiar example of the late President Franklin D. Roosevelt. He was born January 30, 1882 with the Sun at Aquarius 11° *plus*. As he died at the age of 63, his life divides itself, from the point of view of *solar progressions* into an Aquarian, a Piscean and an Arian phase. The first phase ended almost exactly at his father's death (December 8, 1900), after his entrance to Harvard University. The Piscean phase closed and the Arian phase began in the Fall of 1930 when F.D.R. was re-elected Governor of New York with a huge majority. This proved him a success in spite of his grave physical handicap (he had been stricken by polio in August, 1921) and established his readiness to climb further to the Presidency, to which he was elected in the Fall of 1932. At the time he was elected and took office his progressed Sun was on the third degree of Aries which, in the Sabian set of zodiacal degree-symbols,* suggests the identification of an individual with the very structure (thus, destiny) of his natal country.

From the very start, F.D.R.'s chart suggested such an identification. His natal Moon, Mars, Sun and Mercury touched vital centers in the U.S. chart.**

But before the young Franklin could fully realize his destiny, he had to pass through the dreary ordeal of infantile paralysis and through the seeming defeat of all his hopes or ambition that his illness brought to him.

The operation of a "dialectic" sequence of thesis, antithesis and synthesis has been known to philosophers long before it was made popular by the Marxian concept of historical development. In simple terms it means that one cannot fully understand and demonstrate what one's true self and destiny are *(thesis)* until one has passed through tests, trials and tribulations which challenge one's inner Solar (or Soul) purpose and appear to make it unrealizable (the phase called *antithesis*). Then, finally, one *may* emerge victorious and in the end fulfill one's true individual selfhood in a "work of destiny", that is, in a creative relationship with one's society *(synthesis)*.

According to this pattern, the zodiacal sign of the natal Sun represents what a person potentially *is* in essential truth of being. While the progressed Sun passes through that sign (Aquarius in F.D.R.'s case), the person unfolds in some way his or her latent Solar powers (vitality) at the body-level, and at the level of ancestral family-past and native environment; yet he or she most likely does not effectively demonstrate this deep, individual potentiality represented by the Sun's natal position except in an imprecise or shadowy manner.

At best a person senses this inner Soul-truth and destiny as it is *reflected* upon the screen of his or her racial, cultural and religious traditions; thus, as these traditions allow him or her to see it—which may mean in a very distorted, perhaps dark, sense, if the birth-environment is something he or she is *meant to overcome and transform*. Child prodigies may seem to be exceptions; but such precocious children or youths are not actually "individuals"! Rather, they mirror and give expression to a *collective* racial or cultrual trend. They are merely effective mouthpieces for the past, which fulfills itself spontaneously *through* them.

Obviously, the length of this first "progressed Sun phase" depends on the place of the natal Sun in its sign. If it is on one of the first degrees of the sign, this period of self-unfoldment takes from twenty-five to thirty years. If the natal Sun is late in its zodiacal sign, the period is very short. This last instance would theoretically seem the "better"; yet if the progressed Sun enters its second zodiacal sign too early, the individual may not have sufficient time to allow the deep potential of his or her true self to "set", before the contrasting and antithetical trends assert themselves—as we shall see presently.

The Second Solar Period

The second zodiacal period of the progressed Sun may not outwardly be a sharp contrast to the first. In many cases nothing happens that is very obvious in the way of a change in the life-habits or circumstances. What changes is mainly one's basic attitude toward one's life-energy, one's feeling toward oneself and the meaning of one's existence. On the other hand, however, even one's attitude may not change immediately. Indeed, in most instances the change is brought to a focus and made clear around the time the progressed Moon meets the progressed Sun in the second zodiacal sign crossed by the

Sun after birth. This event is what I call the "progressed New Moon", which begins a new "progressed lunation cycle" (a thirty-year process).*** From then on the individual becomes increasingly aware not only of his or her own potential of being, but of the outer social conditions in which he or she has to operate, and (often) against which, or in spite of which, his or her destiny *will have to take form.*

This is the real meaning of contrast or antithesis. Man needs contrast and the play of opposites in order to come to a clear realization of what he essentially is, i.e. of his inner basic purpose for living. His own powers and his will have to fight their way through, if his mind is to become lucidly aware of what his life is "all about". It may be an easy struggle, or a particular person may not be very much of an "individual". He may easily fall into old ancestral patterns of normality, and in such a case, the struggle is merely the usual one of making a living, raising a family perhaps, or in general, of finding a more or less comfortable place to settle in the vast field of society.

In some instances, it seems to start this way; then, after the progressed New Moon occurs in the sign of antithesis, things begin to happen and the challenges increase, often reaching a full climax when the progressed Moon *opposes* the progressed Sun (progressed Full Moon).

In F.D.R.'s life the first progressed New Moon occurred on the last degree of Aquarius when he was just about eighteen years old. It ended the Aquarian progressed Sun cycle; and within a year he entered college and his father died. The progressed Full Moon in Pisces occurred during the Winter of 1914-15. He had been made Assistant Secretary of the Navy in the Spring of 1913, after nearly three years in the New York Senate.

The Piscean phase of Roosevelt's life ended in the early Fall of 1930; but in June, 1929 his second progressed New Moon had occurred at Pisces 28°48'. He had then overcome his ordeal and become Governor of New York State. His new start had become focused. Through his victory over illness, pain and despair he had conquered the adversary (the principle of antithesis). He was now ready for a third stage—the fulfillment of his destiny.

As the Arian period of Roosevelt's "solar life" began, Hitler was also beginning his rise to power. The two lives were strangely synchronized by fate (or world-*karma*). F.D.R. lived to see his progressed Full Moon in the 14th degree of Aries during the Summer of 1944. Victory was by then assured; the decision to develop the atom bomb was made. It was for F.D.R. the beginning of the end. He had done his job and etched the mark of his individual destiny upon world history. He died within a year—after Yalta.

The Sequence of Zodiacal Signs

The signs of the zodiac follow each other in a significant order. Aries is a "Fire" principle; Taurus, an "Earth" principle, Gemini is characterized by "Air", Cancer by "Water". The sequence of the signs is also patterned by the threefold classification of cardinal, fixed and mutable signs. Roosevelt's birth-sign, Aquarius, is an "Air" sign and a fixed sign. When his progressed Sun moved into Pisces, it moved into a Water and a mutable (or common) sign. This change of zodiacal qualities should help us to grasp the meaning of the process of unfoldment of destiny, for the change varies according to the Sun-sign at birth.

The point of focalization of Roosevelt's life-force passed from Air to Water, then to Fire. Interestingly enough he became connected with the Navy when his progressed Sun was in the Water sign Pisces, and he contracted infantile paralysis after swimming in the ocean! Water is a strong contrast to Air; likewise Earth (for instance, Taurus) is a contrast to Fire (Aries)—or Air (Gemini or Aquarius) to Earth (Taurus or Capricorn).

It is not easy to define clearly the meanings of such contrasting sequences, and to show, for instance, how the contrasts Air-Water and Fire-Earth differ. Moreover, the sequence Aquarius-Pisces also differs from the sequence Gemini-Cancer because, though in both cases we have Air followed by Water, Aquarius is a *fixed* Air sign, while Gemini is a *mutable* Air sign, etc. For this reason the best thing is to study many individual cases, and to try to isolate from them some common features; but such a study is far beyond the scope of this article. We can, however, see how the basic principles operate in a couple of instances.

Franklin Roosevelt's basic Aquarian characteristics were clearly visible throughout his whole life, but at first, as his Sun was progressing through Aquarius, they revealed themselves in the superficialities of a youth of "high society", no doubt ambitious and eager to express in one way or another a basic idealism. To such an Aquarian type must come the realization of how far removed the collectivity of his people (the "common" factor in a society) and the traditions of his culture are from the Aquarian dreams and ambitions. In Pisces the progressed Sun becomes, symbolically, filled with the moisture of the racial collectivity, the great Unconscious (so often compared to "the sea").

Pisces is the end of the cycle. The new Aquarian dream must meet this concluding phase of the cycle and the accumulated ghosts of the failures of the past. What happens then decides the future—the Arian future which is then only a *potentiality*. It may or not become actual fact. It can become a positive, creative, initiative reality *only* if the Aquarian "fixed" character remains steady, centered in faith, undeviating in its vision of the future.

When young F.D.R. entered Harvard he entered as well the "sea" of a collective intellectual tradition. It was the turn of the century. Freud was beginning his analysis of the remains in us of social and psychological frustrations and failures; the Curies, Planck and other scientists were opening the doors of the atomic "underworld". By the time young Roosevelt was in Columbia studying law, Einstein was revealing his first theory of relativity— Einstein who was three and a half decades later to urge him, as the President of the United States, to start the atom bomb research project. The Russo-Japanese war saw Asia rising and another Roosevelt intervening to curb Japan's ambition—a fact Japan was not to forget. Then World War I—all the "ghosts" of our Western society rising—and F.D.R.'s own *karma*, the illness focusing upon the individual the pressure which a society in crisis was experiencing everywhere. Indeed, in 1921 when F.D.R. was stricken, the United States had failed, had repudiated Wilson's great dream and the newly attained world-responsibility for leadership.

F.D.R. had to experience all these Piscean travails, for Pisces is the symbol of social crisis, of vast turmoil, of a disintegrating cycle. But he overcame the death of the cycle, and he rose, symbolically, with the vernal Sun, Aries—the fire of renewal or rebirth, the cardinal, actional sign of leadership. The Aries phase of his pattern of solar progression brought him the fulfillment of his youthful Aquarian hopes and ideals, of his undeviating, unyielding ambition to be a "man of destiny".

Further Illustrations

If we took a person born with the Sun in early degrees of Aries (i.e. in late March), this person's progressed Sun would reach Taurus sometime during his mid-twenties. He may have been born with a fiery eagerness to make a new start, to release some new energies, to impress his power and selfhood upon people and upon his culture. This may have meant breaking with family and tradition, and reaching ahead for new virgin fields.

The "virgin fields" in such a person's life are represented by the thirty years during which his progressed Sun passes through the sign Taurus. This is the long period of "ploughing" and "seeding" the Taurean earth. At least, to such an Aries type, this is what his life through his thirties, forties and early fifties is most likely to mean—in one way or another, whether emotionally or intellectually, or through sheer expenditure of self in action. And if the soil is poor or the sower careless or inexperienced, if "weather" is against his efforts or the "seed" is unfertile, then this Taurean period may end in weariness, discouragement, illness or death.

If the Aries-born Sun of will and purpose achieves victory, at least a partial one, then late in the fifties a Gemini period begins: the "synthesis" of Aries-initiative and Taurus-perseverance, of burning faith in a divine Power and of wisdom and compassion learned in the hard experiences of dealing with the "fixed" inertia of Taurus-Earth. Gemini then brings the Aries-born individual to the new realm of Air and mutability, to the level of Mind and of freedom. Aries-Fire rises to the Air-world of Principles and celestial Intelligence.

In closing I shall mention the case of Joseph Stalin who was born with the Sun at Sagittarius 28° 47'. He was therefore only a little over one year old when his progressed Sun reached Capricorn. The result was that he became, as it were, overshadowed by the Capricornian trand toward political activity and "empire building." The Sagittarian influence was superseded and, though his mother had destined him to the priesthood and he studied for a while in a seminary, he rebelled and became identified with a world-cause, Communism. His revolutionary activities started at about the age of nineteen, and he was expelled from the seminary (1898). His progressed New Moon late in 1901 (Capricorn 22nd degree) began his political career in earnest. He met Lenin in 1905.

During the Summer of 1910, the Aquarian phase of his solar unfoldment of personality began. He had experienced in prison the usual readjustment or self-clarifying and individualizing phase of many lives (28 to 30). His destiny was set, operating from then on at the national level. In Aquarius it gained "fixity" of purpose and the ideological quasi-fanaticism in matters of social (or spiritual) importance which is often associated with Aquarius. (Capricorn impels to large-scale *action* and personal identification with a "cause"; but Aquarius seeks the *management* of the powers released by the group devoted to that social, political or spiritual movement.)

Stalin's second progressed New Moon occurred in June of 1931 on the 22nd degree of Aquarius. Seven years before, Lenin had died. Trotsky had been defeated and exiled. Three years later Kiroff was assassinated as Stalin's progressed Sun squared his natal Pluto in his natal seventh House. Then the "great purge" began. Perhaps Stalin developed a persecution mania and a paranoid craving for self-deification. At any rate, his Aquarian period was brought to a close in the Winter of 1940.

Stalin's progressed Sun moved into a fourth sign, Pisces. A very few months later, Hitler invaded Russia. Now that the "Stalin myth" has been shattered by his successors, it is hard to tell how much Stalin was responsible for the stubborn resistance and eventual victory of Soviet Russia. Be that as it may, Pisces, in one of its aspects, is war, because it demands severance from the past. Pisces thus represents the struggle against the ghosts of the past, and often it means becoming overwhelmed by, or at least a mouthpiece for these ghosts.

All such remains of a stubborn past are not bad, of course. But the Kremlin ghosts are assuredly not the nice kind, judging from Russian history; and Stalin may well have been haunted by them. What matters here is that the Sagittarian features of his natal Sun, (which the progressed Sun had no time to exteriorize in Stalin's youth as it passed so soon into Capricorn) found a new way of reappearing in the Piscean period closing his life. Sagittarius and Pisces are both "ruled" by Jupiter, and both common or mutable signs. But for Stalin, the Sagittarian Fire had at the end turned into Water!

The Sabian Symbols for the 360 degrees of the zodiac give for the last degree of Sagittarius the picture of "The Pope, blessing the faithful". Disregarding altogether, of course, the literal reference to one religious organization, we see in the symbol an expression of religious exaltation and quasi-deification, of channelship for super-personal forces. Certainly Stalin, as the much publicized "little Father" to his people, fitted this symbolic picture, especially in his supposedly mellowed and benign pose after victory. He died with his progressed Sun in mid-Pisces, his progressed moon in Sagittarius; the two signs were thus linked in a significant manner.

The correlation between a brief first zodiacal phase of solar progressions and a fourth phase (which requires living beyond sixty) may take many and varied forms; but in most instances the end of the life tends to re-assert in a new way, what had been left rather under- or undeveloped at first, or had been deviated by the pressures of the social-political environment and the instinctive energies of the physical-emotional nature.

Thus flows the life-pattern of solar progressions in its simplest zodiacal expression. The details of the pattern have, needless to say, to be filled in by considering the series of aspects which the progressed Sun makes to all planets of the chart (natal and progressed) as it moves through the two, three or four signs which measure the life-span of man. But this is another story.

---

* *cf.* Dane Rudhyar's *An Astrological Mandala: The Cycle of Transformation and its 360 Symbolic Phases (Random House, New York: 1973)*

**(For July 4, 1776)—the symbol of the American *people,* in contrast to that of the American *government* which can probably best be symbolized by the chart for the adoption of the Federal Constitution. *cf. The Astrology of America's Destiny* (Random House, New York: 1974).

****cf. The Lunation Cycle* by Dane Rudhyar (Shambhala Publications, Boulder, Colorado: 1967).

Book Two

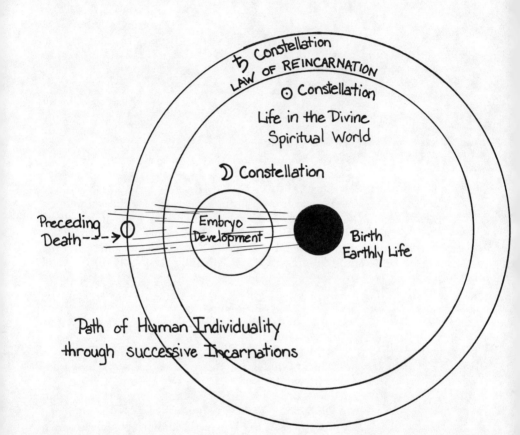

ħ Constellation
LAW OF REINCARNATION

☉ Constellation

Life in the Divine
Spiritual World

☽ Constellation

Embryo
Development

Preceding
Death - - - →〇

Birth
Earthly Life

Path of Human Individuality
through successive Incarnations

ASTROLOGY
by Willi Sucher

There are some people alive to-day who are able to appreciate the starry heavens in a peculiarly personal, inward, and intimate way. When, in moments of solitude and stillness, they look up to the twinkling multitude there is at times the accompanying feeling that the heavens might reveal their penetrative tones and secret harmonies whose personal correspondences are to be found only in the depths of the soul. Those who can sense these cosmic overtones are a gradually decreasing number; such harmonies are part of a stream that belongs to a past increasingly difficult of contact, the more modern science takes possession of the Earth.

Nostradamus, in the sixteenth century, possessed powers of perception which to us are almost incomprehensible. To him, the sky was a script in which he read time-embracing prophecies of the destinies of peoples and generations yet to come—prophecies that continued to be fulfilled up to the time of the French revolution. In him appeared to be stored all the star-lore of the ancient Chaldeans, Egyptians, and Greeks.

In the Mystery Temples the priests, by their knowledge of the stars, unveiled the history, past and future, of the world and of mankind. Only a small part of their immense wisdom lay in a knowledge of the connection between man and the world of stars as portrayed by the ordinary birth-chart. They noted, for instance, the position of the moon, whether it were waxing or waning, in what sign of the zodiac it stood, and so on—further indices of the destiny of the Earth and the character and capabilities of the subject. With the decay of the ancient mysteries the ability of the old initiates correspondingly deteriorated; it especially has been lost in a maze of records, formulae and rules, which, in course of transit through the centuries can no longer be understood. Only the remnants of the wisdom possessed by the ancients in its once magnificent fullness is recognisable in modern Astrology.

The immediate source of the inspiration drawn on by the ancient Initiates is of necessity closed to us. During the last four centuries natural science has become the direction of the search for knowledge—a direction which also set limits to the amount of knowledge attainable by the method. There is no correspondence between modern Astronomy and the wisdom of the ancients. Modern scientific teachings change rapidly, yet the underlying spirit which imbues them—a sincere inner quest for knowledge—is that with which we must approach Astrology if we would recapture the ancient wisdom. For the impulse which urges science is at bottom a natural and discerning love of the Earth—it is true that because of it the heavens have been lost—but they can be regained when science infuses into its researches a knowledge of the Spirit.

In embryology—a science of significance in connection with Astrology— great strides have been made. The origin and growth of both animal and human embryo has been the subject of much laborious research. True, much remains in darkness, especially about early stages of embryonic development, a period of primary importance and of far-reaching effects on the human after birth. Indeed, the question arises whether the actual time of birth (regarded by the ancients as fundamental to their star-wisdom) is not after all of only secondary importance. In studying the influence of heavenly bodies on human beings one may wonder whether the *time of conception* and suceeding embryonic stages are not of greater significance than the constellation at birth? Birth only means that the young life has attained to separate existence; it is released from the mother.

When we rightly comprehend that which has been left to us by tradition we shall see that the ancient star-sages were well aware of pre-natal events in their more cosmic-spiritual aspect. The almost mythical records from Egyptian times speak of the Hermetic star-wisdom and refer to Thoth or Hermes, the legendary founder of the ancient Egyptian culture. Through the clairvoyant consciousness which in those times men still possessed, this wisdom shed light on the horoscope of birth, particularly in the relation of the Sun, Moon, and Earth. From an understanding of those relationships they were able to deduce the *real* beginning of embryonic development and to appreciate the particular aspects which were being woven by the cosmos into the new human organism just coming into existence. Understood in the light of this knowledge, the constellation of birth opens up for us a key to the spiritual nature and powers of the Universe which form and mould the real *being* which man brings with him through the gate of birth into earthly existence.

The constellation of stars at the moment of birth illumines the human being from three aspects; the Moon, Sun, and Saturn in the relation to the Earth. By them, deep spiritual connections are revealed. At the moment of birth the Moon is either visible above the horizon, or invisible below it. Its relation to the Sun is either waxing or waning. With these facts as a basis it is possible in each individual case to go back to the time of "conception". In this way we are led to a certain constellation lying approximately 273 days prior to actual birth, though this period varies in individual cases. The physiological aspect of birth is still very much of a mystery, but those interested in Astrology will probably agree that the constellation at the moment of conception, for the purposes of our present study, is probably of great significance. Under its influence a new life is beginning to take form. Whoever is familiar with the development of the embryo will also agree that the precise moment of conception is vital, so it will be worth our while to study cosmic conditions prevailing at the time. From that moment it will be necessary to study the flowing cosmic life for the next nine months; to observe the path of the Sun through the signs of the zodiac together with those of the planets, their retrogressions and so on, all coinciding (approximately) to ten revolutions of the Moon around the Earth. These Lunar revolutions are of the utmost importance; they are precursors of the subsequent rhythmical epochs of the earth-life to come—*the whole cosmic process is pictured in them.* But besides gaining an insight into the earthly life of the new human being, we shall have a picture of his destiny in which are indicated his potentialities, hindrances and the conditions which will prevail at varying periods of his life. Even tendencies to illness and health will be disclosed. Prenatal cosmic phenomena portray the creative element in the human being, the so-called "etheric" body, which throughout the earth life accompanies the physical body bringing about its development and changes, and guards it against its tendency to decay. All this has very much to do with the moon, for the moon translates the cosmic, spiritual nucleus into events in time. This fact could well be termed the *Moon Mystery* of the human being.

But we are able to go still further. Man's connection with the moon enables us to understand the finer qualities of the organism — including all that which is due to heredity. Man has of course, particular and important relationships with the Sun, not only in its objective sense as a fiery, heavenly body, but in the sense that it is a solar entity expressing itself in an appointed orbit. We know that the apparent path of the Sun is a very important cosmic reality. The Sun-sphere leads us to a constellation which, though it has a mathematical relationship to the birth constellation, is, in point of time, very largely independent of it. It can, in fact, appear either before or after birth but of this greater details will be given in future articles. This constellation has a deep correspondence with the soul and the essential nature of being; it reveals the fundamental outlook on the world. It has already been shown that every possible world-conception and philosophy can be related to one or other of the signs of the zodiac.* Idealism, as a philosophy can be related to Aries, the logical outlook with Jupiter, and so on. If then, man is an idealist, but tends towards logical expression of it, one may say that he has Jupiter in Aries as a spiritual horoscope in contradistinction to the mathematical precision of the ordinary horoscope of birth.

In order to determine this spiritual constellation it was necessary to study actual lives, from which it became apparent that it could be deduced with mathematical accuracy from the constellation of birth. Proceeding from certain facts and mathematical conditions relating to Saturn at the time of birth, a constellation can be found which tells us much about the passing of the human individuality through previous incarnations. This aspect of the heavens stands in almost timeless sublimity above the horoscope.

The diagram will help to make more clear the cosmic relationships and from it we shall try to work out exact details. In the first place we have the acknowledged fact of reincarnation, of the individuality plunging ever and again into epochs of earth-evolution at particular times suited to its development. During the periods between incarnations the soul is preparing for its next earth life. We may, therefore, assume a certain "direction" through all successive incarnations, indicated in the diagram by the line going towards birth. After entry through the gate of birth, nothing remains in the consciousness to remind the human being of his sojourn in more spiritual worlds. Yet there is a way to penetrate the veil of the stellar constellation ruling at the time of birth, the rendering of which tells of the immense preparation which was undergone to make this earthly life possible. This is indicated in the three circles of the diagram.

All this can be found in the mathematical relationships of the constellation of birth. To begin with, light is shed on the prenatal cosmic influences which correspond to the embryonic development. There is also reflected in this constellation expressive pictures of the bodily nature in its widest sense — the destiny which has found concrete expression in the form of the body. This, the "moon-mystery" of the human being, is indicated by the innermost circle in the diagram.

Furthermore, we are given an insight into the life of the human soul in the realms of Divine Spiritual Beings. This is reflected in the Sun constellation. In it is revealed a man's philosophy — the "last echo of his former union with the world of the Gods" — a philosophy which is, so to speak, the inheritance of the Thought of the Gods. (Second circle in the diagram.) Finally, from far cosmic distances, there streams into the birth-constellation from a constellation related to the Saturn-sphere (outer circle), the influences of past earth lives.

Quite another aspect of the human being's relationship to the stars reveals itself in the constellation *at the moment of death.* (Rudolf Steiner very well understood this reality and has pointed out that the "horoscope of death" is of great importance to the individual who has passed again into the spiritual world. He further asserts that the contemplation of the horoscope brings to those still living on earth a beautiful and selfless understanding of the existence of those who have passed on. Contemplation of the horoscope of birth, on the other hand, is too often an expression of human egoism.)

Birth and death may be likened to the rhythm of breathing. In entering into earth-life the individual takes in, as in a mighty breath, the ingredients of the Cosmos and of the earth, in order to form from them his own organism. At death, he breathes out again his being into the surrounding spheres; the physical body is seized by the decaying powers of Earth, his super-physical being he gives back again to cosmic spiritual spaces. Between these two poles of inbreathing at birth and outbreathing at death there is an earthly life which changes and evolves the substances from the earth and from the Cosmos — changes them right down into the physical organism. As a result of past destiny, the individual wrestles and strives with what he has brought with him; that is his task. In order to rise above the waves of outward events and demands, the human "I" must work in the finer spheres of the temperament and inclinations. The human being's tendency towards a certain philosophy of life is an inheritance, so to speak from the gods, but the hard facts of earthly life impel him to widen and deepen his philosophy, to change and develop his point of view, to infuse into it a quality of all-embracing universality. The ensuing developments influence his bodily nature; through illness and the like he becomes other than he was. *The fruit of all these strivings and transformations become visible in the constellation of the stars at the moment of death.*

Spiritual science indicates that, after death, the newly released soul at once experiences its past life as in a picture which passes before it. Many people who have been very near to death and only just saved at the last moment have told how their whole lives, concentrated in their most important points, have stood before them as great memory-pictures. Something like this results from a study of the death-horoscope. In it are inscribed the most significant events in the life of the individual who has passed on.

As the birth-constellation, in the way described, points backward into the pre-physical existence of the human being, so does the death-constellation point forward into the existence of the soul after death. The death-constellation has also an important connection with the pre-natal cosmic events—those that took place during the development of the embryo. But it also points to an event which is related to the constellation of the Sun-sphere about the time of birth referred to above. Just as this latter constellation in the Sun-sphere is a symbol of the dismissal of the soul from the lap of the gods, so in the constellation *after* death is mirrored the return of the soul into the sphere of the gods after divesting itself of the last remains of earth existence. Indeed it is often only long after death that earthly strivings arrive at fruition.

In this constellation, which may appear many years after death, but which arises with mathematical consistency from the positions of the stars *at the time of death,* is raised into Cosmic heights all that is pure and ripe enough to be woven into future forms of Earth destiny.

---

*See Rudolf Steiner, *Human and Cosmic Thought* (Rudolf Steiner Press)

THE STARS AND SELF-KNOWLEDGE
by Dan Lloyd

One of the major tasks of our time is to develop a new star wisdom. How is this to be done?

It seems to me that, to achieve this, we have to understand the nature of the ancient star culture, Astrology, and its modern, intellectual offspring, Astronomy. Naturally, we cannot return to the wisdom of the past for an answer to our quest, nor can we cling to the external means of knowledge on which Astronomy relies for a renaissance of star wisdom. Perhaps we may find clues to the right path if we bring to mind the way in which the ancient knowledge of the stars, now mostly degenerated and trivialised, was acquired.

During the era of the Third post-Atlantean epoch the majority of human beings had already lost their former ability to peer directly into the spiritual world; true, remnants of this atavistic clairvoyance remained, but it was more and more the case that, as man's consciousness became increasingly directed to the external physical world, his perception of spiritual facts and beings waned. Only in the Mystery temples was the contact with the spiritual world maintained, and it was from there that the initiates sent out the impulses for the guidance of their fellows.

In a way that is no longer possible today, owing to the change in man's whole constitution, the initiate was put into a trance-like condition so that, with his Ego and astral body, he could free himself from his physical body and enter the spiritual world. While in this condition, the initiate was unconscious of his experiences in the spiritual world, just as modern man is during sleep today. However, on returning to the physical body, a memory of what he had experienced lit up within him and he could testify to the reality of the spirit.

What did he experience during this out-of-the-body sojourn in the spiritual world? He experienced all that could be communicated to him by the higher spiritual beings connected with the planets of our solar system, providing he had been properly prepared in the Mystery temples for such lofty experiences. The guiding spirits of Mercury, or Venus, or one of the other planets would weave into the initiate's astral body far-reaching secrets connected with the planets and their motions, and these secrets were then carried into the initiate's physical and etheric bodies at the end of his trance-like condition so that they could be revealed to the ordinary day-waking consciousness of that time. It will be clear that such a means of acquiring knowledge by-passed the Ego: it was the astral body which was the means by which the communications from the spiritual beings were transmitted to man.

Everything in the nature of the ancient star wisdom was originally acquired in this way, at a time when the Ego-consciousness had not yet entered into its full inheritance. However, the sublime wisdom of the Ancient Chaldeans and Egyptians began to wane in the course of time as the Fourth Post-Atlantean epoch neared. Only spiritual beings of an inferior kind could be contacted in the old way—and thus the Hebrew initiates, who had to prepare for the emergence of the 'I'-consciousness, rightly denounced divination by the stars.

Man's path now was to lead increasingly away from its guidance by spiritual beings connected with the stars to full freedom in Ego-consciousness. This could only be gained by a total emancipation from divine tutelage. Man had to 'find his feet' in the physical world as an independent being. The ancient spirituality had to die out to pave the way for man's newly-emerging faculty: the intellect. The physical brain finally became the tomb of the ancient clairvoyance.

As the intellect came to greater and greater ascendancy during the Greco-Roman age, all that was left of the former star wisdom was the tradition that man is somehow ruled by the stars. The spiritual beings behind the stars vanished from man's ken, and as he directed his newly-sharpened physical gaze into space, he no longer saw in the movements of the planets the gestures of spiritual beings, but only the expression of mathematical laws. By means of these laws the planetary periods could be calculated, and it thus became possible to study the planetary movements as a means of 'prediction'. Horoscopes were cast, the stars studied, and pronouncements made about a person's future—and thus what had once been a divine science sailed into desolate waters.

This whole tendency was in contradiction to man's evolution towards freedom, for what kind of freedom could man be said to be striving for if his every move could be calculated out of the stars?

A decisive step forward was taken with the Copernican revolution. The Earth was deprived of the central position it had possessed in the Ptolemaic system, and was relegated to a minor role as only one of several other bodies revolving round the Sun. The Fifth Post-Atlantean age had dawned: the age of science, of technology, of man as an insignificant atom in a great hostile world mechanism.

What value had the stars now? The science born of man's intellect produced ever more perfect instruments for studying them as purely external objects in space. Their weight, mass, density, velocity, etc, were recorded and analysed. Whether they were composed of this gas or that was noted down. Some of the more imaginative star-gazers even wondered whether life could exist on some of the other planets, for had not strange tell-tale markings resembling canals been found on Mars, for example?

Elaborate theories about the origin of the universe sprang readily from the pens of eminent astronomers. Light-years became a favourite expression for calculating the unfathomable distances of galaxies and constellations. It was taken absolutely for granted that nothing but physics and mathematics were needed to investigate the heavenly bodies. Since all knowledge of the spiritual had been lost, earthly science was simply projected into the cosmos without any inkling of the fact that what is applicable on Earth loses its validity in outer space in the same way that gravity diminishes the further one goes from Earth. Then along came Einstein with his theory of Relativity and everything was turned topsy turvy. All that astronomers could now say was that when they looked in their telescopes they could see certain light effects coinciding in time in their instruments, but the sources of those light effects might no longer exist, and moreover, they might have ceased to exist at different times!

So from an ancient star wisdom we have come to a halt before a wall. And to return to the question asked at the beginning of this article: how do we find our way to a *new* star wisdom, for quite clearly the impasse in which modern Astronomy finds itself is an indication that new methods are needed to solve the riddle of the stars.

The problem of human freedom cannot be separated from this quest. It is precisely in the modern age, when all vestiges of the spirit have vanished from the human ken, that man can rekindle in himself the forces that will lead to the birth of new faculties of knowledge — faculties that will endow him with the capacity to see again into the spiritual world in full ego consciousness. When man was in possession of the ancient clairvoyance, he could not be said to be a free being, for he could not feel separate from the higher beings who guided him. His individuality was submerged in a group-soul consciousness. In the modern age, however, the intellect has killed that ancient consciousness, which now lies in the sub-conscious realm of man's soul life, and the Ego is master of its own fate. Man now only has reflections of the spirit in his consciousness, not the spirit itself, and so the content of his consciousness is not coercive, as it was in the past. The Age of Technology is the Age of Freedom. And man's mission is now to take the path from the realm of lifeless nature, which is all that the intellect can grasp, to the realm of the living, which can only be grasped by the awakening of higher faculties.

Rudolf Steiner's life work stands as a testimony to these higher faculties. He described the three higher stages of consciousness as Imagination, Inspiration and Intuition, and gave detailed indications of how modern man can undertake the self-development that could lead to their emergence. By attaining these levels of consciousness it will become clear that it is not valid to speak of the stars in the way that ordinary Astronomy does. For it will be shown how the stars are primarily a moral realm and have nothing whatever to do with the lifeless laws pertaining on Earth. In experiencing the stars man will learn how they are connected with his own existence and the existence of all other human beings — from the moral aspect.

If the ancient star wisdom gave man a nature knowledge, and with it a knowledge of how to order his social life, the new star wisdom will give man self-knowledge.

Every night in sleep man enters the realm of the planetary weavings when, with his Ego and astral body, he leaves his etheric and physical bodies lying on the bed. At the same time he lives in the radiations from the metals of the Earth. All this activity remains in the sub-conscious. By awakening Imagination, however, he will perceive with his astral body the various metals of the Earth. And by awakening Inspiration, he will perceive the movements of the planets and fixed stars. To quote Rudolf Steiner: "Knowledge of the human heart arises when we understand on the one side the nature of the radiations which stream upwards from the gold-substance in the Earth and are perceived by the astral body in the region of the heart, and on the other side, when we understand how the forces of will come to meet the radiations from the Sun pouring in from above. In other words, when we can succeed in uniting the radiations pouring downwards from the Sun at the zenith with the forces emanating from the gold in the Earth, in such a way that Imagination is kindled by the gold in the Earth and Inspiration by the forces of the Sun—then we understand the human heart. And knowledge of the other organs too arises in the same way."[1]

Such a self-knowledge will transform man's relation to man and to the world. The cosmos will no longer be regarded simply as lifeless space, but as permeated with the living spirit.

In the ancient Druid Mysteries, before they became decadent, the priests were specially trained to perceive the psychic elements in the light of the sun. Over graves they erected their circles of stones in such a way that the physical light was held up. But their vision had been schooled to perceive the *invisible* sunlight, or rather the spiritual rays of the sun, and according to the season of the year they could discern the qualitative changes—for example, yellow in July and bluish in December. By means of their special darkrooms, the Druid priests could follow the whole cycle of the seasons in the psycho-spiritual activity of the sun's radiance. The language of the heavens was then deciphered and applied to the external practicalities of life.

Similarly, in the Mithras cult, the disciple was taught to perceive the course of the seasons by means of a heart-science, rather than a head-science. By sensing the delicate processes that took place in his inner organism, the whole course of outer nature was revealed. And with this was connected the sun's annual passage through the zodiac.

We must again awaken a feeling for the changing seasons, for the Earth is differently related to the cosmos in the Spring from what it is in the Autumn, and since man is so intimately linked to the Earth and the cosmos, his mood must alter too. "Cosmic experience", said Rudolf Steiner, "leads us out to participation in the cosmos; and only by experiencing the cosmos in this way will we once more achieve a spiritualised instinct for the meaning of the seasons with which our organic life as well as our social life is interwoven."[2]

And what is this cosmic experience? It is the experience man has when he confronts himself in self-knowledge while out of the physical body. He then realizes that he is interwoven with all the mysteries of the zodiac which, instead of being an external display of constellations, is now seen to arise from within in mighty spiritual vision. "And if we seize the favourable moment there may flash before us, out of the inner universe, the secret of Saturn, for example, in its passage across the zodiac. Reading in the cosmos, you see, consists in finding the methods for reading out of the inwardly seen heavenly bodies as they pass through the zodiac. By obtaining an inner view of what we ordinarily observe only from the outside we really learn to know the essence of what pertains to the planets."[3]

It is, then, to such a new star wisdom that we must aspire. External study and calculation are necessary, for we must take all that can be known of both the ancient star lore and modern astronomical knowledge and carry it in our soul, fully aware of their inherent contradiction. This contradiction will only be resolved when the fully-conscious Ego principle learns how to harmonise what comes from the past with what, in the present, is beckoning to the future. New beginnings have already been made by pioneers like Willi Sucher to enliven modern astronomical concepts and so redeem their death-like rigidity. Rudolf Steiner's Spiritual Science is the inspiration behind all his endeavours, and others too have taken up the torch and are shining it on the ancient knowledge to coax forth the spiritual concepts that lie enchanted within it.

All this, however, is but a preparation. The soil is being cultivated and, in due season, the crop will grow. It is the modest hope of all who have undertaken the study of Astrosophy that the crop will prove worthy of its vine, Anthroposophy.

[1]Lecture by Rudolf Steiner at Dornach on January 7, 1923, entitled *"The Widening of Man's Perception"*.

[2]Lecture by Rudolf Steiner in Vienna on September 30, 1923, in lecture cycle entitled *"Anthroposophy and the Human Gemut"*.

[3]*ibid*

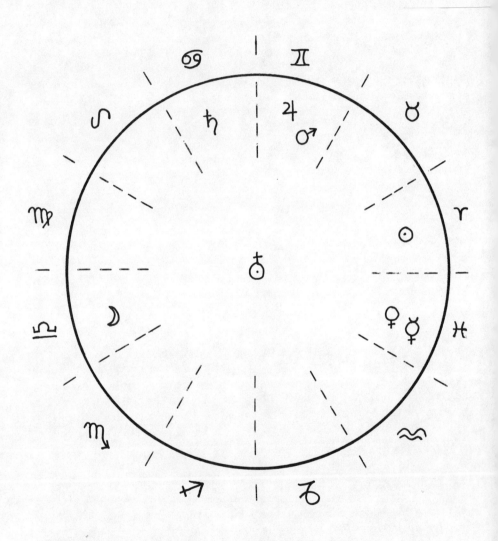

Approximate positions of the planets
at Sunset 3rd April, 33 A.D.

THE STARS AT THE TIME
OF THE MYSTERY OF GOLGOTHA
by Adam Bittleston

This article was published in the 1966 issue of *The Golden Blade* (Shalesbrook, Forest Row, Sussex) and is reprinted here by permission of the Editors.

Only in recent centuries has man learned to look out into the world of space beyond the earth as into an immensity that has nothing to do with his own inner being or his own immediate human concerns. It has now become a deeply-rooted conviction, that space is something in itself neutral and undifferentiated, through which a variety of objects are moving and going through processes which can be described in physical terms, without anything comparable to human purposefulness or human moral judgement. Questions arise about the possible existence of other intelligent beings elsewhere in space; but that the movement of the heavenly bodies themselves concern only the physicist—and not the theologian, for instance—is taken for granted.

In spite of this, continuations of the ancient astrological traditions are widely cultivated, with varying degrees of earnestness. And here the kind of danger which the scientist has tried so hard to keep away from the development of his knowledge—the disturbance of the mind through wishes and hopes and fears—finds endless opportunities. Often an interest in astrology can be maintained in a separate compartment of the mind, without affecting a man's general ideas and beliefs about the universe around him.

When we approach the work of Rudolf Steiner, we encounter a very different spirit. The origins of all phenomena, whether celestial or terrestrial, are sought by him in worlds of spiritual being which he describes as accessible for organs of perception present, though generally dormant, in every man. Through the study of Rudolf Steiner we can understand both the astrological tradition, as having originated in genuine ancient perceptions, and the necessity for an astronomical science which pushed all this aside.

But our relationship to the world of space does not change all at once when we begin to take Rudolf Steiner's statements seriously. Particularly with all that he says about the stars we may notice a remarkable fact: there is not much sense in learning such things in the way we learn things from an ordinary textbook. There are subjects which may be learned at different stages of our lives, without our having to take much account of where we stand in the fulfilment of our individual destiny. But all that Rudolf Steiner has to say needs time; we cannot compel ourselves to assimilate it. An event in our own destiny may be needed, in order to awaken a real understanding in us for something that may have been read years earlier. There may be no evident connection; we may only notice that a detail in some description by Rudolf Steiner has come very much nearer to us. It is indeed easier to see why this should be so when he is concerned with something of which we may have immediate practical experience—for example the education of children or the trials of the human soul—than when he is concerned with the planets and the Zodiac. But as we can observe our destiny leading us externally, taking us perhaps on a journey to another country at a particular stage in our lives, so we can see that men are led differently into the varied realms of understanding. One man may be drawn in his early twenties to seek out eagerly everything he can learn from Rudolf Steiner about the stars. Another may feel clearly that he should leave this particular subject for a much later time in his life. A third may take it up, and accept and value much of it, and yet encounter certain problems which may require thirty years for their solution. For we are concerned with a knowledge which is not colourless or morally neutral; it calls for the activity of all that a man has. And we can come to see that it is possible to find a way between the temptations which beset us only when we try to form a new relationship by drawing upon the inner powers which have been brought to man by Christ through the Mystery of Golgotha. Within us is to be felt the abyss that has opened up between the earthly world and the Divine heavenly reality. And only the power of Christ can sustain the soul in the crossing of this abyss.

Again and again Rudolf Steiner returned to the assertion that the Mystery of Golgotha was not simply an action for the earth, but a cosmic event. It has just begun to strike some men, engaged in the kind of cosmological speculation which considers the possibility of a relationship between man and greater intelligences from other parts of the universe, that such a meeting might have happened at the time of Golgotha. But our conceptions of outer space are in general utterly unhelpful for the comprehension of the Incarnation.

A relationship to space in which man could share with his whole mind and heart and will was sought in the ancient world in the most practical way: by the building of temples. Standing within the temple, or looking towards it from a distance, men felt the holiness of space; up and down, forward and backward, right and left, began to express changes in the aspect of God to man and of man to God. In our time, what we receive from Rudolf Steiner, to begin with only as ideas, can change for us gradually into a diversified sense for the qualities of space, in their relation to our own human form. Our human body is the little temple; Space is the great Temple, the royal Tent.

Within the differentiated space, where every movement has a quality—as of finding or losing, of gaining strength or gaining light—the planets move as in a ritual dance. The more we study the actual movements of the planets, the less they appear like those of a clock, and the more like an awe-inspiring dance, which the onlooker can never wholly grasp. It is possible indeed to calculate backwards and forwards the movements of each of the planets—particularly those which have long been known to man, the major planets up to Saturn. But because the rhythms of the planets are mutually incommensurable, the solar system never repeats itself as a clock so evidently does. Even each single orbit of a planet is unlike every other. These differences are of course to a very considerable degree calculable, on the basis of gravitational theory; but though in this the solar system seems like a great machine, the difference from human machines, which are based on commensurable ratios, should be remembered.

During the last months of his life, Rudolf Steiner wrote about the calculable element in heavenly movements and earthly processes. He described three different relationships which can exist among spiritual beings towards this calculable element, which has come to exist only in the course of cosmic evolution, and which in a future time will cease to be present. There are Luciferic spiritual beings, for whom all calculability is an alien thing. There are Ahrimanic beings, who greedily attach themselves to the calculable, and hate all freedom. The good spiritual beings, with whom man has been connected from his origin, live themselves in freedom, but accept with loving understanding the necessity of the calculable within the universe. At the Mystery of Golgotha, Christ in freedom takes upon Himself the celestial and the earthly necessities.

A path therefore which we can take towards an understanding of the Mystery of Golgotha is through consideration of that moment in the cosmic dance when the Christ enters earthly history. We should not expect this to be an easy path. But we can hope eventually to be led to an insight into the writing of the heavens that is neither egotistical nor impersonally abstract. Always when we are asleep, a kind of echo of the cosmic rhythms is aroused within our souls; we find a right relationship to what stirs within us in the depths of sleep through what we bring from waking life as an understanding of the Mystery of Golgotha.

One element in the constellation of Golgotha is indicated in the Gospels by John the Baptist himself. "Behold the Lamb of God, Who bears the sin of the world." At the festival of Passover the sun then stood, and had stood for many centuries, in the constellation of Aries, the Ram. In the sacrifice of the lamb at Passover, instituted by Moses, the significance of this constellation was reflected. The forces of Aries work from the head through the whole being of man to give him his upright stature. But he should not wear this uprightness proudly; inwardly he is very far from being worthy of it. He can only go forth worthily from the decadence of his inner Egypt if he learns to offer his uprightness to God.

In that Christ becomes Man, the promise of human uprightness is for the first time entirely fulfilled. Christ truly stands, truly walks upright on earth. And He sacrifices Himself, taking upon Himself the burden of all human unworthiness.

When on the evening of Good Friday the sun is setting, the full moon rises in Libra, the Balance. Men have taken the scales as the symbol of justice, even of that human justice which is administered on earth. Before Golgotha, men sat in judgment on the Christ, and condemned Him. But Golgotha is itself the judgment of men, and of the evil which inspired them. The spiritual world would have to condemn man did not Christ now take up man's load of guilt. From Golgotha onwards, the souls will not only enter into the judgment of the moon-sphere; Christ will lead them through judgment towards the spiritual heights.

When the body of Christ Jesus is laid into the earth, there stands high in the southern sky the planet Saturn, in Cancer, the Crab. The forces of Cancer are those which enclose heart and lungs within the fence of the ribs. Living in the immensity of space, we are nevertheless able to have our private world, our inner life of soul. This is liable to seem all too private and self-enclosed. In the ancient Mysteries the pupils learned what this inner being truly is. Within it the effects of long ages of the past reach their completion. A universe dies; another is to come into being. Within the circle of the soul are the seeds of ages to come. All this is expressed in the interpenetrating spirals of the symbol of Cancer.

In the Mystery of Golgotha what had been kept hidden was made manifest. Upon the Cross, in the sight of all, were shown world-ending and world-beginning. The life of the soul depends upon its feeling about this; as is described in the story of the Grail, the wounded soul must feel the sharpest pain when Saturn, who recalls the cosmic past and prepares the cosmic future, stands in Cancer.

West of Saturn, over the Sepulchre, shine Jupiter and Mars in Gemini, the Twins. Through Gemini the form of man receives the symmetry of right and left. From early childhood we feel the wonder of this likeness: and everywhere our thinking begins to delight in the likenesses of things. Socrates, in Plato's account of his death, proves to his pupils that we must have brought the concept of similarity with us from the spiritual world in which we were before birth. Through the concept of likeness we can discern unlikeness as well; each of a kind is also its separate self.

For the Greeks, Gemini were usually Caster and Pollux, one brother mortal, the other immortal. At the death of Castor, Pollux asks for it to be granted that they may continue together; either both in the heavenly heights, or both in Hades.

The mystery which this myth touches is fulfilled at Golgotha. Christ is in truth the immortal Brother determined to share the fate of mortality. The wisdom of Jupiter and the courage of Mars are united in this resolve.

But man on earth does not always love when he sees another who bears his likeness. The Romans looked back upon twins of whom one killed the other. And in Genesis we find brothers, capable of being to each other companion and completion, of whom the elder kills the younger. From that time onwards there sound in the depths of every human soul the terrible words, "Am I the guardian of my brother?" Every shade of indifference, of jealousy, and of hatred becomes possible for man.

The circling planets are visible tokens for spheres of spiritual being which contain evil powers as well as the good Hierarchies. From the realm of Mars there come indeed impulses of strength and courage; but the ancient world rightly saw in Mars a cosmic reminder of forces which treaten to destroy all human community, bringing about endless conflicts among men. There is for example the wonderful passage in the Kalevala where it is described that at the first smelting of iron the hornet's sting became intermingled with it, in place of honey.

Without the Deed of Christ, humanity on earth would have fallen more and more into the power of debased Mars forces. This danger still exists; and we see the achievements of human mathematics, which is a gift from Gemini (for all mathematics is based upon the counting of like units) devoted to making the greatest weapons of destruction. But Christ give the development of the earth a new direction; it is to become a Mercury, a realm of healing. The blood and water flowing from the wound of Christ are to free men from an impossible pressure of egotism, to bring into movement again what in man has become hardened, and to bring about new, spiritual enduring relationships among men.

Before sunrise on Easter morning, the planets Mercury and Venus stand south of east as morning stars. Venus is beginning a period as morning star; Mercury is near its greatest western elongation. They are close to one another, and converging, in the constellation Pisces, the Fishes. On Good Friday evening, being morning stars, they had set before the sun. On Easter morning they could have been visible to the women on their way to the Sepulchre; and whether or not they were seen by physical eyes, their relationship to the stars and to the earth was of endless significance. Within the realm of earth, the Christ has overcome death. To walk upon the earth, and to touch the things of earth, can now have for men a new sense. The forces of Pisces give us feet and hands, those members of the body which come most directly and constantly into contact with the things of earth. The cosmic thoughts which work in human destiny, that are too quick and subtle for our hardened brains, are often carried into effect by our hands and feet. For Mercury to shine in Pisces can now mean something much greater than those qualities of skill and agility which the Greeks often connected with Hermes; it can mean that an individual destiny is brought into the service of Christ's healing work. Venus is Pisces need not impel men to grasp and to hold fast for themselves what they love most; it can work in the journeying feet of the Disciples. The two qualities converge; henceforth real healing can never be a mere skill without love, or real love only a desiring without healing purpose.

All this is to be found if we listen attentively to the Gospel narratives which describe the women at the Sepulchre on Easter morning. It is women who are first able to grasp the fact of the Resurrection. Experience and recognition of the Risen Christ come to the men more slowly; for most of the Eleven, only in the evening. St. John's Gospel says that Thomas Didymus did not "see and believe" until eight days later, the following Sunday. But for all who shared in the Easter experience, the meeting with the Risen Christ was the beginning of a period of intensive learning, of the transformation of their whole relationship to the world, continuing up to Pentecost.

About this the four Gospels say very little. Rudolf Steiner sometimes spoke with great solemnity and earnestness about the teachings of the Risen Christ. Through learning something of this, we can understand very much better the words and actions of the Disciples as they are described in Acts, and much else in early Christian history. For during the time between Easter and Whitsun the Disciples learned to know much more completely Who Christ truly is.

In ancient pre-Christian times a knowledge of the Spirit of Christ had also existed. It was cultivated particularly in those sanctuaries which were concerned above all with the mysteries of the Sun. They spoke of the Sun not as a single phenomenon, but as threefold. First came the external sun, felt indeed much more as a living thing than we do today. In its dazzling rays Luciferic powers are at work, awakening man to the external world, but drawing him away from his divine origin. But behind this abundant splendour men could find a second Sun, a realm of spiritual beings, which manifest themselves through the forms and processes of nature, but are also akin to all that makes the human soul consistant and purposeful. Those beings of this inner Sun who are concerned with the form of Man, the ancient Hebrew wisdom called Elohim; Rudolf Steiner spoke of them as Spirits of Form. But we can think of all the beings described by Dionysius the Areopagite as the Second Hierarchy—-Exousiai, Dynamis, Kyriotetes—and by Rudolf Steiner as Spirits of Form, of Movement, and of Wisdom, as working together in the realm of this second Sun. For them the whole solar system is like a single organism.

But the pupils of the Mysteries were told that they had to seek further, for a third Sun; and only here would they find that being Who gives to man his eternal meaning, Who was called by later times the Christ. In different ways what was known in the Mysteries about the third Sun was imparted in ceremonies and legends to the various pre-Christian civilisations. In Greece, Plato could clothe in philosophical forms what had been conveyed by such teaching; he spoke then of the Idea of the Good, of the Light which shines in the world of reality outside the dark cave in which men must dwell between birth and death. A last great expression of such teaching is to be found in the writings of Julian the Apostate.

That Being Who had once been sought in spiritual heights, towards Whom men had once been able to look back through the gate of birth as the great Companion of their sojourn in the sphere of the Sun, lived in the weeks that followed Easter among the Disciples, bearing a human form in which every trace of death and evil had been overcome. They could learn that He had now made the earth His dwelling-place. And they saw how His power could begin to take hold of man's being in general, beginning with the most delicate processes, to become through the ages more and more evident. They felt how He would work for the redemption of human speech.

During the time from Easter to Whitsun the visible sun moved through the rest of Aries, and through Taurus, to the beginning of Gemini. Taurus, the Bull, is the source of the powers which form the human larynx. In early childhood we see generally the achievement of the upright position followed by the development of articulate speech; Rudolf Steiner described these as gifts of the Christ-power working within the child. And he compares the first three years in the life of the child with those Three Years in which Christ lived as man between the Baptism and the Crucifixion. What follows after Easter is like a great interpretation for the Disciples of all that they had shared in, but had not been able to comprehend, during the Three Years. In our time, too, what we find in the Gospels can often be felt as great questions, which would remain unanswerable without the Resurrection. The words of Christ are expressed indeed in human speech; but how are the ears to be formed, which could hear them?

In one of his accounts of the ancient Mysteries, Rudolf Steiner describes how the asking of questions and the finding of answers were there interwoven with the life of the planets. Deep and earnest questions were entrusted at a particular time to the sphere of a particular planet; and then from another planet in due time the answer would return. Questions which concerned the Archangels, the beings who are active in the development of human language on earth, were entrusted to Jupiter; the answers came from Mercury.

Jupiter completes the circuit of the Zodiac in a little under twelve years. He needs therefore about a year for each constellation. During three years he will thus pass through about a quarter of the Zodiac. Mercury is always near the Sun, and passes through his phases in relation to the Sun three times within a year. Within three months he too, as well as the Sun, can pass through as much of the Zodiac as Jupiter in three years. And we find that this happens during the weeks which follow Easter. Mercury follows just that path, along which Jupiter has come before the Mystery of Golgotha—through Aries and Taurus and part of Gemini—up to Whitsun, A.D. 33.

There is, however, a difference in the movements of the outer and the inner planets. The outer planets, Mars, Jupiter and Saturn, during the period when they are long visible in the night sky, make great loops; they are for a time retrograde in the Zodiac, moving in the direction opposite to the annual course of the sun. Jupiter and Saturn do this yearly; Jupiter generally makes one loop in each constellation through which he passes, Saturn two or three. These movements need not be regarded as only apparent; Rudolf Steiner spoke of the real movements of Sun and planets as lemniscates of a kind, of which we see something in the planetary loops. As a result of these movements, Jupiter will often pass three times through the same point in the Zodiac. Thus we find that Jupiter and Saturn had been at the same points in Gemini and Cancer, at which they stood at Golgotha, already in the previous year, at the traditional time of the Transfiguration, August 6. We can understand that at this moment the event of Golgotha was spiritually prepared at that level of being into which the Disciples are enabled to look, when they see Christ Jesus speaking with Elijah and Moses about His "Exodus" (Luke 9:31).

When the inner planets Venus and Mercury move backwards in the Zodiac for the formation of a loop, this is much less conspicuous, as such movements take place for the most part when Venus and Mercury are too near the Sun to be visible. But Venus on Easter Day is still engaged in such a movement.

From Easter to Whitsun, Mercury moves on a direct course. Halfway through the period, he is in superior conjunction with the Sun (that is to say, directly beyond the Sun) and then becomes an evening star. By Whitsun he has reached deep into Gemini, and stands very close to Jupiter.

During the central period between Easter and Whitsun, both Sun and Mercury work from the realm of Taurus. The Risen Christ implants into human speech the regenerating, redeeming power through which all the dangers that threaten it can be overcome. Without the Deed of Golgotha, the work of the Archangels, the spirits of the Mercury sphere, in the development of human speech would have become impossible. Once speech had been the direct expression of Will; later it was shaped by all the rich variety of man's life of Feeling. But even at the time of Golgotha, and much more in our time, it has become the expression of abstract Thought. This is the death of speech. And it is threatened, just as individual souls can be threatened, by powers of the underworld which would use it for their own purposes. We see to-day how speech can be degraded by systematic double insincerities; used by those who do not believe what they say for those who only pretend to believe what they hear. The age-old work of the Archangels can continue rightly only if they find in human souls genuine picture, living Imaginations of the divine Trinity. These come about through an active understanding of the Mystery of Golgotha.

This begins to be expressed to the world when the Disciples "speak with tongues" at Whitsun. Before this happens the Christ has guarded the inner freedom of man by a deed which it is particularly difficult, and particularly important, for us to understand at this time. Forty days after Easter, He is received into the realm of the clouds; the vision of the Disciples can reach him no longer. Only through this separation could that full sense of individual responsibility mature within them out of which they were to proclaim the Gospel. But this did not mean, as can easily be thought, that Christ then left the earth. Rather did He then impress upon the whole aura of the earth His own cosmic majesty. In everything that lives on earth the effects of His Incarnation would henceforth be present. In sacramental actions the Disciples would be able to make this manifest. But for a time He would be seen only seldom.

The freedom which men would feel increasingly within themselves did not necessarily alienate them from Him, or from each other. But only very slowly did it become possible to understand this freedom. Paul described it in flaming words; and in our time Rudolf Steiner's *Philosophy of Spiritual Activity* is really a theory of knowledge and a resulting ethics of freedom written in accordance with the spirit of Paul. But man has not been able to understand how freedom can exist within him although the world is subject to laws—whether these be Divine or natural, at work in human destiny or in the stars.

When Rudolf Steiner spoke of human freedom, he often described it as something unique in the cosmos, something which men would bring as their particular contribution to the evolution of the world. And yet he spoke also, particularly towards the close of his life, of the freedom of the Gods, of the beings of the heavenly Hierarchies.

Man needs first an understanding of his consciousness with itself, to grasp the freedom for which his being is prepared. Then he can go on to seek within him for powers through which he can encounter beings with a quite different consciousness. Rudolf Steiner once described something like a sevenfold branching of the human "I" through which selves develop in us able to meet the beings of the Hierarchies. That in us which can be the Angel's brother will recognise the Angel's freedom.

The rediscovery of a living wisdom of the stars depends on the one hand upon our feeling for the Mystery of Golgotha, on the other upon an increasing awakening towards the mission of Michael, the Archangel who is the great guardian of spiritual freedom in our time. Michael would have men feel what the starry cosmos has been to humanity in the past, and learn in freedom to bring his deeds into harmony with both the heavenly and the earthly present.

Rudolf Steiner stated that the original Good Friday was on April 3rd, AD 33—this is to be found in his *Kalendar 1912 - 13* and in some of his lectures, as a result of spiritual scientific research.

Historical research has sometimes led to the same date, for example in Dr. George Ogg's *The Chronology of the Public Ministry of Jesus* (Cambridge, 1940), and in his article on *The Chronology of the New Testament* in Peake's *Commentary on the Bible*, 1962, where references are given to writers who disagree. The alternative date in AD 30 seems to have been reached as a result of a misunderstanding of Paul's chronological statement.

Dr. Elisabeth Vreede worked out the planetary position for Good Friday and Easter Sunday during Rudolf Steiner's lifetime, and showed her results to him. They are published in her *Anthroposophie und Astronomie*, Chapter 21. Chapter 5 and much else in her book is also very helpful on this subject. The positions given by Dr. Vreede have been compared with those in *Planetary, Lunar and Solar Positions AD2 - AD1649*, by Bryant Tuckerman, Philadelphia 1964, from which have been derived the movements mentioned here other than those given by Dr. Vreede. Rudolf Steiner spoke of the significance of Cancer in his cycle on *St. Matthew's Gospel* (Berne, 1910, lecture 11) and of Saturn in Cancer in his lectures on the Grail (Leipzig, 1913-1914, lecture 6), now available in a new translation under the title of *Christ and the Spiritual World: The Search for the Holy Grail* (Rudolf Steiner Press, 1963).

A fundamental reference by Rudolf Steiner to the relationship between the Christ's work on earth and the heavenly constellations is contained in his book, *The Spiritual Guidance of Mankind*. For the work of Michael in bringing into harmony human freedom and cosmic processes see Rudolf Steiner's Letters to Members, August 1924-March 1925, published in *Anthroposophical Leading Thoughts* (Rudolf Steiner Press). Relevant passages are to be found also in *The Effects of Spiritual Development* and in *Human Questions and Cosmic Answers*.

JOHANNES KEPLER AND THE
PHILOSOPHICAL DEFENCE OF ASTROLOGY
by John Meeks

One of the most frequent objections raised against the practice of astrology even today is its assumed lack of any secure basis in logic and human reason. As if in utter defiance of the scientific spirit of our modern age, a superstitious element, a half-conscious legacy from the "dark" Middle Ages appears to have survived over the centuries to blossom out again in the form of a vast popular literature, promising power, success and happiness, all on the basis of celestial houses and aspects. And what is more: whoever takes the trouble to acquaint himself with the methods most frequently used in modern astrology soon discovers that only few of its proponents would be capable of pointing out the stars of the zodiac in the sky, or describing, say, the course of Venus' movements and visibility as an evening star. The astrologer's vocabulary is largely Latin, his twelve signs no longer correspond to the positions of the visible constellations; his knowledge of planetary positions is derived from tables, not from observation. Where, then, is the basis in experience which we are justified in demanding from all scientific endeavour? Is it irretrievably veiled in a chaos of half-understood traditions, whose very origins are as obscure as they are remote?

The spoken or unspoken conviction which underlies all astrology is that there are definite and objective correspondences between celestial and earthly events, between the courses of the stars and human destiny, between macrocosmos and microcosmos. As a true representative of the Middle Ages, Hildegard von Bingen (1098-1173) gave expression to this conviction in words which reflect the belief of an age: "Man bears within him Heaven and Earth." For the greater part of medieval civilization this was more than an intellectual standpoint, it was a way of life. Homo caelestis, man as a citizen of Heaven and Earth alike, speaks to us through the sculpture, the painting of the Middle Ages: we feel his presence in the upward-striving forms of the Gothic cathedral, in the music and literature of the time. Not until the very foundations of European culture were shaken at the dawn of a new age, did the traditional lore of the stars become the object of serious philosophical debate.

These debates were waged by some of the most significant personalities of the emerging Renaissance, most of whom stood more or less under the influence of Neo-Platonic ideas. Cosimo Medici, who founded the Platonic Academy in Florence in 1438, attempted to secure the place of celestial influences on the scale of an elaborate hierarchy in which not Christian, but Greek deities occupied the highest orders. In his fragmentary "Book of Laws", Zeus is placed as the highest God, representing Pure Being; Poseidon follows as the Idea of all Ideas and father of the remaining gods; to the third order belong the stars and demons, the former being classified into two groups: planets and fixed stars. The planets alone play an active, creative role. The Sun and Moon in particular have an influence on the mortal nature of man, which they helped to create.

In utter contrast to such a system stand the ideas of Pico della Mirandola (1463-1494), one of the most outspoken opponents of astrology. Pico challenges the element of uncertainty which is always present in the interpretation of horoscopes, and finds no basis for astrology's claim to be a science. He is unwilling to recognise any other genuine influences from the luminaries than light and heat. For this reason he finds no justification in the claim that they exert a different or enhanced influence at the times of particular aspects, such as conjunctions. And finally, he raises the ethical objection, that the free, creative spirit of man may tolerate no dependence on the stars.

Pico's objections are, in fact, essentially the same as those which might be made today by a representative of modern science against the possibility of concrete influences of the stars on earthly affairs. And with some justification. For the great majority of modern astrology is degenerate for the very reason that it revives or preserves more or less ancient traditions while bypassing altogether the debates and philosophical arguments which were current half a millennium ago.

It may therefore be of more than passing interest to look in some detail at one of the most serious attempts to counter the arguments of Pico della Mirandola, made a full century and a half later by Johannes Kepler (1571-1630).

Kepler is remembered above all as the discoverer of the three laws governing the motions of the planets around the sun, later used by Newton to derive his theory of gravitation. It may therefore be said that the whole of celestial mechanics rests on foundations laid by Kepler. While this achievement is universally recognised as one of the most significant in the history of scientific thought, the very considerations which led Kepler to his discovery are often disparaged as unworthy of so gifted a thinker. Kepler was deeply influenced by many of the ideas of Neo-Platonism. He was convinced that the whole of Creation was pervaded by cosmic harmonies, that the universe was conceived according to a divine architectural plan, whose secrets would reveal themselves to mathematical investigation. It was, in fact, this very search which led him to the discovery of the laws of planetary motion. Kepler began his quest early in life by looking for a deeper significance in the relative distances of the planets from the Sun. While retaining the conception of the planets moving along spheres, Kepler allowed these to circumscribe the five Platonic solids, thus deriving the approximate relative dimensions of the planetary spheres. Thus, the Saturn sphere circumscribed a cube, which in turn circumscribes the Jupiter sphere. Between Jupiter and Mars is the tetrahedron; between Mars and Earth the dodecahedron; between Earth and Venus the icosahedron, and between Venus and Mercury the octahedron. This ingenious suggestion, published in the *Mysterium Cosmographicum* in the year 1596, gave new significance to the ancient conception of the spheres, which, since the idea of infinite space had been championed by such spirits as Nicolaus Cusanus and Giordano Bruno, seemed little more than an awkward appendage handed over from classical times.

However, a certain imperfection seemed to be inherent in this grandiose architectural plan. The Platonic solids did not exactly fill out the space alloted to them in Kepler's theory. Why should the Creator conceive a plan of sublime perfection, and yet carry it out imperfectly? Did this in fact prove that the relation to the Platonic solids was mere coincidence?

Kepler struggled for many years with this problem. His discovery that the planets move along elliptical orbits, and not circular ones, as Copernicus had assumed, demonstrated once and for all that the solar system could not be imagined on a rigid, unyielding framework. Its proportions, he saw, depended in large part upon the five Platonic solids, but not entirely. In order to gain a deeper understanding of its nature, it would be necessary to pass over from a static consideration of the planets' distances to a dynamic study of their movements. This Kepler did in his monumental work *Harmonice Mundi* (Harmony of the Spheres, 1618). Here, after a thorough consideration of the geometrical solids and their relations to the sizes of the planetary orbits, Kepler ascends to an exposition of the musical and harmonic aspects of their relative movements. A comparison of these movements with the vibrations of plucked strings provides the key to discovering the cosmic harmonies which they embody. Because the planets are sometimes closer to the sun and sometimes further away, their velocities also vary, giving each, as it were, its own musical scale. The ever-changing aspects of the planets thereby reveal themselves as an unending symphony, which nonetheless, as Kepler himself admits, "can be grasped by the intellect alone, not by the ear."

In the fourth part of his work, entitled "Metaphysical, Psychological and Astrological Book", Kepler ventures an answer to the fundamental question: By what agency do the stars affect the terrestrial world? If indeed the cosmic harmonies are perceptible to the intellect alone, then we have to do with a most exceptional state of consciousness. How can the harmonies and discords of planetary movements and aspects possibly affect the lives of such people as have no inkling of mathematics? Although Kepler did not have a high opinion of astrological soothsaying, he nonetheless assumed that the birth horoscope bears a definite relation in the character and destiny of the person to whom it belongs—quite regardless of whether he himself has any notion of the celestial movements or not. Moreover, years of observation had convinced him that weather conditions were also affected by the position of the planets. Was there, then, a fine material or etheric link in the chain of causality, which stretched imperceptibly from the Earth to the Heavens? This was the assumption which seemed implicit in the work of many astrological prophets, "this mostly degraded portion of humanity, childish and fanciful in its thinking." On the other hand, it seemed to Kepler a sign of superficiality to teach that the Sun as a source of life should have only an external influence, like that of a sculptor upon his stone. He was convinced that all living creatures must partake in the life of the Sun, thus approaching Goethe's insight:

Wär nicht das Auge sonnenhaft,
Die Sonne könnt es nie erblicken;
Läg nicht in uns des Gottes eigne Kraft,
Wie könnt uns Göttliches entzücken?
(Zahme Xenien III)

Kepler attributes to the Earth as a whole, and to all the living creatures which populate it, an instinct by means of which geometrical relationships of the various luminaries are translated into concrete effects. The Earth, which he sees as a living organism, is gifted not only with life, but with a soul, the *anima terrae*, in which this instinct resides. "The whole nature of the lower world", says Kepler, "and the nature of every human being in particular, is formed by God in such manner that it does not comprehend the heavenly forces by means of a conscious perception of the light rays, but rather in a way which is still hidden." (Tert. interv. Pt. 59) This hidden or unconscious perception is grounded in the relationship which connects all living creatures to the world of light, mediated as it were by the soul of the Earth: "Because the most eminent quality among living creatures is a geometrical instinct, which, with their formative or soul faculty is related to the light—it follows that regardless of the outward activity in which they are engaged: whether the plant is growing, whether the animal is asleep or awake, whether man is at war or at peace—that all that they do or leave undone receives its particular form and direction as well as its destiny from the rays of light (proceeding from the luminaries) and their geometry or harmony, depending on their relative movements." (Tert. interv. Pt. 73)

This proposal does away with the need to imagine cosmic influences streaming down to the Earth on some invisible medium—the very assumption which Pico della Mirandola had attacked by maintaining that we can detect no other influence than heat and light. In his article *On the New Star in the Foot of the Serpent-Bearer* Kepler contends with another of Pico's objections: "Pico asks why we should believe that Saturn and Jupiter should have greater power when they stand in near proximity, than when they are separated. I shall answer according to my own opinion, not that of the astrologers. The effect which we ascribe to the outermost planets when they are united, and to which they are not impowered when separated, is by no means a matter of the planets themselves (excepting the pure radiation of light and warmth), but belongs to the nature of the sublunar world. If this effect could be attributed to the planets alone, the claim might be raised that their power is enhanced by their union. However, if they do affect the sublunar world, they do not do so in the manner of active agents of nature, which emanate a certain power, because there is something upon which they can act; they move nature in the same way as the objects move the senses: as light moves the eyes, sound the ears, and warmth the feeling. For of all these things none is weakened if ever so many senses are open to perceive them.... I made use of the comparison with light and other sense-objects in order to explain an obscure process. At the conjunction of two planets it is no longer light, but the relation, i.e. the position which we call 'conjunction', which assumes the rôle of object. Moreover, the sublunar sense must be of the same nature as the object which it perceives. But the object belongs to the class of relations, and therefore sublunar nature must also be gifted with the power to perceive relations. To put the matter briefly: The philosophers measure nature with a short foot; for they do not believe that there is a sense capable of perceiving intelligible things, apart from those which man is known to possess. In this frame of mind they undertake the foolish task of doing battle against things which are obvious.

"May no one harbour the suspicion that I am anxiously seeking out all manner of special subtleties and sophistries in order to brew a remedy for the case of the astrologers, which others have long ago given up as hopeless. I haven't all that high an opinion of astrology,[1] and I have never been afraid to consider the astrologers as my enemies. But constant experience (insofar as such can be hoped for in the natural sciences) has taught me how the sublunar forces of nature are affected by the conjunctions and aspects of the planets, and whenever I resisted, I was forced in the end to yield. But perhaps people will not believe me, because no astrologer has ever brought forth such arguments as mine. Am I the only one who teaches the astrologers philosophy? . . . ."

The question whether there are in fact direct influences exercised by the planets which by pass this geometrical sense is one which Kepler chose to leave unanswered. To mystify such influences by relegating them to a region totally inaccessible to the senses and altogether hypothetical, was as distasteful to him as to Pico. What Kepler above all wished to achieve for astrology, was to raise it out of the mystical realm of the unknown and unknowable to the light of objective, scientific reason and observation. Although Kepler does not specifically touch upon the problem of free will, his view seems implicit in the explanation he gives (again in reply to Pico) for the effect of the birth horoscope on the character and biography of the individual. Here too we shall quote at some length.

"The fact (that there are sensitive regions in the zodiac) is true for the horoscope as a whole, and can most clearly be seen in the revolutions and transits. Whenever a planet enters the constellation which was rising at the time of birth, or else that which was occupied by the Sun or the Moon at birth, the individual is stimulated to devote himself with all the greater energy to the work at hand.

"In general, it can be said that an unburdened and happy life is only possible when the rays and the qualities of the planets correspond with one another in a suitable geometrical manner. This, however, can only come about by virtue of the fact that the character of the heavens as a whole is impressed into the generative, nutritive, formative, sensual and animal faculty of the human being. For the body is too coarsely material to register the so subtle character of a thing which is not tangible, but accessible to knowledge alone. That, I believe, is the reason why the character of the heavens at the time of nativity, after being cast, as it were, into the substance of a person, is preserved through all the subsequent changes which the heavens may undergo.

"Whatever happens to the individual human being, we may assume happens by virtue of the same ability, with which the Earth itself is gifted: namely, that the character of the heavens, together with the positions of the great conjunctions impresses itself into sublunar nature, and remains there for a time. A physician could cite the example of memory, by means of which things past are preserved, as though they were ever present. The comparison is one of close similarity—this is a great wonder! The difference lies solely in the fact

71

that the things which are recalled to memory are offered to the phantasy at once from without, through the five senses, and from within, through the activity of the spirit. The images of celestrial things, by contrast, are impressed into the inner nature of man in some manner through a hidden process. And whereas the contents of memory do not move nature, but the power of the spirit, the character of celestial events does not move the power of the spirit, but nature. Moreover, to the character of things seen, heard or thought in the memory, corresponds the character of the heavens at the moment of birth for that other faculty of the soul. On the other hand a further correspondence may be found between the renewed act of thinking or feeling in the process of memory, which occasions us to recall an earlier thought or feeling, and the new movements of the stars and the passage of planets through their original positions at birth in this other mysterious influence.

"But all of this is an extremely difficult matter, in which it is easy to err, and therefore I do not wish to maintain it with certainty, and am most willing to listen to the opinions of the philosophers."

It is of fundamental importance to the question of freedom that the character of the heavens should impress itself into the instinctive nature of man and not into his spiritual nature. Were the latter the case, there could be no question of free will. Spiritual activity would be nothing more than the automatic fulfilment of norms which have their origin in the celestial movements. If, however, as Kepler assumes, only the instinctive nature is affected, this will only modify the activity of the spirit, and not determine it.

At this point it may be well to anticipate an objection. Kepler, it may be said, grants the possibility of a happy and unburdened life through the mediation of fortuitous stellar influnces. Does this very possibility not make a mockery of free will by granting to some as a free gift of the heavens what others cannot attain through a lifetime of labour? In order to answer this objection adequately, we would have to consider in some detail in what freedom actually consists. For the present it may suffice to point out that happiness and a lack of burdens cannot possibly be the goal of a free human being. If these should be given him without his own doing, he may readily and thankfully accept them, but will never make them the object of his striving. There seems no need, therefore, to see an inconsistency here with the possibility of free will.

The openness with which Kepler writes, his readiness to modify his views, are characteristic for his undogmatic nature. And yet it is possible to stand in awe of the exactness and depth of his philosophical insights. The manner in which the birth horoscope is impressed into the instinctive nature of man to accompany him throughout his life belongs to the most important ideas which Kepler developed. It seems of special significance that this faculty should be the same as that with which the earth-globe absorbs celestial influences. Kepler rejects the practise of making horoscopes for particular geographical regions because these are open only to a part of the heavens; the Earth as a whole, by contrast, is made as an image of the spherical universe, and is therefore particularly suited to receiving cosmic influences. That hidden portion of man's nature which participates in this ability should, we would expect, be similarly open to the cosmos.

In *The Spiritual Guidance of Man and of Mankind* (1911) Rudolf Steiner describes the manner in which the configuration of the heavens impresses itself into the brain at the moment of birth. "If it were possible to remove the physical brain of a human being and examine it with clairvoyant power, in order to see how it is fashioned, one would see that certain parts are seated in definite regions and send forth processes; and one would find in this way that the brain of each human being is different. No two human beings have the same brain. But let us imagine that we could photograph this brain with its whole structure, so that we obtained a kind of hemisphere on which all details were visible. In this way we would obtain a different picture for every human being. And if one photographed the brain of a person at the moment of his birth, and then photographed the sky as well, exactly as it stood over the place of birth, this picture would show quite the same thing as the human brain. Just as certain parts are arranged in a definite way in the brain, so too are the stars in the heavens. Man bears within him an image of the heavens, and this image is different for every person, depending upon the place and time of his birth. This is an indication that man is born out of the whole universe." (Chapter III).

It is indeed striking how closely the results of exact spiritual research correspond to the tentative hypothesis which Kepler brought forward with respect to the instinctive nature of man. His rejection of the idea that the birth horoscope could impress itself in the physical body, seems virtually confirmed by Rudolf Steiner's description, which does not seem to be that of a physical imprint, but of one which reveals itself to clairvoyant vision. In both cases man is regarded as a free being who bears within him a predispositon, determined by the condition of the celestial bodies and the heavens as a whole at the time of his birth.

We have considered a number of Kepler's arguments against Pico della Mirandola's attack on the science of astrology. The question may arise why Kepler, who was by no means a friend of astrology, should rise so passionately to its defence when he saw it unjustly derided? The answer is undoubtedly that for Kepler the true science of astrology was something very far removed from the trade of the would-be prophets and horoscope-maker which he so thoroughly detested. For him its essence was inseparable from astronomy. His life-long striving to penetrate the secrets of the cosmos by means of qualitative, contemplative mathematics, led him closer and closer to that lofty region where the two disciplines meet. His discovery, or re-discovery of the music of the spheres provides a path, albeit a difficult one, to the gradual attainment of a conscious sense for the qualities of the planetary movements.

In this respect Kepler may be regarded as a direct forerunner of Goethe. What Goethe in large part achieved for the organic world and for the world of colour, Kepler achieved for astronomy, and attempted, at least, as a tutor in philosophy, for astrology as well. And so it is not surprizing that Goethe should once have spoken the words:

"One must, after all, choose one's saints. . . . I have chosen mine, and above all others Kepler. He has his own niche in my entrance hall, where his bust is always on display."

73

BIBLIOGRAPHY

Hemleben, Johannes: *Johannes Kepler in Selbstzeugnissen und Bilddokumenten.* Rowohlt Bildmonographie, 1971.

Henseling, Robert: *Umstrittenes Weltbild.* Berline, 1939.

Knappich, Wilhelm: *Geschichte der Astrologie.* Frankfurt am Main, 1967.

Steiner, Rudolf: *Die geistige Führung des Menschen und der Menschheit.* Dornach, 1911 Rudolf Steiner Press, Bibl. Nr. 15.

Strauss, H.A. und Strauss-Kloebe, S.: *Die Astrologie des Johannes Keppler.* München und Berlin 1926.

Kepler, Johannes: *Warnung an die Gegner der Astrologie (Tertius Interveniens).* Ed. Fritz Kraft. München, 1971.

Kepler, Johannes: *Die Zusammenkloänge der Welten.* Transl. Otto J. Bryk. Jena, 1918.

---

[1]*i.e.* traditional astrology

THE ZODIAC OF THE CONSTELLATIONS
BY W. SUCHER

The perfection and the increase in visual power of the modern telescope has produced an overwhelming amount of facts and results concerning the world of the Fixed stars. Modern astronomical textbooks and publications in periodicals are strongly preoccupied with the riddles of the Greater Universe beyond our own Solar System. It has been possible to penetrate deeper than ever into the remotest spaces of the cosmos. Stars and whole systems of Giant-universes have been discovered of which man of earlier ages seems to have had no knowledge. In one sense we have thus learned a lot but from another aspect the discoveries have made—in some of the scientists' own opinions—the universe around us infinitely more complex and more mysterious than it was in the world-conceptions of bygone civilisations. Myriads of unimaginably big star-communities, fantastic conditions of velocity, gigantic processes of transmutation and other facts have been perceived through the telescope or deduced from the observations. Many answers to old questions have been found but it seems that every solution has produced a host of new and still more formidable problems in its trail.

One thing has definitely emerged: our own Solar system has become in the eyes of modern astronomical conception an insignificant grain of dust and even less, as far as quantity is concerned, to say nothing about our poor little planet Earth. The danger is, if one thinks the conclusions through to the end, that life in our small and smallest world appears increasingly meaningless within the greater setting. However, is it really a matter of quantity?

With the introduction of homoeopathy by Hahnemann (1755 - 1843) there has at least entered a challenge on the scene which might help us to solve this problem. Homoeopathy maintains and has proved that substances are still active in dilutions and high potentisations in which their presence can no longer be proved by the usual means of chemical investigation. It seems that the dynamic qualities of the substances are freed to the extent that their quantitative mass is reduced. Hahnemann himself was convinced that the continuation of the process of potentisation and trituration develops a spiritual curative agency by which health can be restored. Is it then an impossible idea that our tiny Solar system is a dynamically integral entity in the tremendous choir of Greater Universes just because its mass and expansion in space is so very inconspicuous? Is it not possible that there exist other systems which also exert on the whole a dynamic influence rather than make an impression by sheer quantity and size?

It will be our next task to find the principles of relationship between the Greater Universe and our Solar system. Earlier we have pointed out that, apart from certain deviations, all the planets belonging to our Solar family are moving on one common plane. Now we imagine this plane theoretically going out in all directions into so-called infinite space. There it would ultimately meet a number of Fixed stars which, seen from the center, would be arranged perspectively in a circle. The outer edge of this common plane is composed by the well-known twelve constellations of the Zodiac. The division into twelve groups is very old. The partition of the year into twelve months rests on this foundation. They are determined by the (apparent) journey of the Sun through the twelve constellations in the course of one year.

However, men have not always combined the fixed stars at the edge of the plane of the Ecliptic according to uniform principles. The Chinese and the Tibetans have also Zodiacs of twelve constellations which seem to originate in the very dim past but the groups and their names differ radically from those adopted for the Zodiac of Western humanity. This is understandable because the Fixed stars are also moving though exceedingly slowly. In fact the expression "Fixed star" is misleading. It is well known, for instance, that the seven main stars of the Great Bear, or Plough, were forming some thousands of years ago a pattern totally diferent from that of the present time because they have in the meantime, moved to different places. Thereby they have changed their relative groupings. Likewise have also the Fixed stars of the constellations of the Zodiac changed their positions so much that the forms which they compose nowadays are not the same as those several thousand years ago. Therefore the imaginations which they evoke in humanity differ according to the age in which they are conceived. The important point, however, is that there existed twelve constellations as far back as we can trace the history of cosmology. They evolve in the course of time which is expressed in the external changes. Nevertheless, a knowledge of what they have been and what they conveyed, as well as an intuitive fathoming of what they aimed at—as far as that is possible under prevailing circumstances—can help us to discern their impacts and propositions, as it were, at the present moment. Therefore the necessity might well arise to amplify, even to rectify some of the notions concerning the constellations of the Zodiac, in order to obtain an insight into their *present* stage of evolution. On the one hand, we certainly do not suggest to bend tradition lightheartedly because in a sense it is a sacred heritage which we need. But on the other hand we must also realise that nothing in this universe of ours is built to remain static for eternity.

The Zodiac which is generally known in Western humanity was slowly developed in Asia Minor during the last few millennia B.C. It came via Greece and Rome to present humanity. One can find the essential aspects of it already in Sumerian, Phoenician and Egyptian civilisation. Yet, one does not really know where its birth took place. It might have been in the highlands of Iran because the word "Zodiac" is possibly a distortion of "Zaruana Akarana". He was the great Father-deity of Ancient Persian mythology. The God of Light, Ahura Mazdao—the Sun Aura—was externally represented by the constellations through which the Sun moved during the Spring and Summer part of the year. Ahriman, the Intelligence associated with darkness and earth-gravity was externally represented by the "Winter-Sun" constellations. Zaruana Akarana made himself manifest through the integrated totality of the Zodiac constellations. He is, so to speak, a higher octave of cosmic-spiritual reality, in whom the unavoidable conflict between Light and Darkness in a lower realm is resolved and redeemed.

The twelve groups of the Western Zodiac are the well known —

Aries, or Ram	Libra, or Scales
Taurus, or Bull	Scorpio, or Scorpion
Gemini, or Twins	Sagittarius, or Archer
Cancer, or Crab	Capricorn, or Goatfish
Leo, or Lion	Aquarius, or Waterman
Virgo, or Virgin	Pisces, or Fishes

With these groups were associated magnificent mythological conceptions which have their origin in the great religions and philosophies of the peoples of Asia Minor and Egypt, of Greece and Rome. The orbit of the Nordic civilisations also harboured the most wonderful and illuminating cosmological mythology. These sidereal aspects intended to express in pictorial conceptions the influence of the various constellations. Astronomy was then still closely associated with astrosophy which was a complex of highly intuitive knowledge about the impact of the heavens on earthly affairs, on nature or on the destiny of nations and communitites. The stars were then still considered to be only the external expressions or gestures of the Divine World.

In the rhythms and movements of the celestial bodies the great priest-sages of long bygone civilisations read the will of the deity. Only relatively late had there been developed from the original astrosophy the complex which is known as astrology. With the advent of the individual—and egoistic—personality rose also the suggestion that the latter is subject to the influence of the cosmic world.

It is obvious that much of that magnificent mythological conception of the starry universe has come down to us in distorted and misinterpreted form. Thus it happened that we have a welter of mythological tradition which does not seem, however, to convey the picture of an integrated whole. One might even arrive at the impression that the sky of these sidereal mythologies has been arranged at random. In speaking of these constellations one hears sometimes the expression "Sky-Zoo", implying that the names of them were chosen rather arbitrarily, and that their arrangement was possibly the outcome of caprice and not of wisdom. However, if one enters more deeply into the dynamic and esoteric background of the ancient zodiacal mythology one can discern that it was the result of a very disciplined and logically comprehensive order of inner, or spiritual experiences of intuitive nature. Certainly, also the extra-zodiacal constellations have their proper places in that majestic cosmic edifice of ancient starwisdom. They are like assistants and heralds of the effigies of the Zodiac. Those imaginations and intuitions stood on a foundation which was totally different from the aspirations and even tasks of modern astronomy. But this need not prevent us from realising that they gave ancient man a means by which he could go through an existence on Earth which made sense.

On this basis shall we consider, together with the Zodiac-constellations of Pisces, Aries and Taurus, the whole complex of the effigies of Perseus-Medusa and Andromeda, above the Zodiac and those of Cetus-Whale and Eridanus, the celestial river, below. Although they are figures associated with ancient mythology, they still carry a message for modern man and can well amplify the meaning of the neighbouring Zodiac constellations.

With Taurus and Gemini is associated, in the Northern hemisphere, the Charioteer, or Auriga with the Fixed star Capella, in some mythologies also conceived as the Divine Smith. Below, in the Southern part of the sky, the Greater Dog, with the brilliant Sirius, the Lesser Dog, and foremost, Orion, the Divine Hunter, come to our assistance, in order to form a conception of the Zodiac constellations above them.

There follow in the Zodiac the constellations of Cancer, Leo and Virgo, most important stages of the Great Circle. The Boötes or Bear Driver, with the star Arcturus, his two Hunting Dogs, and the Greater Bear or Plough occupy a large part of the Northern Sky. They form a magnificent addition to Cancer, Leo, and Virgo. Below the Zodiac we find the Hydra, a long stretched constellation, who has her head below Cancer, whereas her body stretches almost as far as the constellation of Libra. On her back stands the Crater, or Cup, and there perches also Corvus, the Raven.

Very helpful interpreters of the constellations of the Libra-Scorpio-Sagittarius complex are the Ophiuchus, who carries the Serpent, and particulary Hercules, high in the Northern hemisphere. He kneels or stands on the Dragon. Above his head is the Serpent which is held by Ophiuchus. On one side is the Northern Crown and the other the Lyre. Below the Zodiac are the Centaur, the Wolf, and Ara, the Celestial Altar.

Capricorn, Aquarius and Pisces are accompanied by the Eagle, with the star Atair, Cygnus, the Swan, and the big constellation of Pegasus, all in the North. Below, in the Southern hemisphere, we find the Southern Sea, with the Southern Fish and other effigies of significance.

With the help of these companions of the Zodiac constellations we shall be able to discern the great ancient Imaginations and Intuitions much better and also find ways and means to translate them into modern concepts, without clouding over the old traditions.

The constellation of Aries, the Ram. We find Aries on medieval starmaps depicted as a ram, resting on the ground and turning his head back towards the Bull and the other constellations which follow him. This seems to intend to express that the Ram is the first of the twelve constellations, or the "Leader of the Host of the Zodiac" and may go back to the time c. 2000-3000 years ago when the Vernal Equinox was actually situated in it. However, it is also correct from a deeper viewpoint.

Apparently Egyptian sidereal mythology often associated Aries with the bird Phoenix. According to the fable it was a most beautiful bird which lived a long time, according to some statements thousands of years. When it felt its end coming it built itself a nest of twigs and set it on fire as its own funeral pyre. Then, out of the ashes rose a new bird. The life time of the Phoenix was possibly a pictorial mythological representation of definite cosmic rhythms. Some say it was the so-called Sothis-Period. Ancient calendars had to struggle with the fact that the year, or apparent orbit of the Sun, takes 365 and a quarter of a day. For this reason has the modern calendar to insert every fourth year a leap-day ($= 4 \times 0.25 : 1$ whole day), otherwise it would get into conflict with the seasons. In certain ancient calendars, however, one let the

78

year circle, as it were, through the seasons. This rectified itself within a cycle of c. 1460 years, or a Sothic period. In this sense would the association of Aries with the Phoenix mean the end and the new beginning of a cycle of time.

In Greek sidereal mythology Aries was associated with Zeus, or Jupiter. Jupiter was the head of the Olympian Gods. They had come to power against the Titans who were led by Zeus' father Cronos. The struggle of the son against the father took a long time and the fortunes of the war swayed several times. On one occasion the Olymians were almost destroyed by the Titans. They had to flee in all directions to save their skin. Zeus-Jupiter went in a ram's disguise to Egypt and stayed there until the tide had changed. In this disguise he was called Zeus — or Jupiter-Ammon.

There is deep wisdom in this myth. The flight to Egypt wants to depict a connecting-up of the young Greek civilisation with the stream of evolution as it had been manifested in Egypt. Zeus was the inaugurator of that culture which, for the first time, turned deliberately towards the world which flows into man through the senses. "Rather be a beggar in the world of the living than be a king in the realm of the shades" was the basic philosophy of the Greeks. The human brain had then reached the present perfection after a long evolution. This fact was depicted in the ram's horns of Zeus-Jupiter-Ammon of the myth. They were an indication of the convolutions of the brain. Out of this newborn brain-senses-thought capacity the Greek civilisation was able to create that wonderful world of the plastic arts and philosophy.

There is a welter of additional mythological associations concerning Aries. They all point to an inaugurative, initialling or sponsoring spiritual Divine element, working in Greek civilisation, but also in other settings. In Norse sideral mythology Aries seems to have been conceived as Gladsheim, the "glad home" of Odin, the head of the Aesir gods, dwelling in Asgard.

As we said earlier, the constellations in the neighbourhood of the Zodiac-effigies are a great help in the interpretation of the latter. Above and below Aries are assembled constellations which are connected with the Perseus-Andromeda-complex. (They concern, as we shall see later, also the Pisces.) Particularly Perseus in the sky turns his gaze across Aries down to the effigy of Cetus, the Whale. Perseus is one of the 12 great Sun-heroes of Greek mythology. He is the son of Jupiter and Danae. Therefore he is half-Divine, one can even say, a messenger of the Gods. He has taken upon himself a great task for the benefit of growing-up humanity. Equipped with the winged sandals of Mercury, according to another version with the winged horse Pegasus, he worked his way through to the home of the Gorgons. They were 3 sisters, one of them being Medusa, who had the terrifying capacity to petrify and transmute everything that looked into her eyes into stone. Perseus, being well aware of this, approached the 3 sisters not frontally. Rather did he turn his back to them and watched them in the polished surface of his shield. Thus he discovered Medusa, being asleep. He quickly raised his sword and cut her head off. Forthwith he flew away, holding the head of the Gorgon in his hand, before the other 2 sisters could realise what had happened. Thus he delivered mankind from this menace. (We shall hear later on that on the way home he comes to the rescue of Andromeda who is in bitter plight.)

The story of the petrifying qualities of Medusa appears to indicate a danger of a hardening which threatened mankind and which the gods wanted to eliminate through the half-Divine messenger Perseus. It seems to be the danger which arose from the newly-conquered capacity of full use of the brain and the senses, which incurred, and still more incurs in our present age the possibility of completely losing any awareness of the Divine-Spiritual world. It is the age-old battle on the plane of thinking, which in the middle-ages raged as the battle between Nominalism and Realism, and which in modern terms is fought as the war betwen materialism and human endeavours to break through anew to the experience of the reality of a Spiritual world.

Thus we can also understand that an older cosmology regarded the Aries as the region of the cosmic archetype of the head and particularly the brain, though not the earthly reproduction of the latter. Furthermore, we can comprehend on this foundation the symbol which is used by tradition for Aries $= \Upsilon$. From a superficial viewpoint it is, of course, the ram's horns. But from a wider perspective it can be conceived as a sign standing for initiative, inauguration, for commencement of a cycle of development or evolution. An element which has come to rest and completion earlier, which is stagnating, is permeated by a new impact from "outside", or, possibly even attacked and invigorated by a novel impulse. A world at rest and satisfied with temporary completion can be fittingly expressed by a circle, the new impulse by a symbol similar to an arrow-head. Then we come to the following cypher: for Aries. From this aspect we can also understand that Mars (= $\circlearrowleft$) was considered in ancient times to be the "ruler" of this sign, as far as our investigations go also of the constellation. Of course, the affinity of Mars to "signs" and constellations must be interpreted with discrimination.

The constellation of Taurus: This group of stars, together with those in its neighbourhood lead us straight into the ancient Egyptian Mystery civilisation. One of the mainstays of Egyptian religion and world conception was the cult of Apis, the bull-god. He was also called Osiris-Apis, or Serapis, because he was conceived as an image of the soul of the god Osiris. At some time the latter was identified with the constellation of Orion, south of Taurus.

The mythology of Osiris is of the most inspiring help for the interpretation of Taurus and the associated groups of stars. Osiris and Seth were brothers and were at first in full harmony with each other. But later Seth became hostile towards his brother. He decided to destroy him. The legend tells in detail how he succeeded indeed. He threw the corpse into the river Nile which carried it out into the sea. Isis, the sister (or wife) of Osiris found it and brought it back to Egypt. Seth got hold of it a second time and cut it up into pieces. These pieces were again collected by Isis and buried in several localities. Later, temples dedicated to Osiris were built in these places.

Who was Osiris? He was, in the Egyptian Image of the universe, the representative of the creative forces of the cosmos. Isis was, as it were, the Earth Mother who received these forces of creativeness into her being. In Seth (or Typhon) we can see the image of an awakening power in the human race towards independence, acquired by gradual emancipation from the

Divine spiritual world. This power in awakening man "destroys the God". A god cannot die actually but he can die in human consciousness. After his death Osiris became the ruler of the underworld and judge of the souls of the dead. Even if he died in man's consciousness, he still works as cosmic forces into the earth. But man does not recognise anymore the cosmic—Divine origin of earth—matter. Therefore the body of Osiris is "buried" in the Earth. It is the stupendous energy which becomes apparent in the "splitting" of the atom, although this carries the "death of Osiris" even one step further into total destruction. Thus the constellation of Taurus appears to have been experienced in bygone ages as a cosmic region which was an expression of the descent of a Divine impulse and its amalgamation with the Earth being or even Earth substance. The Divine impulse which bestows a new beginning on inert existence we saw in the manifestations of Aries. In Taurus this has now descended one step further and is active as an organising principle in matter. This is also expressed in a Greek myth concerning Taurus. Zeus, whose task it was to inaugurate Greek culture and thereby give a lead to the unfolding of European civilisation, saw once from his heights, so the legend says, Europa, the beautiful daughter of King Agenor of Phoenicia. He decided to take her to his realm. To achieve this he assumed the shape of a snow-white bull and mingled with the herds of Agenor. Europa approached to caress the animal. Finally she sat on its back, whereupon the bull raced with tremendous speed down to the beach, plunged into the sea and took Europa swiftly across to the island of Crete. Thus was Zeus associated in Greek mythology with Taurus, the bull, as before we saw him as Zeus-Ammon in the form of the Aries-Ram fleeing to Egypt.

The Taurus principle of creating and organising the physical realm is very vividly expressed in the story of the constellation Auriga, with the Fixed star Capella, which is situated above the Taurus. The effigy is presented on ancient star-maps as a charioteer. According to some Greek sources he seems to have been regarded as Hephaestos, the Divine Smith of Greek mythology, or one of his sons. Egyptian legends give us more tangible information. It is well known that the Egyptian sanctuaries were orientated—at the time when they were built—to definite Fixed stars. The long axes of these temples which led through gates, inner courtyards and temple chambers into increasing darkness acted like observation tubes. Certain stars rising on the axes or passing over them could thus be observed in the innermost sanctuaries even in bright daylight. One has found that such an edifice at Karnak which was dedicated to the great Egyptian Ptah was probably oriented towards the Fixed star Capella in Auriga. Another temple of Ptah at Memphis was also oriented to the latter already as early as c. 5000 B.C.

Ptah was the Divine artificer who was identified by the Greeks with Hephaestos (whom we have already mentioned) and by the Romans with Vulcan, the Divine Smith, living and working in his forge in the depth of the Earth. (See Proctor: "Legends of the Stars"). According to the legend, he has forged the vault of the heavens and also the golden Scarabaeus, the winged Sun Beetle. The chief priest of his sanctuary at Memphis called himself "director of the artists." Ptah himself was regarded as the father of the gods and he is called in one text: "Lord of Thebes, the great God of the First Beginning." He was venerated as the creator of the Gods, the origin of everything that entered into (physical) appearance, the creator of the heavens, the founder of the Earth, Lord of Life. (Uehli, "Kultur und Kunst Aegyptens.")

With this background we can also understand the symbol which tradition bestowed on us. It can, of course, easily be interpreted as the head of a bull = the animal which, in a sense, is like an expression of the heaviness and yet of the astral volition, as it were, of earth existence. However, it seems to us that there is more: the inert lower existence, expressed by a circle (see Aries), is permeated gradually by cosmic being or a cosmic order indicated by the upper circle.

The Mysteries of "Spirit in Matter" are connected with Taurus-Bull. In the ancient myths we hear the story of the submergence of cosmic-spiritual essence in the material world. A future humanity—which is possibly not very far away from our age—will have to evolve a new "mythology" concerning this constellation if it decides to stand in spiritual freedom and spiritual-moral activity before Taurus. It will have to evolve—of course, on a scientific foundation—a real science of matter and the spirit-essence contained in it. Atomic physics alone can obviously not do it. It rather seems to lead to total destruction if it is not countered by a realistic insight into the elements which man meets in this field. The stages of the development of atomic science were strongly accompanied by planetary configurations in the constellation of Taurus, which is rather illuminating.

Taurus-Bull was in ancient cosmology the archetypal region from which the larynx and the whole organism devoted to production and perception of sound and speech are created. This connection of the Taurus with the cosmic origin of the word is clearly expressed in the description of the capacities of Ptah. Everything that exists originated in him as thought, and his thought—like all his plans and ideas for building and artistic creation—needed only to be expressed in words in order to become "real" objects. Thus is Ptah the Creative Word, some kind of pre-Christian conception of the creative Logos. (See J. H. Breasted, "History of Egypt".) This, too can give us an idea of the hidden potential in Taurus which man will be called upon to evolve one day as a spiritually free being.

The constellation of Gemini: The perspective of Divine creation through the sacrifice of the Divinity which we meet in Taurus is taken one step further in Gemini. There the created world enters a kind of rebellion against its origin. Thus a contradiction comes into being which manifests as world-polarity, for instance, Light and Darkness, Day and Night, Heaven and Earth, etc. Even such a polarity as is displayed in positive and negative electricity is connected with this constellation.

In Greek mythology Gemini, the Twins, are associated with the story of Castor and Pollux whose names are actually borne by the two main stars in that constellation. They were twin brothers, but Castor was a mortal being whereas Pollux was immortal. Once they attended a wedding feast which ended, however, in a fight among the guests. Castor was killed but Pollux survived because he was immortal. He was deeply grieved over the separation from his brother and implored Zeus to restore him to life so he could again live together with him. Zeus was so moved by this example of brotherly love that he consented to Castor's restoration to life, under the condition that both stayed together alternatively half the time in the underworld and half in the light of day.

Another story which expresses an element of contrast even stronger is the Norse myth of Balder. Balder's home was Breidablik which corresponds to Gemini. He was called the Beautiful and his hair shone like sunshine. He was full of wisdom, exceedingly mild and eloquent. Once there was great consternation in the realm of Asgard, the dwelling of the gods. Balder had dreamed that his life was in dire peril. Odin, the All-Father consulted a Vala, a prophetess, and she confirmed the forebodings of Balder. Then the gods sent forth messengers to take oaths from all living creatures, from metals and stones, not to hurt Balder. All things promised but the Mistletoe was forgotten because it was in any case considered to be part of a tree.

There was great feasting in the halls of the gods after the messengers had returned. They threw all kinds of things at Balder because they knew that nothing would hurt him. Hodur, Balder's blind brother, stood aside. He could not see what was going on. In that moment Loki, the Evil One, saw his opportunity to take revenge for earlier mistreatment by the gods. He crept up to Hodur and offered to help him to take part in the great sport which was going on. He pressed a bow and an arrow, made of mistletoe into his hand and guided him to shoot at Balder. The arrow pierced Balder's body and he fell dead.

In this story the Opponent against the god of light—in a sense an equivalent figure in Norse mythology to Seth in Egypt—uses the handicap of blindness to realise his evil schemes. The blindness of Hodur can be interpreted as an expression of the beginning estrangement of the created world from its Divine origin. This fact of the moving apart of the worlds of Creation and of the Creators was strongly experienced in ancient Persion civilisation which was inaugurated by the great Zarathustra. Originally the universe was united in the Father Deity Zaruana Akarana whose external manifestation was the Zodiac. (As we suggested earlier, the word Zodiac might be a corruption of his name.) But then a division occurred. Ahriman became lord of Darkness and he dwelled in the interior of the Earth. In the heights of the cosmos dwelled the forces of Light under the leadership of Ahura Mazdao, the Aura of the Sun. And man was called upon to bring light into darkness by tilling the soil. Organised agriculture had its foundation in this mighty cosmic Imagination.

This mythology upon which a whole civilisation had been built is clearly associated with the constellation of Gemini. The Vernal Point, i.e. the crossing point between the equator of the Earth and the ecliptic, projected into the heavens or, in other words, the locality in the Fixed star Zodiac in which the Sun apears to stand at the commencement of Spring was then in the

direction of Gemini. Experience demonstrates that these everchanging association of the Spring Sun with the Zodiac constellations exercises a decisive
impact on the march of civilisations.

There was, however, also consolation in the great conflict which is indicated
in Gemini. Below the latter is Canis Major, the Greater Dog, with the well
known Fixed star Sirius. In Egyptian mythology we find Isis, the sister and
wife of Osiris, identified with this star. She was the great Mother deity who
remained after the death of Osiris with the Earth. Even as the spiritual
darkness spread on our planet, caused by the growing estrangement from the
Divine world, Isis still preserved the spark of Divine wisdom in humanity
through the cultivation of the Mysteries. She nursed and brought up Osiris's
son Horus who became the avenger of his father's death by the hand of Seth.
He destroyed him in mighty battles.

For the Egyptians this star Sirius was the guarantor that even in the spirit-
estranged chaos of the Earth was ever present cosmic order and relief.
Whenever Sirius rose in the course of the year before the Sun they knew that
the river Nile would begin to rise and bring life-giving flood to their parched
fields. Sirius, which was also called Sothis, was also used to keep the calendar
of the Egyptians in harmony with the heavenly rhythms caused by the fact
that the return of the Sun to its original position, or the "year", needs 365¼
days, their nominal year moved ahead of the seasonal year by a quarter of a
day annually. (Our modern Gregorian Calendar effects the correction by the
institution of the leap day.) After 1460 years it had gained a complete year,
and nominal and seasonal year corresponded again. This was called a Sothis
Period.

As all things and beings in the universe develop and thereby change their
nature, so do also the constellations. Already the great Zarathustra perceived
that the "Twin" in the heights of heaven, Ahura Mazdao, moved down
towards the Earth. In fact there exists in ancient Persian literature a prophecy
which seems to point to the Incarnation of Christ. In other words, the ancient
Persian saw in Ahura Mazdao the Cosmic Being of Christ. He left his lofty
abode, the Sun, in order to perform on Earth the Great Deed of Redemption.
Then, Lucifer took over the Sun which until then he had shared with Ahura
Mazdao. Thus, the constellation of Gemini-Twins came to signify a most
dramatic Triad: Lucifer in the Heights, Ahriman in the dark depths of the
Earth, and Ahura-Mazdao-Christ between them, keeping them in their bounds,
even redeeming them. This became then an earth-historic reality in the
Temptation-scene which is described in the Gospels, following onto the
Baptism of Christ Jesus.

In ancient cosmology Gemini-Twins was associated with the polarities in
the human body, as for instance, right and left side of the body, right and left
arms, and also the head-limb polarity. This was still the aspect of the unequal,
assymetric Twins which nevertheless are inseparably united. Thus
can we understand the symbol used for this constellation, a "higher"
and a "lower" world, joined together by a "backbone" or spinal cord.

The constellation of Cancer: Although this is relatively a small constellation with few conspicuous stars, it seems to have been regarded in ancient cosmology as important. In Greece it was considered to be the Gate of Incarnation of Man, whereas the opposite constellation of Capricorn was the Gate to the Gods, after death. This perspective appears to be a logical continuation of the spiritual implications concerning Gemini, the Twins. There we encountered the great estrangement of Heaven and Earth which manifests in countless spheres of human existence. Here, in Cancer, the Crab, the two worlds have now come completely apart which is also expressed in the symbol which we use for this constellation: ♋ . The two spirals move away from each other and leave a gap or abyss between them. In the symbol for Gemini, the Twins, the two worlds are still connected with each other.

According to the perspective of this constellation, man, who has descended from a world of Divine-Spiritual Being, enters through the Gate of birth into an earthly existence in which he has at first no recollection of his prenatal experiences. He is deeply involved in building himself an earthly "house" in which he can fulfill his tasks. Therefore Cancer is associated in astrology with the "house", meaning everything that facilitates his incarnation, parents, home, environment, etc. This was also expressed in the association of Cancer with the archetype of the chest of the human physical body. It is the "house" of the heart and of breathing.

However, man enters the physical world through incarnation, following a definite aim. This is expressed in another myth of Greek origin, although its meaning is difficult to discern. Cancer was connected with Bacchus or Bacchos, the god of wine. The introduction of wine to human consumption was intended in ancient times to help the awakening of the human Ego. In the impact of alcohol on the blood was called forth as a re-action the awareness of Self. This then was the meaning of temporary severance of man from the Divine world by his incarnation. Of course, modern man must seek the realisation of his Self with different means. The old methods and·practises provoke in a modern humanity intolerable obstruction of the development of egohood. This is also indicated in Cancer. About this change we shall speak later.

The separation of Earth-man from the spiritual world was expressed in Norse mythology by mighty imaginations which were also connected with *Cancer.* This is the story of the great Guardian Heimdal and the Bifrost Bridge. Once upon a time there existed a bridge which was built of air and water and protected by flaming fire on its edges. Bif-rost means "rainbow". It led from Midgard, the dwellings of the human race, to Asgard, the abode of the Aesir, the gods. Heimdal, son of the waves, was its guardian. He dwelled in Himinbjorg, "the ward of heaven" or the highest point of the bridge.

Then the Twilight of the Gods occurred; the great battle of Ragnarok was fought, when all the sinister enemies of the gods rushed up in open rebellion against Asgard. The fire giants, the Muspel, stormed over the bridge to invade the dwellings of the gods, and the bridge was burned down. Heimdal himself, who destroyed the evil Loki, was killed by the latter in turn. He, like most of the Aesir, died at the hands of his enemies.

Thus there was no bridge anymore between the human world and the realm of the gods or the spiritual world. After a certain moment in history man was unable to reach out to the reality of that spiritual world. This is what the story wants to tell us. And the connection with the dynamics of the constellation of Cancer, as it is expressed in the symbol we use, is obvious. There still existed, however, an awareness of these higher worlds which had withdrawn from the reach of man and which is expressed in the upper of the two spirals of the symbol. This can be seen in the connection of Cancer with the Scarabaeus in Egyptian mythology.

The scarab is a beetle which makes perfectly rounded pellets of dung in order to deposit its eggs in it. The unceasing labour of this insect appears to have become for the Egyptians a symbol of the ever-recurring victory of life over the forces of death and decay in the universe. Stone-Images of the scarab were laid on the mummies to make sure that the souls of the dead could advance to new life. The little pellets which the beetles made were conceived as symbols of the cosmic forces which cause the Sun to rise every morning anew.

Thus is the constellation of Cancer also connected with the life-renewing cosmic powers and beings which manifest themselves, for instance, through the workings of the Sun in the universe. This was not just a kind of lyrical beautification of what the Egyptians saw in the sky. They had still the capacity to experience hidden or spiritual realities in the heavens. Along such lines it must also appear plausible when we hear that the leading Spirit of the Universe entered material Earth existence. This happened in the Incarnation of Christ.

Even as humanity acknowledges the historicity of the Christ Events, it is nevertheless divided in opinion concerning the dates. However, we see good reasons for joining those, among them foremost Rudolf Steiner, who advance the idea that Golgotha took place on April 3, 33 A.D. In that moment Saturn had moved to the Eastern edge of the constellation of Cancer. Mars had also moved into this group of stars, and Jupiter was to follow at Whitsun of the same year. Thus we would have found Saturn in Cancer during the major part of the "three years" of Christ's ministry. On the other hand we are aware of the fact that in Christ there appeared on Earth, in a human body, the mighty spirit of the Sun, who had hitherto guided evolution from that lofty abode and whom Zarathustra had perceived and called Ahura Mazdao. Humanity had lost before the Advent of Christ contact and access to the spiritual world. Christ came as the Redeemer and Builder of a new bridge, in the place of the old Bifrost Bridge which had perished according to the story of the Twilight of the Gods. Thus the history of the heavens became Earth history, and the visible configurations in the sky appear as the reflection—and confirmation—of spiritual facts and realities.

The constellation of Leo, the Lion: In contrast to Cancer the Leo group is a very conspicuous constellation, which figured as a lion in all ancient civilisations of the Near East and the Mediterranean space. It was associated in ancient cosmology with the heart and the totality of the circulation of the human body. This was expressed by the symbol which is used: , a gesture starting from a center and moving in a majestic sweep towards the periphery. Thus the periphery was conceived to be intimately conected with the center, and vice versa. The rhythms of the great cosmos reflected themselves in the rhythms of earth-events and -creatures. This was a certain consolation for a humanity which had to live with the perspective of the "broken" bridge of Cancer, as described in Norse mythology. The life of the cosmos was still pulsating through earth-existence. It was realised by actual experience that, for instance, a cycle of time such as that of day and night on the Earth corresponded to or reflected one cycle of a year in the cosmos.

Thus we can understand what the Prophet Ezekiel means (chapter IV, 6) concerning the prophecy about the fate of the Hebrew people and Jerusalem. "I (Jehovah) have appointed thee each day for a year." Likewise were also the movements of the planets through one degree of the arc of their orbits conceived as being reflected or represented in one year of the Earth. This was born out of the ancient clairvoyant perception of the relationship between cosmos and man. There is still a certain validity in this. We shall come back to it later.

In Greek mythology Leo was associated with one of the twelve labours of Heracles, the destruction of the Nemean Lion. This animal had jumped down from the Moon and was destroying beasts and men of a huge part of the Earth. What made it worse was that it was invulnerable against any weapon in human hands. Heracles simply crushed the animal in his mighty embrace and thus strangled him. Then he stripped off the skin and clad himself in it. This is how he is usually depicted: clad with the lion's skin and carrying a mighty club.

This myth wants to tell us more than meets the eye. The lion came down from the heavens, it is a cosmic power. We can even think that it had a connection with the constellation of Leo. Heracles overpowers it. He masters these forces by using the strength of his own ego-capacity. This is the meaning of using the lion's skin as a cloak. He has become a "lion" (of cosmic-human power) himself. This is also the meaning of the lion in coat-of-arms of royal personages, etc.

The suggestion of the Heracles-myth of the Nemean lion would then be that a heroic human being can still reach out to cosmic-spiritual power and sustenance, even if the bridge of direct access — see Cancer — is destroyed. To be heroic means in this setting to be in full control of self or to have acquired this control by occult training, in other words, to have attained initiation. This is further amplified by the characteristics of the main Fixed star in Leo, Regulus, according to ancient conceptions. Already very early we find proof that it was considered to rule all the affairs of heaven as an absolute monarch. It kept the other stars in order. In Babylon it was Sharru, the King, in India Maglia, the Mighty, in Persia Miyan, the Center. There is the suggestion that the name Regulus is connected with the concept of regal power.

In the association with regal splendour and ritual, still prevailing in certain coronation ceremonies, etc., we see a definite Leo-manifestation of ancient order. All ritual and ceremony, particularly in connection with the institution of royalty, was originally meant to be representative of cosmic-spiritual power on Earth. Hierarchical order of royal courts, even if it still appears in connection with religious institutions, was supposed to evoke in the human being mighty imaginations of the Divine Hierarchies in the heavens. Thus was regal power originally meant to establish cosmic order in human society and thereby maintain its integration. Also the Round Table of King Arthur is an Imagination of the transplantation of cosmic order into earth conditions. The famous round table at Winchester in England is a table-top of 18 ft. in diameter, divided into 25 sectors, one for the King and 24 for the Knights belonging to the order of the Round Table. It is obvious that the 24 seats were representative of the 12 constellations of the Zodiac (= twice twelve). In fact, a myth of King Arthur tells that once he ascended to the Seven Kings of the Septentriones (the stars of the Greater Bear), he was taught by them the secrets of cosmic order with the commission to establish the same order also on the Earth.

We said earlier that the constellations grow and evolve in the course of time. The great turning point in their evolution, similar to the Earth and to humanity, was the Mystery of Golgotha. From then on it appears to become increasingly difficult to connect, for instance, the ancient meaning and interpretations with the constellations of the Zodiac. Leo is no exception. Their gradual transformation, which must be contemplated and established with extreme esoteric tact, will come chiefly through matured human spiritual-moral Inspiration and Intuition.

When we discussed the constellation of Cancer we said the main part of the Three Years' ministry of Christ was accompanied by Saturn moving through this constellation. Immediately after Golgotha it entered Leo. By the time of Whitsun it was already there and it stayed in it for about 2½ years. This was the time Saul-Paul persecuted the young community of Christians until the mighty experience of his conversion, which is described in chapter 9 of the Acts of the Apostles. After that he became the great apostle of Christianity in the Western world.

The story of Paul is like a new prototype of the spiritual potential of Leo. At the gates of Damascus he experienced the Divine cosmic Being, the head of the hierarchies of the Sun and thereby of the whole universe, Who had entered the physical world through the body of Jesus. He recognised in Him the One who will step more and more, as the representative of all the spiritual Hierarchies in the place of the ancient manifestations of Cosmic Power as it was, for instance, implied in Leo. Through the direct experience of that renewed cosmic power in himself ("Not I, but Christ in me") he had the strength to bring the message and the conviction to his contemporaries and to posterity, on his journeys through the Mediterranean area. Thereby he gave the ancient symbol of Leo—probably not at all by doing it consciously and deliberately—a new meaning. From the strengthened center of his own being he moved towards the periphery.

The Constellation of Virgo. This configuration of stars is represented on most ancient star-maps as a winged, angelic figure. In the famous Zodiac of

Denderah in Egypt it appears as Isis or Hathor, holding or receiving her infant-son Horus into her arms. In Greece she was associated with Demeter-Ceres and Persephone. In the right hand she holds the Fixed star Vindemiatrix, which means grape-gatherer, and in her left hand she carries the star Spica, a sheaf of wheat.

Below the constellation is the long-stretched effigy of the Hydra the Serpent. Its head is below Cancer and from there it reaches as far as Libra, the Scales. Upon its back stands the Crater, or Cup, and the Corvus-Raven.

Above is the constellation of Bootes with the star Arcturus. It was often regarded as the Bear Driver because it seems to chase the Great Bear in the Northern sky. But he has also been represented as a Herdsman or Ploughman. This would coincide with the fact that in some parts of the world the Great Bear was conceived as the Plough. This aspect is of great importance. We shall presently discuss it.

We add to this background another important fact: During the ancient Persian civilisation, which was inaugurated by the great Zarathustra, the Summer Solstice (= highest positon of the Sun during the year) took place in the constellation of Virgo. The vernal Equinox then still showed the Sun in the constellation of Gemini.

It is not easy to integrate the welter of mythological association of Virgo and the constellations in its neighbourhood into a congenial and comprehensible whole. They convey the appearance of an agricultural community but this is only the surface. The deeper concerns are not of a "commercial" nature, as it were, but a matter of transformation, even of transubstantiation. This is already expressed in the connection of Virgo with the Summer Solstice of Ancient Persian civilisation. The Summer Solstice was in bygone ages experienced as a great turning point. From the moment of Winter Solstice the Sun was rising ever higher in the space above the horizon. The ever more ascending disk of the Sun seemed to support, enhance and accelerate the life of the Earth and its living creatures. Then, from Midsummer onwards, when the Sun fell back in space, day by day, the life processes on the Earth appeared reversed. Man himself had to rely on his own capacities. He felt he had to awaken and develop his own consciousness particularly towards Michaelmas. Of course, these rhythms still work nowadays into man's life but they are obscured to a great extent by the artificiality of modern urban conditions.

In ancient Persian times this turning point in the year was ruled, as it were, by the dynamics of Virgo. Earlier we have pointed out that this civilisation was inspired and organised by the Zarathustrian world-conception of the polarity of Ahura Mazdao, the Great Sun Aura of the light-filled cosmos and the dark forces of Ahriman dwelling in the interior of the Earth. The ethical implication resulting from it was to overcome the darkness by letting the light stream into it. This could be done by tilling the soil, and thus organised agriculture came into being. But it has also the deeper meaning that each single plant which man cultivated was a shaft of that cosmic light streaming down to Earth from Ahura Mazdao. Thus, the ancient Persians experienced agriculture and all that was connected with it as a means of transforming the

Earth.

This is even more strongly borne out in the myth of Horus. We mentioned already that in this portion of the Zodiac of Denderah appears the effigy of Isis receiving Horus into her arms. Horus is the son of Osiris, who was "killed" by his brother Set, or Seth (Typhon). The latter was identified in the heavens with the constellation of the Hydra, below the Virgo. After Horus was grown up he fought against Seth-Typhon. In mighty battles he defeated and destroyed the latter. But several times Set rose again, always in new disguise. Finally he transformed himself into a terrible serpent (= the Hydra) but now he met his definite destruction by the hand of Horus. In the course of these battles Horus, who was then called Hor - hut (= Horus of the city of him who spreads his wings), received the symbol oỉ a winged Sun-disc, which was affixed to all temples as a sign of the overcoming of the Evil in the world.

The story of Ceres-Demeter and her daughter Persephone describes a similar conflict which was, however, resolved in different ways. Persephone, or Proserpina, played once with her friends, the nymphs, in a meadow. Suddenly Pluto, the sinister lord of the underworld appeared and took her away by force to his dark underground abode. Long Ceres (=Virgo) searched for her child until she learned from a river god where she was retained. But Ceres also realised that Pluto would never let Persephone go. In her grief she neglected the task to permeate the Earth with the streams of cosmic life. Nothing grew anymore on the planet, and famine threatened the dwellers of the Earth. Zeus had to step in, and he decreed that Persephone should return from her dreadful abode to the upper world. But, alas, she had already eaten of the food of the underworld. Thereupon she was permitted to return only half a time, some say only during the six light months of the year, and then return again to the sinister palace of Pluto for the dark season. Demeter-Ceres instituted the Eleusinia, festivals held at Eleusis in honor of her daughter and herself, to commemorate her long search for Persephone.

A helpful contribution to the comprehension of the dynamics of Virgo is the mythology of Bootes and neighbouring constellations. Bootes meant "Ox-driver", not bear-driver, as it is very often interpreted. According· to Greek mythology he was the son of Demeter. After all his possessions had been stolen by his brother, he was forced to support himself by cultivating the soil. For this purpose he invented the plough. Thus does he now stand in the heavens, with his two oxen—which according to other versions are his hunting dogs (Canes Venatici)—and the Plough (also known as the Great Bear—Ursa Major). Thus we find here a motive which we met already in connection with the Ahura Mazdao—Ahriman perspective of Ancient Persia: The forces of Evil are overcome by "tilling the soil", by letting the life-giving light of the heavens stream into the darkness, even by turning the evil away from its path of destruction and using it for the good. For in ancient Egyptian mythology Ursa Major belonged to Set-Hydra. It was called the "Thigh of Set" (Lum, "The Stars in Our Heaven").

All this is very well corroborated by Celtic Star Mythology. The Great Bear was there "the Chariot" or "Arthur's Chariot." It was and still is also called "the Plough." King Arthur was definitely associated with the Great Bear or

"Plough". The name "Arthur", like that of his Gaelic equivalent, "Airem", means "Ploughman". (See Charles Squire, "Celtic Myth and Legend".) On the other hand, the name "Arthur" might well stem from the Welsh "Arth-Uthyr" which means "Great Bear". Arthur is not the name of a single individuality but is rather a title, or degree of initiation. There seems to exist an ancient legend according to which "Arthur" received a kind of initiation by the seven Kings which are represented by the seven main stars of the Great Bear. (See Fiona Macleod, "The Septentriones".) Arthur and those around him destroyed the ferocious monsters which still populated the Earth as remnants of watery, vapory Altlantean conditions in bygone stages of evolution.

The complexity of the mythology of Virgo is best resolved by studying its archetypal connection with the physiology of the human body. This constellation has been considered since the most ancient times as the cosmic origin of the digestive system, particularly the tract below the diaphragm. There the mysterious transformation of substances takes place which man takes into his organism as food. He certainly needs these processes of breaking down and conversion of the physical material for the maintenance of his own earthly existence. But thereby he performs also at the same time a kind of etherising service with regard to the substances of the Earth. The amount which the human race has eaten and thus transubstantiated in some fashion since it is obliged to do this must be colossal in sheer quantity. In this context the transforming, ever changing dynamics of the constellation Virgo is unmistakenly apparent.

However, all the transformation enacted in the human body and in the world which emanated originally from the spiritual regions beyond Virgo aim at the accomplishment of evolutionary goals. Mythology expresses this by the imagination of the Child which often bears representative characteristics of the soul of man on its journey through the vicissitudes of earthly life, and invariably gets into conflict with the evil in the world which is then overcome. Thus the road into the future is freed from obstructions. The great imagination in chapter XII of the Revelation of St. John presents such a perspective. The "woman clothed with the Sun, and the Moon under her feet and upon her head a crown of twelve stars is an image of what man of the future can become who has fully realised in himself. as a Self, the spiritual potential which is hidden "behind" the region of Virgo. Then will the spiritual fruit or essence of man be born, once material being and limitation will fall away from him. "And she brought forth a man child who was to rule all nations with a rod of iron, and her child was caught up unto God, and to his throne." The dragon with seven heads and ten horns stood before the woman, to devour her child and thus obstruct the road into the future. But he and his host was defeated by the Archangel Michael and his angels.

With all these mythological implications we can now make an attempt to understand the symbol which is used for this constellation. In all the other

symbols which we have encountered so far, we can detect a meaning but this one seems at first impenetrable. However, this is understandable if we realise that we are here facing the deepest Mysteries of existence and life on Earth, the perspective of slow evolution towards a non-material future, the existence of Evil which constantly tries to obstruct the forward road.

In ancient times when the Mysteries—the cognition of the spiritual secrets of Man, Earth and Universe—were still intact, a human being who endeavoured to approach them was obliged to take a long and often tedious road of cognitional and moral preparation. In a general sense one can say that he had to ascend over three stages of inner evolution, or advance through "three gates" of revelation to ultimate initiation. These three gates seem to be indicated in the symbol of Virgo but have been somewhat distorted in the course of tradition.

But what did the neophyte meet once he had entered through the third gate? He met the Serpent. In the case of meeting the material and yet so mysterious reality of Virgo in the human form as the region below the diaphragm, the imagination is quite obvious. The intestinal tract can appear like a big and long serpent. With regard to the Mystery of Life, as Meaning and Aim of existence and evolution, man met the Serpent of Wisdom, but he met also the Serpent of destruction and evil. We need only to think of the Serpent of Paradise. This was Lucifer who can lead man to enthusiasm and exalted wisdom, but also to rebellion against the Godhead and downfall, experienced in human sickness and death. The realisation of Truth through the Mysteries of Life and Cosmic evolution was, and is, the protection of the human being.

The constellation of Libra, the Scales: We said that Virgo can be conceived as a representation of the portal to the Mysteries. It points in two directions. If we follow the constellations backwards from Virgo to Aries we find, so to speak, the reflections of the Mysteries of the Cosmos. These are expressed in mythological pictures of the kind which we described in connection with Aries, Taurus, Gemini, Cancer, mainly the destinies of the deities, as it were. In Leo we find then mainly an enumeration of the requirements which the human being needs to fulfill to go on that journey.

On the other hand, Libra represents the threshold which man has to cross in order to penetrate to the Mysteries of the lower world as it were, that is of the soul of man and of the Mysteries of the Earth, of the elements, etc. In order to enter this world he must practise balance of soul, because in the depth of his own being he meets, apart from his immortal entelechy, also destructive forces. At a certain stage he is confronted with the Mysteries of Death which will lead him to resurrection in everlasting spiritual life. This is the stage of Scorpio, the constellation following Libra, the Scales.

Libra is a relatively small constellation. It does not contain particularly bright stars. This might be the reason why its mythology is not very distinct. At one time, before Julius Caesar, who reintroduced it into the Calendar, it seems to have been ignored altogether, or combined with Virgo. There are suggestions that long before this it was regarded as an Altar, a Lamp, or even an image like the Tower of Babel. This is rather interesting and would, in a sense, confirm what we said earlier. An altar on which an act of religious ceremony is performed is a portal or threshold to an invisible, Divine world. A ritual is a presentation of spiritual facts.

Likewise was the Tower of Babel such a threshold of gigantic measures. We know that these "towers", or Ziggurats, were, in a sense, the equivalents in the valley of Mesopotamia of the Egyptian pyramids. But these towers were a kind of step-pyramidal buildings. Terraces, which, according to their varying colours were dedicated to the planets, led up to the top terrace on which a sanctuary stood. This was a kind of astronomical observatory. From there the priest-sages followed and calculated the movements of the planets which were regarded as gestures of the gods. Thus the "Tower of Babel" was indeed a threshold to the Divine world. The employment of this symbol for Libra would suggest that this constellation was experienced as a "Threshold".

This aspect of Libra was also expressed in Egyptian mythology. There it was represented by a feather against which the souls of the dead were weighed. They were brought by the dog-headed Anubis into the presence of Osiris who sat in the judgement seat. Before him stood the *scales* on which they were weighed in order to find out whether they could preceed to the higher realms of spiritual experience. This might be the background of the symbol which antiquity has bequeathed on us for the Scales:

Above Libra is the head of the Serpens which is carried by Ophiuchus, a mythological complex about which we shall speak later. Still higher is the Corona Borealis. According to the myth this was the crown which was presented by Bacchus to Ariadne, the daughter of Minos, a King of Crete. In his domain was the famous labyrinth which harboured the ferocious Minotaur. Crete was in those days so powerful that it exacted tribute from Athens. Every year the latter city had to send seven youths and seven maidens to Crete to be fed to the Minotaur. Theseus, the son of the King of Athens, was once one of the victims to be sent to the island. However, before he was taken to the labyrinth, King Minos' daughter, Ariadne, fell in love with him. She decided to save him from the terrible fate of being imprisoned in the maze in which the Minotaur was housed. Once the victims were in that subterranean structure, they could not find their way out, and eventually the monster caught up with them. Ariadne gave Theseus a ball of thread and a sword. He was to drop the end of the thread as he entered the labyrinth and unwind the ball as he went along through the passages. Soon he was confronted by the monster which he killed with his hidden sword. And now he was able to find his way out of the subterranean maze by following the thread of Ariadne. On the way back to Athens the triumphant Theseus abandoned Ariadne. According to another version he had to yield her to Bacchus who demanded her as his bride. Bacchus presented her with the crown as a wedding gift which nowadays appears in the Northern sky.

In this myth is represented the deeper, spiritual significance of the Grecian civilisation. The latter was associated with Aries, for the Vernal Point was in that constellation during the Grecian Age. Opposite it was Libra, which was then the Autumnal Equinox. The preceding civilisation of Egypt and Chaldea was guided by the Vernal Point in Taurus, as we said earlier, and the Mino-Taurus of Crete was, so to speak, the image of a terrible remnant of the earlier impact into a later age in which it was not anymore justified. The Minotaur lived in the labyrinth because the Aries-potential of the new capacity of thinking and use of the brain was at first bewildering. Man was in danger of losing his way. He needed the thread of logical thinking, of the right sequence and co-ordination of perception and concept. Greek thinking was different from what we generally call thinking nowadays. From what we have as heritage by such thinkers as Aristotle and Plato we can surmise that they had still in their thoughts a strong and direct awareness of the reality of a spiritual world. In this sense is the Crown of Ariadne, Corona Borealis, an amplification of the nature of Libra being a portal to the world of the Spirit. She who saved Greek thinking from being overwhelmed by the atavism of the Taurus had earned the crown, because she had saved what was supposed to be developed ever more into a new approach to the Spirit, congenial to the newly conquered power of Egohood.

The constellation of Scorpio: We pointed out earlier that, having come from Virgo which represents the Mysteries of Life and through the Threshold of Libra, we face now in the heavens the representation of the Mysteries of Death. The symbol which we use is ♏ or ♏⟋. We can understand the arrow which is attached. It was probably an image of the scorpion's sting. However, the prefix which looks like the letter "m" is a mystery. We found the same symbol being used for Virgo and there we suggested that it can represent three gates or portals leading over three stages of an inner, esoteric development to the spiritual Truth and Reality. Thus we could read the symbol of Scorpion. The soul would find a double perspective beyond the last gate: The arrow or spear which points upwards, wants to lead on the the realms of the spirit. The arrow pointing downwards warns of death as an end in itself.

Both aspects were expressed by ancient mythology concerning Scorpio. In Egypt it was associated with the commencement of the reign of Typhon, or Set, the murderer of Osiris. It was then the constellation in which the Autumnal equinox took place.

The Fixed star Antares in Scorpio was looked upon as the Rival or Equal of Mars. The latter was, and still is, considered to be the ruler of Scorpio. In Central Asia Antares was known as the "Grave Digger of Caravans" (see Lum, "The Stars in our Heaven").

The association of Scorpio with the experience of Rising to the reality of Spiritual or Eternal Life is not so obvious. This is understandable because these concerns were closely guarded secrets of the Mysteries and of Initiation. The neophyte who proceeded after long preparation to the final stage of Initiation had to go through a three-days death experience which was brought on by physical means. After that he was led back to life and had now a direct knowledge of those spiritual realms which man enters only after death at the end of his life in the body. This knowledge enabled him to master the problems and tasks of life through inner enlightenment which was in keeping with the great spiritual perspectives of world evolution.

Particularly the constellations above the Scorpion express this aspect. There is, first of all, the effigy of Ophiuchus which means "the Man that holds the Snake". In Greek mythology he was connected with Aesculapius, the son of Apollo and god of healing. Holding the Serpens he is a living representation of the caduceus, the wand of the Healer-god Hermes and the ancient symbol of the medical art. Thus Ophiuchus-Aesculapius was, so to speak, the great God-Initiate of the mysteries of healing. His skill was so great that he restored many to life who had already died. Thereupon the ruler of the world of the Shades complained to Zeus because he did not receive enough human souls into his realm. Zeus destroyed Aesculapius by one of his thunderbolts but he placed him in heaven where he can still be seen as the constellation of Ophiuchus. His life-restoring capacity is in its proper place in heaven, not on the Earth.

Still higher in the Northern hemisphere is the constellation of Hercules. He steps or kneels on the Dragon who has the Pole of the Ecliptic in his grip. Next to his right hand are the head of the Serpent which Ophiuchus holds, and Corona Borealis. In his left hand one finds on old starmaps Cerberus, the threeheaded Hound of Hell, a monster which Hercules brought up from the underworld in the course of one of his famous twelve labours. Also the Lyra is on the left side of Hercules.

To be quite correct this is the Hercules who was transplated to heaven by the gods after his death, according to the myth. Thus we find here again the motive of death and its transcendence. However, we detect more. We are learning by way of mythological imaginations *how* to transcend death. As we said, Hercules stands on the head of the Dragon, like a pre-Christian St. George. The Dragon is in mythology and legend always the representation of that element working in man which attempts to hold him bound to the Earth and its gravity exclusively, to make him a servant of matter, and above all to eliminate with every conceivable means all notion of the reality of the world of the Spirit. If this power succeeded, then death would persist beyond the end of the earthly career of man. On the other hand, Hercules holds off the Serpent above his head with the club in his right hand. This is the power in man which would misuse man's egotism, his pride and arrogance, to rebel against the Divine world, to seek to establish his own Kingdom in the universe, apart from and against the great aims of cosmic evolution which the Divinity holds out since the beginning of Creation. If this power were to succeed man would die an eternal death in utter isolation.

Man who decides to transcend death must ward off the two powers which are lurking in his own being to destroy him and build on his destruction their own Divinity-estranged cosmic Kingdoms. This was age-old knowledge and wisdom of the ancient Mysteries. For those who had learned to "read," it was even visible in the heavens in the effigy of Hercules. Rudolf Steiner depicted it in his great 30-foot-high wooden statue which he carved. It shows in most expressive forms the anti-powers, Ahriman and Lucifer. These are their ancient names. A mighty figure whom Rudolf Steiner called the "Representative of Mankind" (in whom one can see the Christ as Archetypal Being) steps between them. His gesture seems to be one of assertion of the Greater individuality of man, of that individuality which identifies itself in full consciousness and spiritual freedom with Evolution as the Divinity holds it out. Through this gesture Ahriman and Lucifer are banned to the domains in which it is their allotted task to work. Lucifer, the proud spirit, falls to the Earth, Ahriman is banned under the Earth, into the realm of gravity. This statue can be experienced like a modern and christianised representation of Hercules in the sky.

Hercules—or, the Representative of Mankind—would then identify himself with the aims of cosmic evolution. Indeed, this identification is implied even in an external sense in the constellation of Hercules because in it lies the so-called solar apex. Modern astronomy has found that our Sun is not standing still. It moves in space and takes the Solar system along on the journey. The aim of this movement seems to lie in the constellation of Hercules, in the near neighbourhood of the Fixed star Omicron Herculis and Lambda Herculis. (See Richardson, "The Fascinating World of Astronomy, p. 209/10.) And this is the solar apex.

To the left and right of Hercules are the Corona Borealis and the Lyra which we mentioned earlier. They explain, in a sense, how Hercules can meet the two dangers which he confronts, Draco-Ahriman and Serpens-Lucifer. Corona Borealis, the crown of Ariadne, we discussed earlier, in connection with Libra. Ariadne symbolises those soul-forces which give Theseus the capacity to find his way and maintain his integrity in the labyrinth of the newly conquered potential of the brain and the senses. There is lurking destruction if man relies only on that which is inside the orbit of this physiological domain. To meet this attack of Lucifer he must develop capacities which transcend intellectual, statistical thinking.

The Lyre, or Lyra, to the left of Hercules does not only concern the complex of Scorpio but also Sagittarius which we shall have to discuss later. It does tell how Hercules meets the danger coming from Ahriman. Certainly, in the heavens Draco's, the Dragon's, head is held down under the foot of Hercules, and his hand has a firm grip on Cerberus, the threeheaded Hound of Hell, another symbolic representation of Ahriman. But the Lyre can tell us how to meet these attacks constructively.

The Lyre is said to have been invented by Mercury. Later on it came into the hands of Apollo who passed it on to his son Orpheus. The latter played upon it so masterfully "that even the most rapid rivers ceased to flow, the wild beasts of the forest forgot their wildness, and the mountains came to listen to his song". (Proctor, "Legends of the Stars"). The nymphs came to listen and one among them, Eurydice, was particularly enchanted. Orpheus made her his wife. But one day she was bitten by a snake and died. The unhappy Orpheus ventured with his lyre into the sinister regions of Hades, in order to effect her release. Pluto, the lord of the underworld, and those around him were so enchanted by the music which was streaming from the magical lyre that they permitted Eurydice to return to the living. There was, however, one condition: She was to follow Orpheus on the way to the upper world, but he was not allowed to look back to her. He saw daylight in front of him when, forgetting the condition to which he had agreed, he glanced back to make sure Eurydice was really following him. As he did so, she shrank further and further away, irresistibly drawn down again to Hades. After the death of Orpheus his lyre was carried to the heavens and this is the constellation of Lyra.

We meet here the motive of the overcoming of death, although Orpheus does not appear to have fully succeeded. But he at least pacified with his instrument the sinister power of Pluto. In this sense does the Lyre also belong to the complex of the constellation Scorpion and its environment.

Why had this Lyre such tremendous magical qualities? It was no ordinary instrument; it had been invented by Mercury, possessed by Apollo. In other words, it was a cosmic lyre upon which sounded the Harmonies of the Spheres. And this was the secret of its power, of its death-transcending magic. Thus it is placed on the left side of Hercules, indicating that with it he overcame the Ahrimanic danger, for Ahriman is, in a sense, the lord of death.

What are the Harmonies of the Spheres? Earlier, we tried to work out a concept of the spheres of the planets. They are the areas which are contained within the orbits of the planets. The latter are, in this sense, only the visible messengers of the invisible spheres which were experienced in ancient times, still in Greece, as the dwelling and working places of Divine Spiritual beings. We can know that also the souls of the departed live in these spheres. As we have pointed out earlier the latter are set one within the other in perfect harmony which expresses itself, for instance, in the harmonic mathematical progression of the distances of their orbits from the Sun. This then is the Harmony of the spheres. To know and realise their spiritual reality and their inhabitants is the meaning of the Lyre, or Lyra of Apollo-Orpheus. Over him who "possesses" it death has no power.

The constellation of Sagittarius, the Archer: This constellation is depicted on classical star-maps as a centaur, a mythological being with the body of a horse and a human upper part. He is usually armed with bow and arrow and seems to aim at some object in the neighbourhood of Scorpio. There exist, however, also other representations which show him carrying a lyre.

Another centaur can be found in the Southern hemisphere, the Centaurus, a rather large and conspicuous constellation. Unfortunately, it is so far South that it cannot be at all, or only partly, seen in Northern latitudes. It is below the Hydra and surrounds the famous Southern Cross on three sides. In Greek mythology this constellation seems to have been associated with Chiron, the great centaur who educated most of the heroes of Greek antiquity. He was an adept of medicine and music.

The Sagittarius was connected with the centaur Nessus who played a decisive part in the story of Heracles. He was killed by Heracles for attacking his bride.

Who were the centaurs? Centaurus, the ancestor of this race, was the son of Ixion and a cloud. Therefore, we should not imagine him as an ordinary human being. He, and also his descendants, carry the heritage of the ethereal element of the clouds and the peripheral atmosphere in their bodies. On the other hand their ancestor Ixion had been banned by Zeus to the darkest part of Hades, Tartarus, for an unpardonable offence against Hera or Juno. There he was bound to a constantly revolving wheel of fire.

Thus the centaurs unite an amazing contradiction in their bodies. On the one hand lives an almost heavenly element and cosmic wisdom (as in the case of Chiron) in them. This we see represented in the horse-body. The earthly part, as it were, appears in the image of the upper human form and, particularly the head. In other words, we realise in the centaur an image of an early stage of man's cosmic biography. He was then still permeated very strongly by the cosmos and its rhythms. In a sense, it is implied that the body of the horse still reached far out into the cosmos and moved on the firmament. Only with a small part of his being he submerged in earthly substance. This is the centaur's head.

Heracles is in the myth constantly involved in the destiny of the centaurs and always is obliged to fight against them. On one occasion he accidentally kills Chiron, his own tutor. We have mentioned already that he also killed Nessus. Once Heracles came with his newly won bride Deianeira to a river. Nessus who lived there, used to carry travelers to the other shore. Deianeira sat on his back to ride across when the centaur decided to gallop off with her as soon as he had reached the opposite bank of the river. Heracles, who had stayed behind, soon became aware of Nessus' intention. A moment later Heracles brought the centaur to the ground, pierced by one of the hero's deadly arrows which he had dipped in the blood of the Hydra, or Lernean Serpent.

This was, however, the cause of Heracles' own death some time after. On some occasion he was entreated to robe himself in the blood-stained garment of Nessus, not knowing its origin. No sooner had he put on the gown when the poison of the Hydra, which had been mingled with the blood of the centaur, began to eat into the body of Heracles. The torments became so unendurable that he decided to end his life. He burnt himself to death upon a mighty pile of wood. But his noble soul was caught up to heaven by Zeus where it is now visible to all as the constellation of Hercules.

Thus is Sagittarius, the Centaur, a dynamic representation of early stages of Man's Becoming. Heracles, whose effigy in the sky stands like an external reminder of man's cosmic prototype and future spiritual aim, as we said when we discussed Scorpio, kills, or overcomes the centaur in himself. He does this because his task is to become an earth dweller who realises his Egohood. For this reason must he sacrifice his own cosmic heritage, the body of the horse, man's deep ancient and egoless involvement in the cosmos.

However, he has also to pay for his achievement of Egohood by emancipation from the cosmos. The death of the centaur in him becomes the cause of his own earthly death, though he is raised afterwards to the heavens. But now he is a member of the cosmos as a being conscious of his own, higher Self. This is the tremendous evolution which is implied in the story of Sagittarius-Nessus-Heracles. It is at the same time the eternal interpretation of this constellation: Ascent to cosmic Egohood over long stages of sometimes painful catharsis and ceaseless endeavour. Thus we can also understand and accept the symbol which is used for it. And furthermore, we can also comprehend why it was regarded since ancient times as the cosmic-archetypal region of the thighs of the human body. From Aries to Virgo we see a gradual turning to an inner world, in a physiological-archetypal sense, until in the Virgo region of the human body we are confronted with a sphere which reaches a culmination of isolation from the external world. After that we find already in Libra the beginning of a turning again to the external world. And in Sagittarius the physiology of the human body definitely orientates itself through the thighs towards the surface of the Earth.

The constellations of Capricorn and Aquarius: The two effigies are closely interconnected. Capricorn appears to have inherited some of the twofold aspects of Sagittarius: It is usually depicted as an ibex, a rare animal which lives only in the highest mountain-regions of the world. Yet, instead of hind legs it has a fish's tail, indicating that, though it lives in extreme altitudes it nevertheless reaches down into the watery element. The fishtail lies under the Aquarius; in fact is is submerged in the water which flows from the urn of Aquarius, the Waterman. This water forms the "Sea," as it was known in Chaldean astronomy. It is composed of the constellation Eridanus, the river, the Southern Fish (Pisces Australis) and Cetus, or Whale.

In Greek mythology we find Capricorn regarded as the Gate of the Gods, as the opposite constellation of Cancer was the gate of birth, or descent of Earth-man. In Norse myth it was associated with Alfheim, the dwelling of the elves or dwarfs. They were divided into white elves and black elves, both being great artificers who were ever employed by the Aesir gods. They made such wondrous things as the sword of Odin, the ship of Balder, etc. However, the black elves were enemies of the Aesir-gods and were wont to work destruction. In India this constellation was depicted as the Makara, a sea-monster, which was, however, the steed of the great god Varuna, of whom we shall speak in connection with Aquarius.

In all these mythologies we discover the double aspect which we mentioned above. Thus we can well say that this constellation appears like a connecting link, or a kind of mediator between heaven and earth. Indeed, the horns of the Ibex are like antennae which receive the elements of the cosmos, and the body, particularly the fish's tail, transmits then to the "waters of the deep."

The nature of the heavenly gifts which the Capricorn-Ibex receives from above is well represented by Cygnus, the Swan, and Aquila, the Eagle, in the sky above this part of the Ecliptic. The latter constellation was in Greek sidereal mythology the Eagle of Zeus. Cygnus, the Swan, seems to have been simply the Bird, living high above Earth-weightiness.

With this background we can understand the traditional symbol of Capricorn and also its association with the knee of the human body. The knee-pan

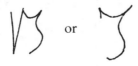

carries the full weight of the upper part of the human frame, and yet, it makes possible a flexibility which lets man walk gracefully and in a harmonious rhythm.

Whereas we have in Capricorn a representation of the portal to the cosmos, so does Aquarius, the Waterman, reflect something of the splendour of the cosmos itself. In Indian cosmology this constellation was Varuna, the great Indian God, who was second only to Indra in importance. He seems to have been the same who was recognised in Ancient Persian world conception as Ahura Mazdao, the great Aura of the Sun. He was the guardian of Rita, the cosmic order, and had created the rhythms in the universe, like day and night, the seasons, etc., which are all made by cosmic rhythms. The opposite, "nonrita", or An Rita, became in later days "one of the commonest words for untruth and sin" (Basham, "The Wonder that was India"). Likewise was the Opponent of the Cosmic order of Ahura Mazdao, Ahriman, regarded as the father of the lie.

In Greek mythology Aquarius was associated with the goddess Hebe who provided the Olympian gods with nectar and ambrosia, the heavenly or cosmic food which gave them eternal youthfulness. For some reason Hebe lost her high office. Some say this happened because she became the bride of Hercules, after he had ascended to heaven. Therefore Zeus had to look for another cup-bearer. The Eagle (constellation Aquila) was sent down to search for a substitute. He found Ganymede, the son of a King of Troy, and he carried him on his wings up to the Olympus to take over the office of Hebe. Thus a mortal had become the caretaker of the food of the cosmos, a tremendous change and perspective of a future relationship between man and the cosmos.

Above the Aquarius is the *head* of the constellation of Pegasus, the winged horse. He had been created by Neptune from the foam of the salt sea. Thus he rises in the heavens from the part of the sky which the ancients called "the Sea". He lived in the sacred grove of the Muses where he had kicked open the fountain of Hippocrene, the fountain of poetic inspiration.

The horse in mythology is an image of intelligence. For instance, the four horses in the Revelation of St. John (chapter VI), the white, red, black and pale horses are perfect illustrations of the Divine Intelligence which will manifest in corresponding future ages of evolution. The winged Pegasus belongs to a similar category of Cosmic Intelligence. It will endow man who turns to him with Inspiration. Any deed of man, not only poetic creation which rises from such Inspiration, is a manifestation of the Cosmos on Earth. In actual content and effect, as well as timing and rhythm, inspired action of this nature can become a humanised and individualised realisation of the cosmos of the stars and its functions. Often men might not even be aware of it. However, the future will demand more and more conscious action from man as a preparation for distant stages of human and cosmic evolution. This is the message of Aquarius-Waterman.

Thus we can also understand the symbol of Aquarius: the Waters of the

deep reflect and become even one with the Waters of the heights. Furthermore, we find the dynamics of this constellation at least indicated in the corresponding physiological counter-image of man's body. In the opposite constellation of Leo we found the archetype of the center of man's circulation, particularly of the heart. In Aquarius this stream of the circulation comes to the periphery of the body, to the "cosmos" of the environment.

The constellation of Pisces, the Fishes: Like the opposite constellation of Virgo are the Pisces in Greek Mythology connected with that Divine element in the cosmos which is represented as of female being. However, here it is a story of persecution and oppression, and following rescue. Once when the Olympian Gods had to flee from the wrath of the giant-monster Typhoeus or Typhon, Venus and her son Cupid changed themselves into fishes in order to escape the persecution. These are the two fishes of the corresponding constellation in the heavens which are connected with a ribbon of stars.

The most illuminating information we obtain from the story of Andromeda, whose constellation is above Pisces. She was the daughter of the King Cepheus of Ethiopia and his Queen Cassiopeia. Both their constellations can be found in the Northern sky, above Andromeda. Cassiopeia was beautiful,and one day she claimed that she was more beautiful than the daughters of Neptune, the Nereids. The latter complained to their father who rose in anger from the sea and sent a monster, the Cetus, or Whale, to Ethiopia. (His constellation can be seen below the Fishes.) The ferocious creature soon laid waste to the country. King Cephus had to consult an oracle and was told that the only way to appease Neptune's anger was to sacrifice his daughter Andromeda to the monster, the Cetus. The suffering of the population became so great that the reluctant King had to give his consent. Andromeda was brought to the seashore to be chained to a rock. The Cetus approached already to devour her when Perseus came flying overhead on his way back from the expedition in the course of which he had killed the Medusa. (See description of the constellation Aries.) He realised at once the plight of the maiden and, exposing the severed head of the Medusa which he carried in his hands, he swooped down on the sea-monster. It was instantly turned into a huge rock, for Medusa's head had still the power to petrify everything that met its gaze.

As always in mythological representations, the female element is an expression of soulforces, either of human nature or cosmic beings. Andromeda is obviously associated with the human soul-element because her parents are humans who attract, as Cassiopeia, even the wrath of the Divinity. However, she is of outstanding qualities as her effigy in the heavens demonstrates. She stands there with outstretched arms, chained to a rock. But the fixed star Alpheratz which marks her forehead belongs also to the body of the Pegasus. Thus the latter constellation seems to rise up out of the head of Andromeda.

We have earlier pointed out that the image of the horse in mythology means Intelligence. The Pegasus, however, is winged, or Divine-cosmic Intelligence. Thus Andromeda appears in the heavens as a representation of human soul-forces which are the bearers of cosmic, not narrow earthly, Intelligence. They are chained to the rocks of material earth-existence and threatened by monsters who dwell in the twilight of an atavistic-watery element. But they are rescued by the half-Divine hero Perseus who has overcome the powers of petrifying Earth experience. This is indeed a tremendous picture of the situation in which the soul of man found itself in ancient times. But at the same time it contains also a mighty perspective of future stages of human evolution.

In the preceeding constellations we saw the possiblity of a magnificent rise of man to a new relationship with the cosmos and the Spiritual world beyond it. In *Sagittarius* we are confronted with the mighty battle of man for the realisation of his Egohood. In *Capricorn* we witness then the struggle to find the right relationship between the human microcosmos, endowed with Self-hood, and the Macrocosmos. In *Aquarius* we are then witnessing the begin-nings of the new union of man with the Macrocosmos (see the story of Ganymede, the *human* cupbearer on Olympus). Now in *Pisces* we face simply the question why this evolution should take place, what its cosmic purpose is supposed to be. By submergence in the physical-material element, by being chained to the rock, by great suffering man will be called upon in the end (Pisces is the "end of the Zodiac"), to transform the Earth, to redeem its inhabitants in the Kingdoms below him, who were drawn into his destiny.

We have heard this message of transformation once before, in connection with Virgo. But there it was the transformation inaugurated by the Gods in order to make of man the instrument which he is expected to become. Now, in Pisces man stands alone. Along a painful road has he come to the realisation of his Self and the cosmos. As much as he can unite himself, as a Self, with the cosmos, so much can he enact and perform that great deed of redemption and transformation. This is the story of the potential of Pisces.

On the background of all this can we discern a meaning in the traditional symbol for this constellation. In Gemini we found the world above and below, the heavens and the Earth, the division into the manifoldness of beings and objects of what once was united. ⚥ This must "in the end" become brotherhood of universal Love: a standing side ♉ by side to achieve the goal. We can thus also understand the association of this constellation with feet and hands, because there are the periphery or "ends" of the body, and also, with our hands shall we be able to accomplish that great work of redemption. ♓

Book Three

GUIDELINES ALONG THE PATH
OF THE PLANETARY ASPECTS
by William Lonsdale

As long as we conceive planetary aspects to be abstract geometric, numerological, or harmonic relationships between physical planetary bodies in euclidean space, we will continue to miss their point, their real significance. When contemplating living realities, we must find our way out of mechanistic thinking to imaginative perception. In spiritual spheres, two realms intersecting are more than two solids with vast emptiness between them. The mode of interaction becomes just as formative as any supposed fixed identity of the given components. Simply put, the planetary aspects are just as fundamental a reality as the planets that are aspecting.

The lazy mind tries to set up each variable to be considered as "just-like-before", so that Mars is always Mars, acting, asserting, and the like in some primitive heedlessness; Saturn will be Saturn, blocking, restricting, causing congestion and problems; and a square between them, like all squares everywhere, gives poor Mars even more headaches, crushing its free spirit, hindering it by cumbersome considerations, loading every action with Saturnian leaden obstacles. Actually, if Mars were merely Mars-as-ever, the problems invoked would be far more severe and couldn't lightly be noted by the expert astrologer. If Saturn undeviatingly brought Mars down, it would indeed be a simple world. If squares were always busy blocking and straining just like that, anybody could easily get a fix on how planets interact, and the simplistic descriptions that fill Astrology texts would be universally acknowledged as accurate and the definitive word on how each aspect manifests every time it comes up. Everybody would be happy with the new social science that was once the sacred science of Astrology.

Squares and every other aspect represent a spiritual reality. Only our deepest understanding can grasp how they operate in any given context. In order to begin to move toward the time when astrologers will realize this and develop themselves accordingly, I propose here to suggest a few new ways (and some very old ones) of looking at each of the more powerful planetary aspects. Not only will we move beyond "malefic-benefic" considerations, we will also show a kind of cosmic movement from one aspect to the next that can become a means to experience all the powerful aspects in a truly artistic way.

We start with the reality in front of us that cannot be denied. The square aspect points to the areas in each individual's chart in which internal and external factors combine to render him out-of-touch with any sustaining whole. A square severs the person from himself, from the life around him, and from any Higher Reality. It places him tight up against the brittle surface of existence, depriving him of any relief or release. Through his squares, the individual is stymied, hyper-sensitized, forced to face the dilemma of his insufficiency, his helplessness, his atomization. The planets that are squared will not flow together unless one goes through a new development, unless one can kill off within oneself that which causes the situation to be this way and replace it with forces that arise from one's innermost depths.

This is a hard task, rendered more difficult by the common level of agreement to ignore each others knots and binds and pretend they're not there. We give little encouragement to go down into one's squares and work them out. It won't make one money or friends. It doesn't seem necessary, for everyone carries around these problems. However, the squares you have are uniquely your own, they operate within your own being and cause you tremendous pain and deprivation, preventing you from being able to activate a lot more energy and awareness. How do they do this?

Whenever two planets disrupt one another's flow, they do it thoroughly. For example, let us take Saturn squared to Venus. Now keeping in mind our suggestion that there are many ways any aspect can manifest, let's try to get a basic sense of what might happen in the life of someone with Saturn square Venus that is different from what happens to those without the aspect. Venus generally allows one to feel comfortable simply being oneself, responding to life from one's own heart center, giving appreciation for all that pleases or fulfills the self, sharing a sense that people in relation to each other can feel good and can naturally flow together, without demanding or expecting more from one another than each is ready and able to give. Venus tends to be good-humored, gracious, forgiving, unself-conscious, and self-sustaining. On the other hand, Saturn impels one usually toward the most intensive, sharply defined, purposeful, and hard-driving expression. Saturn presents one with the dilemma of identity and destiny, the morality of perseverence and responsibility being superior and infinitely preferable to monentary experiences and easy-going propensities. Saturn demands that one dwell in the core of oneself and that the course in life be undeviatingly true to "who-one-really-is." Saturn tends to be stern, systematic, orderly, insistent, and penetratingly powerful.

It would be easy to make it seem as though these two principles are alien to one another and to explain what may happen in the square aspect between them by their fundamental incompatibility. But this would miss the point of the square and would also fail to give equal weight to the experience of those with Saturn in other aspects to Venus. No, these two principles can form many different kinds of relationship. The point here is that with the square aspect, there is an absence of relationship in the positive sense, an almost total thwarting of one another precisely because a relationship cannot be established. For the person with Venus square Saturn, the Venus function, which has to do with positive or at least mutual relationship, is dammed up by the Saturn function, which tends of its own nature to deprive one of superficial reassurances. Thus, Saturn tends to get the upper hand most of the time here. For women, this can be particularly devastating. Venus is naturally constellated in a woman, that is, there is little in a woman's make-up to lead her of herself to resist or distort Venus and much in her make-up to lead her of herself to realize Venus fully within her daily life experience. Saturn squaring Venus freezes the usual rewards of a Venusian affirmation of what is encountered and substitutes insistent inward criteria. Women with this aspect often find themselves unable to partake in loving sharing from an unself-conscious goodness of heart. They want and need more, far more — there is the yearning in them for a confirmation from others of their inner worth, a certification of the core reality they are trying to come into touch with. Yet it is in the nature of Venus to draw to the self only what is commonly agreed upon, what everyone accepts beforehand as socially fruitful or beautiful. Saturn in such a woman signals a need to get down into greater depths while Venus will not allow it, except in serious and purposeful group situations, and will instead signal to others that they should ignore Saturn's pressure and generate the accustomed behavior that will make everyone feel good without having to go into the intricacies of deeper identity questions. What happens when another person encounters conflicting signals such as these? If, as we said before, people generally agree to ignore and overlook these difficulties in each other, then the other will in most cases go blithely along, pretending the Venus square Saturn person isn't sending out the signals she is indeed sending. This superficially pleases Venus, but Saturn feels betrayed, and freezes the situation. This means that while everyone acts as though nothing has happened, the turning aside of her deeper needs takes the wind out of Venus square Saturn, makes her feel uncomfortable while others seem per- fectly fine, leaves her with a sensation of being alone and remote and untouched by what is happening. In compensation, Venus may try all the harder to act perfectly normal, which may render this person's social behavior exaggeratedly congenial, reassuring, and smooth. This tug-of-war goes on and on, with different results in each person, but in some fashion simultaneously driving one further and further inward on oneself in a bare, desolate unease, and propelling one more and more outward to compose the appearances with perfect aplomb, perhaps overdoing the latter into an immaculate surface sheen and unfailingly correct deportment, or some such compensation. Where is the person herself in the midst of all this? Confused, divided, touchy, disquieted by something that does not seem at all obvious or clear. Where can she go from here?

This is the real issue. What can people do about their squares, those areas of their life-expression in which they seem to get the worst of everything, where nothing seems to work out right, and yet in which everyone acts as though none of this were actually going on inside of each other? Is it a social issue, a personal one, a cosmic one? Are the solutions psychological, spiritual, pragmatic? What is the dimension or scope of the square situation?

There is nothing cosmically wrong here essentially. It may well be that the individual with Saturn square Venus is not intended to fulfill Venusian expression in a natural, spontaneous, unhindered fashion. The presence of the aspect indicates that this most direct and simple phase of expression has to be qualified by profoundly discordant considerations. A different manner of woman may be forming in the cauldron of Saturn in square. But to get there, she first may have to witness and be seized by a conflict, a feeling that something is lacking, so that she can begin to find the missing link within herself and bring it forth as a new creation. If life went on splendidly, how would she be alerted to the reality that a part of her remains unborn? Real change always represents a struggle, a battle, some inertia to be overcome.

Let's apply this kind of analysis to another square, Jupiter square Moon. The Moon ordinarily is one's immediate touchstone of livingness, the feelers one puts out to sense the situation one is in, the attitude one adopts to make the most of what is happening, and the sensitivity which leads one to internalize those elements of experience that strike a resonant chord. The Moon harbors life, cradles it within, and sends it out again marked indelibly with one's personal touch. It is adhesive, repetitive, predictable, and yet in the moment fluent, pliable, in rapid flux. In relation to all this, Jupiter represents the inner picture of direct experiences and particularly of further possibilities that leads us out of ourselves into fulfilling all that we are here for. Jupiter designs a plan that will accommodate any new developments, but that will guide us unfailingly (hopefully) in the direction that is essential for us to be moving along. In our Jupiter phase we glimpse the overall picture and act accordingly. Jupiter is grand, dramatic, sweeping and yet quite applied, sharply attuned, even commonsensical. Jupiter in many ways is the most complete and whole planetary principle.

Together, Jupiter and the Moon have a lot to share. For this reason, the person with Jupiter square Moon is particularly acutely deprived, for in one of the areas of human expression that can be most enterprising and delightful, those with this aspect feel left out, being forced to follow a separate track of their own whose destination is somewhat unclear. Jupiter presses at the gates of the Moon, trying to pry open the lunar shell, to let in more light. The Moon often refuses to budge. Here we have the drama of an habitual mode of behavior (Moon) that is in stark contrast to hopeful sparks and magic moments (Jupiter). Whenever this person can bring forth their best on an occasion in which greater values or archetypal issues are evoked, a whole other side to the nature is revealed than would usually be possible in the course of everyday living. One could almost say that he lives for such moments, knows himself best at these times and gauges his progress accordingly. In many cases, the Jupiterian dimension will be epitomized less by actual experiences than by what goes on within imaginative, reflective intervals. But whether projected outwardly or otherwise, there is something about such people that seems special, even extraordinary, and they like to present or picture themselves as set apart, distinguished, amazing. The everyday level seems insignificant by comparison. However, their Moon's revenge will be swift and all pervasive. Mundane situations that call out pedestrian capacities and common skills crop up to dominate the consciousness. He who would like nothing better than to advance in heroic strides across the stars is forced to endure grosser realities almost excessively, or so it often feels to Jupiter square Moon. In ordinary life, he may meet up with continual rebuffs. Why? Because he is exuding disdain for lesser considerations in just the way that's guaranteed to draw them to him. And at his best he knows that these tests are what he needs, that only as he manifests his finer qualities in the least of situations is he living up to his true promise. Keeping this in mind all the time can be very difficult as he so yearns to expand, to defy the odds, to go all out and perform the impossible. The possible stands waiting, and in it lie the great lessons for those with Jupiter square Moon.

To take one final example, Mercury square Moon can show us something of the more constructive side of squares. Mercury moves quickly amongst the planets, forging key connections. It wants merely to take things apart and then put them back together again, continually and gladly. Its function is to focus on what is encountered and keep it going in whatever fashion seems possible or desirable. Thus Mercury is protean, opportunistic, keen-edged and interested in whatever presents itself. The Moon has already been described.

Mercury can adapt to anything, even squares, and is generally the least troublesome planet in square formations. This is particularly so in this aspect. A frisky, fresh what-can-I-get-away-with wit and spark is evident here. These people seldom resist the chance to test the boundaries of any situation that threatens to become stagnant, checking everyone out and keeping things straight. A twinkle of mischief gets them into and out of a lot of amusing situations. However, there is a lot more to the aspect than this. Positively, the interplay does not seem to get too heavy, as Mercury and Moon engage in banter and by-play, generating more exuberance than anything else. The Moon is brought out of its accustomed complacency to mix with ongoing situations more resiliently, which these people usually need to do. The workout their Moon gets may open them to experiences they would otherwise feel too stiff to move into. One of the evolutionary strengths of square aspects is their ability to plunge us further into life, to correct deficiencies within certain planets, to deepen, broaden, and extend our frame of reference. However, they generally do this at the cost of considerable pain and inner growth. This is the case here in a less dramatic form than we've so far seen. In many people with Mercury square Moon, a gnawing need to belong, to be part of what is happening, forces them to overcome an inherent sense of being different or isolated, an aloofness, or strangeness, that is too much. Often groups and social situations present quite a challenge for them to "come to life". Their teasing wit is now revealed in a different light. They often come forth out of themselves by leading with a Mercury, throwing out a comment or quip or provocation. If they get the desired response, they're off with the current, a real part of things. Here the square functions to remold one's behavior in highly necessary ways.

Now that we have glimpsed a few possible manifestations of square energy, we can take a closer look at the spiritual principle of the square. What is really happening in these aspects is that wherever we have squares, we have severed the golden cord that connects us with the surrounding spiritually sustaining forces, and been plunged into materiality to such a degree that we no longer identify with anything about ourselves that might take us out of the bind we find ourselves in. That bind is that the unregenerate facets of our own nature rule, rather than the essential selfhood. Past defeatist attitudes and a host of costly decisions have bound us to the wheel of life without any map back to ourselves. Because the most pressing difficulties are difficult to own up to within our own being, most people act as though life, other people, fate are doing this to them, while actually it is they who are doing it to life and to themselves as well.

There is a kind of healthy padding that our constructive forces, exemplified by trines, sextiles, and conjunctions, build between the soul and the body. When this becomes thin and worn down by our negativity, the soul becomes too closely imbedded within and dependent upon the physical body. Our vitality begins to ebb and we become overwhelmed by a sensation that instead of being one unified selfhood, our ego is coming apart and crumbling into a host of little fragmentary selfish "egos". To some extent the central selfhood in this instance can scarcely be felt, we experience an inner negation, and we find ourselves becoming an island within ourselves, isolated and cut off. Only the strict limits of manifest, physical fact seem real or accessible to us. When in this state, we are visited recurrently by shocks or jolts that come right in on us, which are intended to wake us up and stir us to action, to changing ourselves, to caring. Unfortunately, very few can respond with full openness to such signals, for one feels weak and not strong, out-of-touch with one's sources of energy and awareness, at the mercy of external impacts. Usually we put up protective barriers, which may include the whole array of psychological defenses, and most particularly a retreat into passivity, apathy, defensive withdrawal, provincial self-serving attitudes, self-doubts, bottomless fears, and perhaps a melodramatic acting out. When imprisoned in our own bodily nature, we seem to become blinded by the wall of the body, and in a restless groping, we cannot penetrate to any depth of human experience, everything becomes transient and superficial, and we distance outselves from what is happening as though we were superior to such unsatisfying experiences, often mocking the edifice that we ourselves have constructed. We feel then that what is out there and coming in on us is not enough, that we can't reach it anyway, that it isn't really there, it's not worth our while, it's just not enough to keep us going. At this point one has undermined not only one's own integrative faculties, but also the entire world around one, seeing little validity in anything, inside or out. Finally, when entrenched within this impoverished state of consciousness, we are drawn to the strategy I call The Big Lie. In order to survive at all intact, we maneuver surface appearances in an attempt to fool the world. Now we play out one kind of behavior on the surface, appearing to conform completely to every least standard of normality, while another thing entirely happens within our own depths, as we stand far removed from ongoing events, not experiencing with any real involvement anything of what we are projecting. This is rockbottom, and yet it is a very common state to be in in our world of today, whether individually or collectively. Squares are very much the aspect of our times, the dark secret we all share and hide from each other.

The only way I know of that can take us out and beyond this quagmire is the way through direct experience. Only if we can immolate ourselves in things as-they-are, keeping ourselves fully open to all the sense information coming to us from without, can we take the next step toward self-vanquishing. An alchemical transformation of weakness and self-loss into strength and power awaits us. The challenge materiality faces us with is to found the self on one's own inner sensibility and no longer on external criteria. We are being forced down to something indestructible at the foundation of our selfhood, a Living Power that can only be rekindled within our depths if we are able to remain within ourselves, to feel and sense life freshly once again by being there with what is happening. A person who has gone through this awakening of the individualized will, the initiation of our times, can bear the weight of incarnation. He or she can love in freedom, not coerced or determined in activity by past associations or assumptions, but rather present utterly out of free inner choice. Where once we were divided, our Mind tugging us one way, our Heart another way, we now become united with ourselves, with the world around us, and with the higher worlds that stretch endlessly beyond, in loving knowledge.

Opposition aspects share with the square an intensive focus outwardly on sticking to the realities of this world, together with the gnawing inner necessity that we go through a major life change if we are ever to deal rightly with whatever life experience comes our way. All intensive aspects, including the quincunx, which will be discussed later, as well as semi-square, sesquisquare, and biquintile, precipitate this inner call to make a different person of ourselves. However, no other aspect matches the irrevocable life-or-death urgency of the square.

The opposition aspect points to those areas in each individual's chart where he finds himself at a crossroads in his journey through life, calling for a pause to take stock of himself and decide which way to go. His dilemma is complicated by the many factors pressing to be taken into account, the multiple range of possibilities that lie before him, and most of all his own inner uncertainty. He tends to be of several minds, divided loyalties. Which is the right path?

For those individuals who have moved forward with undeviating inner purpose each step of the way up to this point, any moment of reflective pause can be taken in stride and made the most of. They review their priorities, assess their alternatives, and whether through rational or intuitive means, arrive at the best decision they feel they can make under the circumstances. These are people who view the reality outside of themselves objectively and clearly, and who look at themselves as well straight in the I.

Our world today is full to overflowing with those who have wandered far from this ideal. If unconscious factors have been consistently undermining one's ability to deal with inner and outer reality, if one has been unable to maintain one's grasp of immediate realities, if one scarcely knows who one is or what one is in fact dealing with at any given point of issue, the opposition aspect can tear the self apart.

Most of us are of divided minds concerning most of what we do. Part of us pulls one way, another part in the opposite direction, a third part off on a tangent from either of the first two. We won't let ourselves be, yet we lack the courage to confront ourselves with whatever deeper issues may be at stake. We are flooded with pictorial impressions that we can't tune out, but which never become entirely alive and real for us. We stand bemused, uncertain and unresolved, and feel restless yet vaguely indifferent. Nothing as decisive as the square crisis is there to force us to get down to basics.

Let's see how this works out in a given instance. When Saturn opposes Mercury in the birth chart, several possible difficulties can arise. With oppositions more than any other aspect, the specific manifestations span a vast range, for we are here dealing with a subtle inner realm. We have seen Saturn tending to drive us in upon ourselves and Mercury to keep us moving forward, improvising and making and breaking connections along the way. In the opposition aspect, Saturn is seldom as powerful and in command as in the square, while Mercury has its greatest trouble finding connections with any planet so far away at the opposite end of the zodiac. Therefore, clear and sharp directives from within are seldom forthcoming with this aspect.

Individuals with Saturn opposite Mercury sense that they are operating "in the dark", that there are many factors involved in any given situation of which they are unaware. As a result, they are never sure that they know what they are dealing with, and what is expected of them. Often they will look to others to reflect back to them something of the direction they should go in. However, Saturn insists on a strictly accurate, high-quality fidelity to the inner reality, and so they will not be open to just anybody who happens along (although Mercury would prefer to be). They will feel drawn mainly to those who exert special authority, who seem sure of themselves, who cannot be denied. And when furthest removed from their own inner stability, they will do anything necessary to ensure a supply of whatever promises to give them a fix on their own state of mind.

At times forcefully pushing away those who threaten to get too close, at other times ardently hanging on every word of those who seem to know them better than they know themselves, such is the seesaw they can't stop riding. What are these compulsive patterns really about?

In essence, Saturn in this aspect insists on a guarantee that whatever tangent Mercury is moving along give proof of some greater validity. Saturn whenever necessary, to make sure of this, steps all over Mercury, putting its stamp on everything Mercury reaches toward; the rest of the time, Saturn lays back and refuses to identify with most of what Mercury is able to bring. Because Mercury is in astrology the fluid agent of interrelationships with each other being we meet, this results in human contacts being very tricky and changeable. A person with this aspect seldom feels assured that any given relationship has validity in its own terms. And since one's own Saturn usually stands far apart from the moment's encounter, one desperately looks to the other person's immediate behavior either to prove everything is coming along splendidly, or to undercut any connection whatsoever. Simply put, those with Saturn opposite Mercury tend to set other people up to be everything and nothing for them, applauding others excessively when they perform on cue and retreating entirely when the desired responses are slow in coming. The only contacts that form exceptions to this are powerful, magical connections, which may be simultaneously feared and greatly desired; and entirely unstirring connections which may leave one feeling empty and very alone.

One further twist complicates relationships considerably for these people. Mercury can be as dubious about Saturn as Saturn is about Mercury. Since Saturn represents the inner purposes of a given lifetime, any clash with its real needs will be thoroughly devastating. Mercury expresses its counterforce to Saturn by crowding Saturn, drawing to the self all manner of bizarre situations and encounters, leading inevitably in perverse directions; and then at other times Mercury will try to deny Saturn's heaviness by dissipating and making light of those contacts that Saturn may deem deeply meaningful. The proliferation of peripheral connections keeps these people busy extricating themselves from entanglements and snafus. The dissolving of soul ties, or perhaps constant testing of them can be far more painful. When Mercury withdraws its support from Saturn's efforts, this means that no matter how deeply Saturn opposition Mercury people may feel involved within a particularly significant relationship, sooner or later they will tend to provoke a severing of that tie.

And everyone involved is then left dazed, wondering what happened.

The only way to reconcile this split within one's own being is for both Saturn and Mercury to yield up their doubts of one another and false egoism toward the greater good of the whole person, and in particular toward each other's free expression. This can be brought about when the individual with this aspect wakes up to realize the pattern he or she has been weaving and resolves to correct it. With opposition aspects, this is essentially all that is needed. Oppositions hinge completely on inner attitudes. Saturn should back off when appropriate, permitting any given encounter to unfold of its own free momentum. Mercury should get out of Saturn's hair, allowing whatever ties have been able to form in a deeper fashion to go as far as they are destined to go, free of pranks and provocations. Once they have begun to give each other space, Saturn and Mercury can even begin to assist each other. Saturn can bring strength and inner clarity to the most casual rapport, while Mercury can defuse and bring light to overly intense situations with its ability to enjoy life from a neutral perch. This kind of repolarization will take time, as the rut of self-undermining generally proves slow to give way, but a keen awareness of exactly what ones attitudes are doing to oneself as well as others will lead one along the road toward claiming a greater inner freedom.

The oppositional dynamics can be seen in a more positive light through the opposition of Jupiter and Mars. We have seen Jupiter to be the planet of plans, scope, dramatic broader purposes. Mars can now be seen as the force of direct impetus toward specific objectives. Mars scans the terrain ahead, sees what forces are at work, and propels itself along the sharpest projectile it can find straight through the middle. For Mars, the only thing that really counts is to "get there", along the way repelling any opposing forces, and rallying whatever forces can be of assistance. Mars is pungent, clear-headed, strong, and entirely intent. It knows no bounds and often blunders because it operates in such one-pointed and naive fashion. In a very real sense, Jupiter and Mars form diametrically opposite principles, so the opposition aspect between them provides an excellent example of the drama inherent in all oppositions. Among the famous people with this aspect are: Sir Thomas More, Gandhi, Nietzsche, Richard Wagner, Karl Marx, Swami Vivekananda, Greta Garbo, Sarah Bernhardt, H.L. Mencken, Nicola Tesla, and Sigmund Freud. A formidable group!

Jupiter tends to be at its strongest in opposition aspects, bringing out the best in the opposition. Standing in polarity to Mars is ideal for the kinds of lessons Jupiter is here to point toward. There is something outrageous and also something very bracing about people with Jupiter opposite Mars. What is most outrageous is that they are never satisfied, never content to be who they are and do what they do. Many with this aspect feel impelled to be a conscience of their times, a spokesman for an important cause, a gadfly exposing what others may find more convenient to overlook. They work tirelessly for what they judge to be the collective good, but seldom dutifully and routinely. They cannot resist prodding, pushing further, forcing an opening of peoples' eyes. However, when acting on their own behalf they may seem blind, deaf, and dumb, their great insight and drive doing little to transform their own being. As a result, Jupiter opposition Mars folk may endlessly berate themselves for all their failings. Something in them seems to resist any attempts to embody the ideals they cherish.

Why is this? For all the general appeal of their inspiration, they are actually great partisans, pushing what they believe in, trying to stamp out what they abhor. But what they abhor has a strong beach-head within themselves, and that is what they are really trying to overpower. They may be the champion of great reforms or performer in larger-than-life dramas, but whatever they do or say, they remain their own most critical audience, for they cannot get out of their systems the opposing view point to the one they so avidly proclaim.

Here is an inner split that takes the form of an exaggerated outer certainty combined with an agonizing inner doubt. What if they are wrong? How can they deal with the possibility that the enemy within is in the right?

What is happening here astrologically is that Jupiter prevails over Mars in the outward expression, but Mars remains powerful as the opposing force deep within. A balance can be struck here only by acknowledging the split and making room for Mars to have its say. Mars is strictly the warrior, seeking to fight the good fight. But Jupiter's cause is too much for Mars. Jupiter enlists all available life forces in behalf of what is deemed socially relevant or effective. Mars backs off from Jupiter's sweeping priorities and pushes forward on its own narrow way. Mars goes for what is straight ahead. To follow Mars at all, the ambitious all-or-nothing demands of Jupiter must be moderated and then spiced with a dash of impassioned "this-is-what-I-want-to-do-because-I-want-to-do-it." But this Martian self-will will only be given outlet if personal desires are allowed their validity alongside "what-is-best-for-everyone".

What is bracing about these people is that at each point along their path in life, they are capable of magnificent attainments despite and because of their inner division. Because of, in the sense that the tension generated by the untapped Mars within spurs Jupiter opposition Mars people to a great ability to reach people. There's an urgent stridency to their performance, as though their whole manner suggests: "It must happen now or else." One of the intriguing qualities of the opposition aspect is that especially in modern times the most magnificently evocative and persuasive expression can come from someone wracked by suffering, who is fighting within themselves amongst the forces and issues at stake in the larger community, and trying to channel these consciously and objectively. Nevertheless, while they are sure to provoke a response, and to tap into the common reservoir, the energies that Jupiter opposition Mars people are playing with make it very hard for them ever to feel at peace or to understand all the forces at work in themselves and their world. Unless they can find it within them to balance the claims of the opposing planets by permitting all parts of their being to come forward and find their audience, even the morbid, the forbidden, the unregenerate.

One final example will fill in more of the overall picture of the opposition aspect. With Jupiter opposite Sun, we come to a highly significant aspect, for here is our first approach to the Sun itself. If Jupiter represents our overall plans and life momentums, the Sun epitomizes all that we bear within ourselves as self-conscious ego beings. The Sun is our vital spark, the proud fiery heart of our core manifestation. With the Sun we are radiators of freedom, as fact and as potentiality. We love, we proclaim ourselves, we fulfill that which we are. The Sun is dynamic, life-instilling, courageous, and great. It is the one point among the planets where our higher selfhood shines forth undiminished.

Those with Jupiter opposite Sun cannot bring forward their solar being directly. Jupiter for them dominates the night sky, shining independent of the Sun, and they find themselves impelled to focus on a Jupiterian rather than Solar self-expression. This means that the fine clear self-confident strength of the Sun gives way before the aspirations and ideas of what the self is intended to become, which Jupiter is so fond of. It should be noted here that the Sun overpowers other planets that fall within its conjunction, but is itself left in the background in its oppositions. And since Jupiter is at its most powerful in the opposition aspect, Jupiter opposite Sun is the quintessential example of the Sun being "eclipsed" by a planet that is large and bright enough in its own right to be the center of a person's life concerns.

Individuals with this aspect tend to identify themselves by what they can manifest in the world that is positive and "correct" rather than by who they are inside. They want very badly to please, to make an impact, to be seen in a favorable light. They find it very difficult to stand within their own boundaries and radiate from there. Instead, they must come forth and justify their existence by the good that they do for others.

This kind of thing can render a person highly susceptible to environmental influences. When it is unclear where the self ends and the world begins, the effect can be that one becomes hyper-expanded into the surroundings, one becomes one's world. A number of problems can arise at this point. A few examples: Vicarious experience becoming more important than one's own sense of oneself; a need to throw the self off, to make light of the self at its own expense; an acute embarrassment at being a self at all and therefore a need to prove that one is merely acting the way anyone would act under the circumstances. In whatever form this takes, the problem essentially is: Only perfect fulfillment of the Jupiterian potentiality allows the person with Jupiter opposite Sun to feel good about themselves at all. And anyone, anything in their world can call into question the validity of what they are expressing to such a degree that these people will surrender their center to whatever center seems stronger or more justified. Then, in reaction against this tendency in themselves, these people may manifest their Sun compensationally as an exaggerated bravado and self-importance, masking the fear of being carried away by others.

Whenever Jupiter opposition Sun people meet conflicts and disappointments, their way of overcoming is to gird themselves to being even more incredible and dynamic than they were before. They take on too much, martyring themselves to life's difficulties, relying on their own efforts exclusively. They lack the ability to give and take fluently as all flows one way.

The path through this thorny dilemma is a long and hard one. This aspect represents a profound challenge. We are here offered the possibility of a genuine self-transcendence. This can dawn only if we can develop a dual awareness, a higher perspective by which self and other are simultaneously illuminated. There is an unconscious fear with Jupiter opposite Sun that if one focusses too much on self, the world of the others will be neglected. In compensation, one may retreat too much to the self and try to fend off the world. But if one can be awake to the needs and desires, the expectations, and the points of view of everyone concerned, self as well as others, then one can span a much larger range of being and truly be free of self. One cannot overcome the self by trying to leave it behind, to stamp it out, to deny it. In the moment of simultaneously knowing the reality of one's own being and intuiting whatever other realities are present, one becomes the opposition, penetrating to a real experience of the whole situation. No longer afraid or playing tug-of-war to plug in gaps here and disengage over there, one finds at last that each opposite reveals the other to itself, that one can be oneself as well as one's performance, and pierce to being more than self or performance, to be that which streams through all that we are, all that we do, and all that comes before us as life-experience.

The opposition aspect is a paradox. Contained within it are innumerable seemingly contradictory extremes, forces, points of view, facets of life. The poet Keats once described "negative capability", the essential capacity of the poet as "being in mysteries, uncertainties, and doubts without any irritable reaching after fact or reason." I think this capacity is what the opposition aspect is intended to cultivate in us all. Although I have spoken throughout this section in terms of resolving our oppositions, in a larger sense this is not the point. Rather, through oppositions we are brought in touch with the parameters of the whole, in order to draw us forth out of our limited conceptions of ourselves and of our world. It is in the opposition aspect that two planets draw each other out to view and experience a whole other side to life than they would ordinarily be open to.

This means that whatever planetary functions we have involved in oppositions are being invited to expand to a broader perspective; in other words, that parts of our being are being shown more about themselves so that they can become aligned to other parts of our being, so that we can recover our wholeness, our balance, our essential purity. If we use the wrong means to accomplish this, we only make matters worse. It will do us no good to figure it all out, to analyze perpetually, self-seriously, awkwardly our own predicament. This process merely perpetuates itself ad nauseum. It will equally do us no good to attempt to protect ourselves against the expansion that is knocking at our gates by enveloping ourselves in a scaffolding of assumptions, expectations, anticipations, and demands. We cannot guide our progress by enforcing self-created barriers and rigid criteria for what we will take in.

These wrong means represent attempts to deal materialistically and intellectually with a challenge that calls for a spiritual response. All oppositions face us with the question: Can I extend my sense of what is real and significant for me, to encompass all that is actually there round about me and deep within me? Can I merge my being with the being of the world? Can I make a home for myself in this world?

For each I, the stakes are that if I refuse or am unable to take this inner leap, there will always be a false note ringing loud and clear through all my experiences. Only part of myself will be fulfilled by any given experience while part is submerged or left restless and dissatisfied. I will set up the same relationships, the same situations everywhere I go, generating futility and gnawing self-doubt always. As this becomes a matter of habit and routine, I will then grow drowsily oblivious, sinking into a slothful indifference that no longer bothers even to ask why life lacks savor. I will find myself unable to concentrate entirely on anything, as the opposites, like two thieves, pull me far from my center. No longer thinking or questioning or venturing forth out of my narrow self-imposed confines, I will become a person of small vision, obtructing my own way ahead by all the facets of life that I am no longer able· to see. Bogged down in little matters of small consequence, exteriorized to such a degree that everything outside seems enormous while my own self-image shrinks and shudders, I will dwell utterly within my own confused projections, never contacting life directly. I will have become what I imagined myself into being.

Contrastingly, if I can rise to the opportunity to see that everything that ever happens to me is a lesson meant to bring me more in touch with myself, then I will stand above all afflictions and fears. When I am anxious, disturbed, carried away in the rush of daily life in a complex civilization, it will be clearly my own choice, the product of all the crossroads I've been unable to move through. I will bring myself to accounting in the light of the other, I will realize what everybody and everything is trying to tell me. Beginning to stand back from my own tendency to react and compensate for the reflection I am given of myself, I can start on the long painful road back to self-integration. The first major step is to purify and cleanse myself of my assumptions and loaded demands, to render habitable my inner household. After a while, the healing and protective cosmic forces which I had repelled from myself in my eagerness to be self-reliant and cleverly on top of every situation, will come to my aid, wrapping me within my own sheath against the world, yet in the same motion opening me to a loving experience of the outer world, to an embrace of that within all being which corresponds with my own inwardness. As this peaceful seclusion deepens, spiritual maturity can be fostered. Now I know no matter what happens. The myriad jagged fragments of the past now fall into place, reveal their inherent order. With my basis intact, I can operate in complete freedom, attuning myself to experience with extraordinary aptitude. Having attuned myself to the spiritual worlds, I can now operate in the material world without onesidedness. At last my part in daily life is reconciled with my sense of belonging to the eternal, my material commitments are balanced with my spiritual development. It becomes clear in the end that polarities are perfect complements, that opposites are made for each other, filling out the picture, giving the creative stimulus that can only be provided by that which is other. Each moment provides a fulfillment, a step forward in a long-term process, one that can never end. We have taken one giant step forward into incarnation, and we stand at the threshold of life's greater mysteries.

The intensive aspects, long referred to in astrological tradition as "malefic" or "hard" or "inharmonious", generally seen as "afflictions" we must bear for some strange reason, are difficult only because we have made them so. Over unimaginable stretches of time, humanity has fallen again and again into pitfalls that have become imbedded in us as our squares, oppositions, and quincunxes, as Saturn, the Moon, Neptune, and Pluto. We never knew any better. We are now moving into a time in which we do know better. Increasingly, it is agonizing to anyone awake enough to observe how wrong choices are indulged in by people who do indeed know better. Ignorance can no longer be bliss.

Few individuals actually realize their intensive aspects. Most of us flounder in collective seas, never perhaps even going as far as has been dramatized in this article. Instead we hover in the safe middle ground, lukewarm, hoping to avoid having to go through what our astrological configurations indicate. And up to a certain point, it is more prudent to think as everyone does, and to accept the meaning that others do, than to venture forth on unknown seas without a guide. Yet we do have a Guide and many guides, and as history shrinks to one moment of truth, only if we have the courage and clear vision to reach out toward that Light, will we have a chance to go on to greater lessons ahead. The intensive aspects, our private secret nightmare, are also the troubles we have most in common with all of humanity. Where we are most drawn in on ourselves, we encounter the other being, wandering through the same mist. The myth of our own separateness dissolves and we are left with one world, straining and aching to expand or to explode. There is nothing else going on anywhere.

We now come to the radiating aspects, the trine, conjunction, quintile, and sextile. As soon as we begin to consider what happens in these aspects, our scope expands, possibilities and opportunities appear in all directions, and we open wide, relax, and feel good. In these aspects we are graced with all the more positive and gratifying experiences that we can move into. But equally importantly, these point to the areas in our lives in which we stand back inside ourselves looking on while outwardly relating to those around us. Thus, with the radiating aspects, we are free to explore and discover the world around us endlessly, while directing this process from a calm and clear inner center. It is when we are both detached and engaged that we can feel whole and act accordingly, for now the blinders are off and we can see who we are and what we are doing here.

The trine aspect epitomizes all the best of the radiating processes. Abundant light streams through the trine, illuminating life with a warm glow. We find ourselves partaking of, responding to, giving and receiving all that each moment brings. We are full of inward joyful strength, which we naturally move to release and spread toward the periphery, toward whatever is there to absorb and reflect back our goodness. We swim with life's current, participating, involved, animated, eager, almost breathless. There is a momentum surging through that draws us into creative, expansive interaction with those around us. All we want to do is to be happy and to make others happy, to heal and to bless, to release into the moment and hold nothing back. And yet, an aspect of ourselves stands apart, utterly detached, monitoring all that comes our way, channeling whatever attracts us toward where we would like it to go.

Of course, even this seemingly blissful, almost paradisical, situation contains within itself the seeds of unrest, and can be abused. If we become infatuated with our own precious bubble of delights, we may addict ourselves to all good things, and begin to arrange our world so that we never have to deal with anything else. We become insulated, self-reinforcing, aristocratically disdainful of those who are missing out on what we have. Perhaps we then cannot resist creating artificial patterns in our lives that perpetuate what we have grown accustomed to as pleasures, and soon we are no longer actually experiencing anything growthful. We become rutted in a solipsistic haze of assumptions; life is "groovy" but it's always the same groove.

The most discordant trine of all is probably that between Saturn and the Moon. The Saturn-Moon function seems to be quite alien to the trine experience. It's almost as though Saturn and the Moon want to quarrel or polarize or cause each other problems, and this aspect doesn't allow them the friction and tension to do so. Saturn generally arranges life strictly according to a pre-conceived pattern, while the Moon operates in terms of whatever feelings and impressions happen along. Thus, they pull in conflicting directions. The trine aspect between them, instead of reconciling, harmonizing, or easing this situation tends to confuse and dull the impact of such a conflict. People with this aspect often find themselves permeated by energies with which they have difficulty identifying. Much in their life seems to happen to them instead of coming from them. They may not be sure why it's happening or even what is taking place. All they know is how it feels inside, and at their furthest remove they lose touch with this as well. What began as a fuzziness around the edges of reality has saturated their world with doubts, with a sense of meaninglessness, and even with an emotional coolness and defensiveness, a keeping everything at considerable distance from the self.

How can all this come to be? The Moon in this case is avoiding the challenge of Saturn by becoming somewhat passive and mute, leading the person with this aspect away from identifying with the action and events of the life and toward a vaguely uneasy self-preoccupation. Saturn sidesteps this maneuver by withdrawing its inner sense of selfhood almost completely from the scene, reacting by crystallizing a distance from experience that makes any deeper involvement impossible. It's almost as though the Moon and Saturn were engaged in a competition to see who can pull the self more thoroughly away from lively joyous participation in whatever experience has to offer, which is the true trine heritage.

This inability to be with oneself in the here-and-now as life unfolds, illustrates the most devious and disappointing elements in the trine aspect. The Moon and Saturn are each eluding, escaping from, coasting along the edges of each other's realm. When an individual lacks sustainment from the two most fundamental structural components of his inner being, he will end by compensating for this in various ways. First of all, lacking strong motivation to stand behind and back up his own objectives in life, he will become dependent on others to provide the needed spark. He may secretly resent them for this, or excessively obligate himself to others, or need them to approve of, to certify his every move. On the one hand he may feel the need to be enveloped in a whirl of good feelings and to cast a cloak of good intentions about everything he does; on the other hand he may turn icily anti-social, retracting from intimate contact, trapped in a brittle shell of self-sufficiency. A false note sounds through both the compulsive need to be liked and respected, and the out-of-reach harshness and strangeness. Both seem equally unreal.

Secondly, those with this aspect often act as though what is happening is never really happening to them. They seek out object lessons for others, for people in general, but seldom get down to any realization of how what comes into their lives is a reflection of who they are and what they have to work on within themselves. Trying to breeze through the most incredible situations in open-eyed innocence, they miss out on the messages life or other human beings try to send their way. They hear only what they want to hear and see what suits their fancy and their fantasy.

Trine aspects engender a consciousness that is out on the periphery of life-events, scanning, flashing, touching upon the general currents. Self-conscious-ness that is awake and focussed usually is attainable only by working through ones intensive aspects. Here in the trines we see things broadly, looking for what will take us further, seldom staying with anything long enough to develop real self-knowledge. Diffuse impressions are fine and in many ways helpful in some areas of life, but Moon to Saturn is not one of them. The Moon and Saturn thrive on squares (where they give each other no end of trouble) and to some extent oppositions (where when all else fails hard work brings positive changes). In viewing Moon trine Saturn, we have seen the distortions of the trine aspect. Even here, however, the brighter side of the trine can shine through. A softened Moon-Saturn drive makes for a gritty willingness to endure and to make the best of whatever odd karma besets these people. Although they may not be fully aware of what they are drawing to them and what it really has to do with them, they can excel at getting in the spirit of it anyway and developing humor, unexpected insights, and a certain ready courage. Resilient in defeat, self-deprecating when things run smoothly, they run counter to normal expectation consistently. The trine spirit shows through in a characteristic bemusement and wistfulness that refuses to get too caught up in the stark facts that weigh others down.

In Jupiter trine Venus we find the opposite of Saturn trine Moon, in which two planets that have a lot of talents and virtues to share come together in the harmonious trine. It can almost be too much of a good thing. As most typified by women with this aspect, there is a classic beauty, charm, and attractiveness here quite frequently. She can be lovely, effervescent, wondrous, fair. A sparkling magnetism makes everyone feel good about her, drawn to basking in her presence. She is fun to be with, flattering, bubbling with good spirits. She likes to think the best of others, to bless them with her approval. Even if she is not quite so well-endowed she strikes a resonant chord in those who can tune in to her. She is "something special." However...

The finest jewel needs an appropriate setting. If others fail to notice her, if her unique attributes are not valued highly enough, she may begin to lose some of her luster. Further, if mundane situations prevail and little attention is paid to the lighter side of life, she may fade into the background, falling into daydreams and chronic yearnings that seem far from ever being fulfilled. She cannot always shine in everyday matters, for that is not her element, she needs the best to be drawn out of her, complemented, offset. In a suspended reverie, she waits for Prince Charming, is Cinderella, Snow White, Rapunzel.

Clichés these may seem, but for her they are very real. She is a magical being, alive when everyone is at their best, warmed all over when she feels the direct nourishment of expansive, creative human sharings. Discord unbalances her, she is hurt by meanness, appalled at crudeness and insensitivity. She maintains the highest standards and cannot stomach prolonged exposure to anguish and deprivation, in others as well as herself, especially if seemingly arbitrary and perverse. She wants and needs life to be wonderful.

It's easy to see that anyone so poor at enduring obstacles and misfortune, so eager to reinforce the pleasant and turn off the unpleasant, can set up some fairly one-sided situations. Nobody can really be themselves if they're too busy trying to arrange the appearances to look good. It will have to be appearances because reality will seldom consistently live up to the demands of the person with Jupiter trine Venus. More seriously, her assumption of the proximity of the longed-for infinity can get her in real trouble. She may reassure herself when life rests on an even keel by holding herself captive to her ideal of what might happen next, who is bound to come her way once she gets through the immediate situation. She is thereby setting herself up for bitter disillusionment. The archetype she fashions in the intimate garden of her imagination is far more real to her than flesh and blood people with their flaws and quirks. If she retreats entirely into her fantasy kingdom, she may spend many years enchanted and very far away. The world will be the darker for lack of her radiance.

The Jupiter trine Venus individual can draw upon the finest qualities of both planets to realize her inner potential and come to life. Jupiter grants us the gift to foster constructive life-forces in all that we put our hand to. Venus shows us how to love that in the other which wants to develop and unfold itself. Together these two planets carry a feeling for what is beautiful, a human touch, a genius for drawing out the best in whatever is encountered. The true Jupiter trine Venus function is to be light-bearer, dispelling gathering clouds of darkness and the accompanying anxiety and fear by shining forth all the strength and courage that can be mustered. If a Jupiter trine Venus woman believes in a man, she can be his muse, his support, the one who brings him back to life. If a Jupiter trine Venus man finds something he can trust and respect in another person, he can give them a reflection of themselves that bolsters their confidence and renews their ability to go on. Most of all, when anyone with Jupiter trine Venus finds someone who can take all the love and glad spirits that they have to give, then the overflowing bursting gushing smile and magic touch will never quit until that other has been transformed by being irradiated with living light that beams directly into the darkest depths of soul and says "Yes!"

Our final trine is Mars trine Sun, an aspect which perfectly epitomizes the genius of the trine. Those with this aspect want to pour forth spontaneously of all that is within them. Their natural impulse is to be uninhibited and unself-conscious, to make everyone feel that something vital is happening and that there's more than enough to go around. They glory in being irrepressibly themselves and are clearly at their best when they are free to be so. They cannot contain their nascent wonder, their high spirits. They can be outrageous, childlike, and tremendously refreshing. Most wonderful is their ability to cut through hypocrisy and sham, to say what's on everybody's mind, to release pent-up tensions. Blatantly, overwhelmingly, they are who they are and they want to have the kind of good time people can allow themselves to enjoy only when they feel comfortable enough to forget themselves, and when, no longer bound by their personalities, they can let go and really live.

Alert and ready for action, at the edge of their skin hopping about, these Mars trine Sun people can get away with almost anything. The Sun is the principle of being-true-to-self by dynamically expressing all that we are. Mars dares us to do what we want to do, regardless of mitigating factors. The combination makes for a rare charm. When we meet someone who's going to do what they like no matter how we react, usually instead of reacting we stand back to admire and support their efforts. This is especially so when as in this case the person is a natural, more provoking than intimidating, more primal than manipulative. We become swept along in their momentum, perhaps despite ourselves. Quintessentially Mars trine Sun folk are highly contagious enthusiasts and effective catalysts, carrying their world a bit further than it would be otherwise likely to go.

This aspect too has its pitfalls. There can be tendencies to overdo or underplay the energies involved. Because these people are always poised on the ragged edge of "too much", they can easily fall in. Scarcely moderate in any of their actions, when they get carried away with themselves they call up in others instant barriers and reactions. There seems to be little defense possible against such a tidal wave, and so the audience may in self-defense come back at them in a way calculated to neutralize their impact. If this works, it knocks the wind out of overeager Mars trine Sun. If it fails, everyone feels uncomfortable, awkward, even the Mars trine Sun dynamo.

Very common is the tendency to try to pull back and be less overpowering for a while. The saddest story with this aspect is the tale of those who learn to calm down and act normally. They can even become tongue-tied, circumspect, distrusting their own impulses. Such feelings cut them off from others, shut them up inside, and leave them pervasively resentful. At their worst in this direction, they can poison their whole being with their brooding sense of belonging nowhere on earth. Once mired in this cosmic funk, they are stuck usually until something in their environment catches their eye and rekindles their enthusiasm, or else after a long recuperation, they step forward again more painstakingly careful this time about whose feathers they ruffle.

In some cases, the extremes of plaintive estrangement and reckless head-first plunge into life are necessary for the personal growth of those with Mars trine Sun. They may capture others' interest more when they are incredibly up or dreadfully down than when they're somewhere in between. And they have a nature that is drawn far more to extremes of any kind than to tempered mediocrity. One feels with these people, if with anyone, that discouraging or denying them is a minor crime, that they should be free to get into whatever mischief their impulses lead them through, unhindered by others' well-meant advice and precautions.

An incidental by-product of the Mars trine Sun tear through life is that anyone else within shouting distance can benefit from having a little hype rub off on them. Those under the influence of the Mars trine Sun force field are quickened in their ability to be alert and awake, to pay attention to their own force of being and to bring it forward straight and unadorned. Of course, Mars trine Sun may at any point have the reverse effect, so dominating the center of attention that nobody else's urges to expression have any room to be heard. And such is the chance one has to take being around such people. Such also is the chance Mars trine Sun has to take, betting that being oneself will work out somehow, knowing that any other way throws up a tangle of complications.

The trine aspect lifts us up and out of ourselves, treating us to the exhilaration of emerging from ourselves into the greater life spread out all around us. As we emerge, we find ourselves drawn into a dance with other people who want to share our fun. There is so much to experience "out there" in the world, so much that we can never get enough. And yet, the trine is not merely the aspect of spreading out. The most crucial parts of the trine experience can only unfold within our own being. The in-breath that balances the sweeping outward reach of the trine can be every bit as complete. It needs to be if we are ever to find peace in the midst of an active contemporary Western existence.

Awareness of the spirit within is the fruit of a realization of one's trines. The feeling of well-being that is generated inside ourselves when we are quiet and still is as joyous as any excitement we can generate by outside stimulus. This feeling and awareness come when we absorb and assimilate what we have gone through outwardly. It's unfortunately true that very few fulfill this facet of the trine experience. Most of us externalize all our gratifications, sensing our own being as something smothering, to be thrown over for the sake of outer rewards. We are all nerves, restless in our limbs, hurrying from one entertainment and diversion to the next to avoid facing our own true being. Thus, for the vast majority of humanity, trines chart the superficial groping after evident pleasures of the moment, while the inner being starves. We like them because they seldom in themselves prod us or remind us of what we are doing to ourselves. But as we fritter away our vital reserves, waste our good will on surface pleasantries, and exhaust our tremendous wells of enthusiasm in nervous activity, we ensure that in future lives the squares and oppositions will catch up with us to force us to reconsider our priorities and become different people. Conversely, unless we work on the squares and oppositions we have now, any trines we have cannot really bear fruit, can never be the joy they were meant to be. Anyone bogged down in the lower regions of their being cannot rise into the higher regions in spontaneous free exuberance.

Astrologically, most trine aspects represent the fulfillment of the forces of a given element, whether fire, air, water, or earth. Two or more planets in the same astrological element, trining one another, open up a space in which a given element can be fulfilled. The effect is usually positive in terms of that element. For instance, if the Mars trine Sun dynamic is keyed into fire signs, the propensity in that aspect for propelling the self forward regardless of anything is accentuated. The earth element would tend rather to bring with it an inner demand that one ground the aspect in constructive attainments from which everyone can benefit and through which one can deposit one's enthusiasm directly and effectively. Air is the element most characteristically aligned to the trine possibilities, so that a fluent pliable expressive ease often pours through air trines. Water trines are also archetypally expressive, bringing in more of the universally human benefits than any other element, along with more of a sensitivity to the inner qualities that need to be developed if any trine is ever to fill all the space it's meant to.

As ever, there are negative and positive possibilities inherent in the emphasis on a given element. We become dangerously one-sided if we propel ourselves and much of our world into a given element at the expense of the opposing elements. If, however, we can do our very best openly and freely, and allow everyone else and everything around us to do the rest, then the given element will find its finest and truest expression. The four elements flow into and interpenetrate each other, and none can be fulfilled integrally unless all are lived into rightly.

Ultimately, the issue with trines is whether we will move in a small or large parameter, whether our ego-strength will be sufficient to carry us further than a self-congratulatory maintaining of certain characteristic stances on life. Only those who are relatively free of petty fears can allow the streaming, coursing vitality of the trine to permeate their being. Only those who feel secure in themselves can allow themselves to live, to respond joyously, to forget and thereby remember themselves. Can we give and take with those around us, this moment pushing off against obstacles, the next moment flowing outward into free mind space? Can we maintain our inner equilibrium, our delicate poise, so as to stay with precisely what is happening while its happening? Or will we back down, equivocate, bluff, rush here and there, going nowhere fast, but looking good all along the way? Those who pass the trine test prove inwardly strong in situations of extreme flux, as well as effortlessly giving when others need to be drawn out of their binds. Those who flunk never get down to anything in their lives, showing much promise but not quite knowing what to do with it. Both smile, but one from deep within, and the other like someone pursued and feverish.

The conjunction aspect represents a whole other level of life-expression. With it we come to the pinnacles of our being. In our conjunctions we stand strong and certain, for all of life is with us to back us up. We carry a collective thrust through into direct action. Something needs to be done, in which further forward progress is crucial, and with this aspect we respond by bearing a seed-potency starkly and single-mindedly to its destination. In a sense, it's as simple as that.

Generally, astrologers note something of this level of expression for the conjunction and leave it at that. The only problem is that conjunctions are much more involved than this. Specifically, the conjunction manifesto that we must mobilize toward direct activity propels us out as far as we can move beyond ourselves. Conjunctions, more than being mere points of emphasis where we demonstrate active presence of being, are those areas in any chart in which we have the choice between great heroic strivings and losing our center in being drawn out further than we are able to sustain inwardly. Our conjunctions challenge us to enact free deeds in the world, to make way for the fire of spiritual purposes to pour through and tansform us in all that we do. They demand every bit of energy, consciousness, and moral force that we've got inside, and more. If we can live up to their high calling, we evolve into purveyors of genuine life wisdom, warriors for mankind's future, seed-men for all that can come to be. But if we either back down in weakness and lack of will, or surge forward uncontrollably, intoxicated with the power that we can assert, then we betray our own innermost being as well as the winds of greater possibilities blowing through our lives; and we stand revealed as asleep or deluded, as incapable of rising rightly to the occasion of merging with universal being.

This highest, purest, clearest aspect of all demands of us rhythmic synchronization if we are ever to learn how to bring pure spirit through into the material world. Only a strong individuality can stand within the fiery cauldron of higher beings and emerge to be a worthy instrument of their work here in the world. The creative potential of cosmic warmth has to be stepped down to normal levels to be effective. The energy needs to be adapted, compromised, tested, leavened, metamorphosed and then once again brought forth to the heights, now charged with a new potency out of the surge of human wills on earth. To attempt to achieve this inevitably involves us in as many setbacks as encouraging developments, in endless ups and downs. Somewhere along the way, most of us lose ourselves. We become immersed, entangled, identified with the action itself. We rush into momentary impulses, we are drawn out on the slightest whim, we begin to hit snags, and every obstacle forces a reaction. Only those of us who train ourselves to wait in stillness for what is intended to unfold can begin to learn how to let the fire and the winds out, and then let them in again. Patiently dwelling within, casting aside lesser disturbances and hindrances, sticking to what is absolutely primary, we can steer clear of the myriad distractions that threaten to engulf us. With firm confidence, heels-set-on-the-ground, we can withstand the overwhelming force of what wants to stream through us and help to channel it to where it is most needed. The fires of the gods must have earth-worthy vessels if they are not to scorch our world.

Whether we are ready to take on the collective destiny or not, conjunctions in each chart will be points of emphasis of our will-to-be. The intensity of this force can vary to an even greater extent than we find with any other planetary aspect. For those who cannot pull themselves together to make any significant impact on the world around them, a sad little trickle of wishfulness and frustration is all that can be detected as a sign of their conjunctions. They will feel buffeted here and there, swept along life's seas, in bondage to anyone stronger than they are, helplessly projecting their own latent ego-strength onto others who can better carry it through. They may divert their will to coasting along and fitting in with each ongoing momentum that they encounter, sublimating their inner fire to its purposes. For those who are too much for themselves, who have too strong a selfhood that needs chastening, the mark of conjunctions is a torrent of self-will and agitation and push, manic self-assertion that can become quite destructive. These choleric tyrants are filled with supercharged dreams of glory and transfixed by each moment's magic, persuaded that whatever they generate must be magnificent. Perhaps a few of the weaker "conjunctives" will latch onto the strong ones, giving them an ecstatic reflection that confirms their every notion about themselves.

What is constant in all manifestations of the conjunction, and what must be emphasized in discussing examples of this aspect, is the feeling that it is simply a given that the way one is is the way life needs one to be. We sense in a conjunction that whatever impulses or energies are involved must be perfectly aligned to everything that is going on. Whatever conjunctions bring us to do and be seems natural, inevitable, and right. Who we are and what our life situation encompasses tend to converge. We find ourselves at the center of a whole radiating sphere, the focal point of whatever wants to happen in group process. Our dramatic performances convey to others: "This is the way we all feel, isn't it?" In tune with the whole, for better or for worse, we are who we are and can be no other way. Everything around us in all directions constantly changes and we ourselves are ever fluctuating, shifting, moving. Yet the central fact that remains the same is that we stand with our conjunctions at the forefront of events, and maintain our position as though we have always been there and always will be.

When Mars and Mercury come together in a conjunction, they stimulate each other continually. Mars wants to thrust us into the thick of life-involvements but then persists in attempting to carry us onward to some goal. Mercury is equally eager to be immersed in the life that comes our way, but Mercury is happy following out each moment's impulse wherever it may lead. The quarrel Mars has with Mercury is that Mars is impatient to "get on with it" and Mercury couldn't care less where experience is headed so long as it stays interesting. Mars loves to lay it on the line to Mercury that "we've got to move on" and Mercury delights in parrying this with its enthusiasm for what is already happening. The net result is that whatever aspect they share, Mars and Mercury are at each other all the time, complaining, remonstrating, persuading. Most aspects between them are therefore difficult, in that Mars and Mercury manage to keep people so busy that they cannot forge a vital link with their experience, being too caught up in analysis, intentions, and cross-currents to penetrate to the essential significance of what is going on.

Here the conjunction shows to its best. It is planets like Mars and Mercury that really come across in conjunction aspects. This combination makes for a fascinating effectiveness, a rare ability to pierce to the heart of events, to glean a great deal from all that one participates in and then to move on with a minimum of strings attached or loose ends to attend to. At their best, those with this aspect exhibit a positive genius for putting their point across, for accomplishing what they set their mind to, and for getting away with doing it precisely as they see fit. They come across to others in a way that is almost guaranteed to neutralize opposition or controversy. When Mars conjunct Mercury people are going strong, they will carry their whole world with them on their every impulse, for they are perfectly in tune with the pulse of the times, their actions are strikingly, sharply relevant, exquisitely timed. Their whole manner and approach captures, epitomizes, clothes what everyone is going through so as to draw forth its salient characteristics and finest potentials. In complex social situations, they keep their cool, hold to what they deem important, unflappably maintain an adherence to sound basics. Sometimes they seem like the only people around who make any sense, who can be entirely naturally themselves, yet in such a fashion that the greater reality is revealed through them. What could be more appealing?

When Mars conjunct Mercury people are alert, bright, and clear enough to embody the most progressive and positive social currents, they can soar impressively, beyond others' second-guessing and backbiting. However, there is something provoking about anyone who charts such a smooth forward course, and if they should falter, a counter-pull can begin to assert itself quite rapidly. Those with this aspect tend to be a bit self-righteous in proclaiming the truth, in asserting what is vital and what is not, in pointing out fresh perspectives that they are sure everyone has been neglecting. A sign of imminent danger is when this conviction that they are right moves toward a crystallization, a dogmatic ideological position. They can easily slip over the line toward sententiousness, lapsing into merely repeating what they've always known to be true, trying again and again to prove that there can be no other way. Infinite variations on this theme are possible. They may, for instance, turn reactionary, or mix fanaticism with paranoia, or stand pat and start sounding banal, outdated. Whatever the particular form of deviation from fluid functioning, what occurs essentially is that their mental image of themselves as special messengers for what needs to be revealed, undergoes a hardening into a fixed role calculated to ensure the self the type of audience that can only reinforce all one's fondest dreams and notions.

This fall into egoism is an impaction, a sterility or paralysis that neutralizes whatever good the Mars conjunct Mercury person has ever been able to do. It stems from Mars and Mercury crowding, piling on top of, and thereby disrupting and cancelling each other's activity. There is always a danger in the conjunction of the planets involved overwhelming and hyping each other, clamoring to impress and virtually take the other one over. The closer together the planets get, the less room they have for independent maneuvering. If the planets in a conjunction have the scrappy, conscious, sharply pointed energies of a Mars and Mercury, ideally they will be able to stir one another to their very finest expression in a kind of wonderful mutual stimulus and reflection, a perfect matching of energies and consciousness. However, neither planet is inclined to wait around for calm reflection, both being eager to make their points in the immediate thrust of the here and new. It is therefore crucial that those with Mars conjunct Mercury cultivate every ounce of objective perspective on their own personal expression that they can possibly muster. One can be sure that any but the weakest Mars conjunct Mercury person will be able to come across to others as though they have indeed become familiar with and gotten a handle on many of their own idiosyncrasies. But genuine self-knowledge requires far more discipline than the busy Mars conjunct Mercury personality can usually muster. And what it most significantly requires in this instance is setting the mind and body into right alignment, usually by grounding the mental energy in a healthy physical expression. When body as well as mind can carry through what one inwardly intends, the quick thrusts of Mars conjunct Mercury will mature into right action, rather than rotting into easygoing self-reinforcement. The individual with this aspect is the only one who can decide which he is really doing.

The other two conjunctions we will take up here are Solar aspects to the two closest satellites of the Sun, Venus and Mercury. Neither planet can get far enough away from the Sun to form any other major aspect (geocentrically). Worthy of note is the medieval notion that any planet that came near the sun was burned up in its rays, known as combust, but that any planet coming within 17′ of the Sun was cazimi, that is, became very strong and central in the life. Thus, traditionally the Sun has been seen to dominate other planets in conjunctions, but with a different twist in very close conjunctions. We will proceed here with the hypothesis that the Sun does indeed come into its strongest expression in these conjunctions, and that it enlists Venus or Mercury to perform a special role in carrying out its purposes. The question of cazimi, just as all questions of orb and variation in influence cannot be gone into here.

Individuals with Venus conjunct Sun tend to be thrust forward by circumstances to set an example, to represent something special to their fellows, to embody a collective aspiration or ideal. What is of personal concern to them is usually important to those around them. They are so archetypally resonant as myth-figures that it may be difficult for any but those closest to them to see through the image to the person underneath. These are people who are easy to like and to share with, but hard to get to know.

The quality they exude from the beginning of their lives is that of a Venus and Sun that have been so fused that few have ever seen them as anything other than beautifully, splendidly Venusian. Since Venus is the planetary principle that makes us inclined to be loving and accepting of others and eager to share our good feelings with whomever we feel drawn to, anyone so blessed as to fall within Venus conjunct Sun's loving gaze is likely to be glad they did. Wonders, charms, enchantment abound there. But let us cut through this splendor to see the real individuality behind the pleasing demeanor.

Those with this particular aspect prominent in their make-up often feel imprisoned within their own good nature and popular appeal. Any tendencies they have to celebrate themselves, to love being the way they are will be accorded a positive mirroring. They know so well how to please, how to get on someone's "good side". However, if they themselves become enchanted by the reflection others give them of any particular facet they express, this can greatly hinder their progress, because they then feel drawn to repeat their success and to develop an image of themselves as identified with whatever particular facet they happened to express. A frequent pattern is that of develping a quick reputation for this or that, and then knowing no way to get out of perpetually confirming and embellishing the reputation.

If they are physically attractive, their outward appearance may become so statically imprinted as everyone's sense of who they are that that is all they seem to be. If they are mentally brilliant, this can be their endlessly reinforced trap. Any gifts or talents easily become a fixed mold. Almost anything Venus conjunct Sun folk present is susceptible to becoming idealized and frozen in place.

Two virtues will be needed to counterbalance this impressiveness. Most essential is a certain innocence or candor or simplicity that forms an invisible shield to protect one from the severe narcissism that can so easily crop up here. This narcissism takes the form of coming to believe that they in themselves are the one being admired, rather than serving as a convenient focal point for collective imagery and wish-fulfillments. This at its worst degenerates into a self-indulgent spoiled notion that they can do no wrong, that whatever fancy they fall into must be divinely inspired and ordained.

Secondly, it is necessary here to be able to put oneself at a distance, to grow beyond needing others' acclaim, so as to start to fulfill the heart of the Venusian promise. If they work at this, they will be able to reflect back to others the flattering energy that has been sent to them, to give it away graciously. Any woman with this aspect will have to work particularly hard to steer clear of ego-reinforcing syndromes if she is to fulfill her potential of being an open vessel for cosmic love to pour through and to irradiate the surroundings. Pettiness, lazy luxuriousness and finding oneself sharply limited to personal experience as one's sole guide and frame of reference are some by-products of abuse of this aspect. He or she who fulfills the promise here will be able to shine forth a healing, restorative warmth and love toward anyone in need and will step beyond personal preferences to embrace the divine child wherever encountered, emerging from extended childhood herself into the joys of ripe self-giving.

Our final conjunction is Mercury conjunct Sun. I'll limit myself to a few words on this aspect when within a five degree orb. It's important here to deal separately with Mercury rising before or after the Sun. First we'll take up Mercury fast or rising before the Sun or earlier in the zodiac.

When Mercury becomes intimate servant of the Sun in a given chart (Mercury conjunct Sun) and when Mercury rises ahead of the Sun in the zodiac, we have before us an individual who feels it to be his business to cause trouble, to set himself up as a fool or gadfly or dissenter in order to change fixed points of view. He runs counter to form, inverts or reverses the usual order and mode of perception. When in staid company, he may act outrageously and when bizarre behavior is taken-for-granted, he may uphold solid values. Constantly adapting himself to situations, he nevertheless must go against the grain and do what is least expected (except when we expect him to do this, at which point he will act predictably). He does not want to be caught, pigeon-holed, or assumed to be anything other than he is. And he may spend much of his life running back and forth, trying to keep moving fast enough in one direction to counter-balance his previous movement the other way.

Interestingly, the person with this aspect is seldom sure that he is in the right, dispite his strongly provocative behavior. He is very much the experimenter and is usually willing to turn around and try out the opposing view. All that he is really asserting is his right to see life through his own eyes, and to keep moving with the changes that he encounters. Once this is evidently accepted, he may visibly relax. However, he generally makes it difficult for anyone really to accept him as he is, for what starts out as necessary survival strategy often becomes mischievous and even perverse. Some with this aspect delight in undermining whatever situations they find themselves in, making themselves look ridiculous, and disregarding everything other than their own impulse, which is to do whatever they can to shift the odds or catalyze disturbances. Here the more destructive potentials of Mercury and of the conjunction aspect come forward. Mercury when negative amorally presses again and again for trivial relief or release, no longer knowing why or gaining much from it, but compelled like an out-of-control mechanical toy to wreak havoc. Conjunction aspects at their worst leave us stranded out on the surface of life, feeling that we have no way back to center. The intrinsic worth of our friends or of our experiences eludes us as we naively, impulsively act out.

The finest expression of the Mercury ahead conjunction to the Sun is a humorous, light touch that disarms, but does not presume to judge or dismiss or take up set positions. People with this aspect can be wonderfully alive to the touch or inspiration of the moment, of the other, of what wants to happen. When free of mental assumptions, they can move fluently through their lives, showing everyone what it's like to combine courage with humility, spontaneity with responsibility.

Those with Mercury conjunct Sun with Mercury rising behind the Sun are slower to leap into experience, as they tend to be busy absorbing all their impressions and confirming their fondest suspicions or hopes. These are people who will see what they are prepared to see. Their Sun dramatically blocks their Mercury so that whatever they need for personal development dominates perception and communication. Although there may be a pronounced attempt to penetrate to what is real, usually what is convenient or self-reinforcing or momentarily fascinating stands in the way. They may feel better if they can develop a comprehensive system of understanding that puts any immediate impressions into perspective. But any but the perfect belief and conviction can seem like a sham to them, for only what they know is right is even remotely viable as far as they are concerned.

Essentially the Mercury behind people are bent upon discovering for themselves what is really going on, checking out all data on the basis of their own experience. It is important for them to learn in the process to assume nothing whatsoever, to be willing to re-examine cherished notions, and to open to fresh points of view. Whenever they reiteratively assert what they have always known, they are in danger of stagnation. But if they can throw over whatever proves no longer useful or relevant, they can time and again renew their point of view at its roots. Then what they have to say about all that goes on around them will find ready ears, and they will know livingly what they know, no longer needing to defend or enforce it at others' expense.

With the Mercury behind the Sun position, we find a fascinating consistency between whatever those with this aspect imagine or project, and what then happens to them. There is a self-fulfilling prophecy at work here, in which their thought-forms to a considerable degree create their reality. Whenever their attitude is one of pugnaciously holding to previous patterns and fundamental assumptions, they generate an endlessly repetitive life situation. Whenever they see through to what is freshly unfolding in the moment, although they may not feel as secure and sure of their own position, their receptivity draws to them all that they will need to move forward. They are not ones to make rapid progress, but any willingness to engage in an open-ended dialogue with life will reap abundant fruits in the long run. It is entirely up to them how far they will be able to go with this.

In both the Sun-Venus conjunction and the Sun-Mercury conjunction, it seems at first glance as though the Sun subordinates itself to the other planet. In the case of the Venus conjunction, all we spoke of were Venusian qualities and issues. With Mercury, similarly, mental forces predominated. If one looks further into this, however, it becomes apparent that the Sun is powerfully present in both instances, and is in fact directing the expression of Venus and Mercury. The personal, direct, unavoidable charms of the Venus-Sun celebrator of life are Solar in their radiation. The insistence on seeing the world through one's own eyes in the Mercury-Sun aspect indicate a Solar self-sensitivity. In these conjunctions, Venus and Mercury do not disappear or even fade, but rather they are enhanced and deepened while becoming almost entirely subordinated to Solar purposes. This means in practice that conjunctions involving the Sun revolve around the stark destiny of the individuality, and never wander very far from this critical focus.

To sum up, conjunctions are aspects of the moment, looming into focus and then receding into the background. They invite us to rise to the challenge of the occasion, to assert and exert our own innermost being, and to recognize and respond to the wholeness that we encounter. Their fluctuating, mobile rhythm can always tempt us toward the extremes of too great an extension of our being beyond ourselves, or of shyly hesitantly enfolding the self in inhibitions and doubts. In the one direction we take on too much and cannot integrate our experience, while in the other we take on too little and lack nourishment for our selfhood to grow and develop.

Most importantly, the conjunction is the one major aspect in which who we are inside and what we meet outside in our life circumstances tend to converge to a point of identification. Whatever we carry within ourselves here has its direct imprint. If we are mean-spirited, with our conjunctions we manage to poison the atmosphere around us, to contaminate others with our

133

meanness. If we are brilliant, we light up the world. If we're strange, uneasy, alienated, we cast a spell of doubt wherever we go. If we are working through a great deal within ourselves, we implicate our whole world in our struggle. All of what we are is on the line, right there in our conjunctions.

As we come to experience and know this reality, we learn the lessons of autonomous individuality. We begin to see that we really are in control of what happens to us and even to a considerable extent to those around us and that nothing can stand in our way unless we let it. This brings in its wake an immense feeling of responsibility, as we realize we must be the ones to spearhead any change that is to take place. We stand erect facing the Sun and breathe deep of its life restoring rays. We are nothing but ourselves, with no place to hide and nothing to do but be true to that within us which is divine. Joining forces with all-that-is, unbound and strong, we reach for the sky.

The quintile aspect, formed by honeycombing the zodiac into five hexagonal segments, is the first "minor" aspect we will explore. The minor aspects mark specialized, intensified inward qualities that can prove spectacularly wonderful or agonizingly disasterous, as well as a vast spectrum between. They represent particular challenges an individual is faced with in terms of unfolding capacities for the sake of the whole of life. The quintiles, septiles, and quincunxes that we take on bear little relevance to fulfilling or realizing ourselves in the usual personal sense of this. They open up an extra dimension of chart interpretation.

Because of the transcendent focus of these "minor" aspects, only the more depth-centered or cosmically-oriented astrologers have generally said much about them, especially in the instances of the quintile and septile. Unfortunately, this leaves us with somewhat idealized pictures of them. We will attempt here to present a more balanced view, one that plumbs the depths as well as the heights of these aspects, revealing their creative dilemma.

In a sense, the quintile and septile represent extra-dimensional variations on the theme of the conjunction aspect. The quintile of 72 degrees (plus or minus 2 degrees), is a beautifully smooth and flowing energy stream that can rise to miraculous inspirational heights or can degenerate into acute psychological distress and exaggeratedly idiosyncratic tendencies. It is the gift of the quintile that with this aspect more than any other, we can freely bring forth who we are our own way, and usually meet with an enthusiastic response to what we express, encouraging us to go further. What we bear within us in our quintiles tends to be just what everyone had in mind. We seem to know what is best, truest, most central for everyone, and to be able either to supply this ourselves or to further its dissemination in our world. Our whole manner of coming across is unattached, fluent, luminously alive, bouyant, free. We demonstrate a knack for embodying the very finest in each of our actions. Rarely will anyone or anything get in our way, so it would seem that all we have to do is what comes naturally, and then sit back and enjoy the bounty of the fully lived life.

If only anything in this world were that simple! Our old adversary, petty egoism, here can drastically alter the wide-open prospects we glimpse as ideal. We have a dramatic choice in our quintiles whether to give forth spontaneously of all our best energies and awareness, or to exult in our own glorious impressiveness, in our triumphant ability to wield power and influence. If we choose the former, in the act of self-giving we can forget ourselves utterly, making room within ourselves for what lies outside ourselves. Others viewing the spectacle of someone who in their best moments is not at all hung up in self-consciousness will not hesitate to open themselves completely to the impulse that emanates from him or her. All those who are receptive can visualize themselves in the performance of the quintile person, with nothing in the way. On the other hand, if we take advantage of our privileged vantage point to assert our sense of self-importance or to force our own ideals and standards down others' throats, we render ourselves irrelevant to the evolution of humanity. Anything we push with our quintiles that is in the direction of a playing up to or manipulation of others, a pretense or subterfuge or loaded self-promotion, will eventually lead us into a cold, calculating ruthlessness that sees only its own advantage. At the end of this line, we martyr ourselves to our own errant genius, and cannot resist dominating whomever we can and proving our superiority at every opportunity, pushing harder and harder till we fall in a great heap and bring those who fall under our spell down with us.

A third alternative to reverential self-surrender and arrogant presumption is there for those who lack the ego-strength either to perpetuate the self or to overcome it. Most people with quintiles in their make-up will never do very much with the quintile potential. If we cannot contain and inwardly encompass this ultra-refined energy stream, we tend to spill it out all over the place, to dissipate its intensity. We feel agitated, exposed, over-extended, and itchy. Vacillating between flowing out uncontrollably and shrinking back into our shell of reserve, we become engulfed in the surge of events, to be thrust out of ourselves and then thrown back, over and over again. We experience all this at best half-consciously, seeing it mostly through glazed-over eyes of incomprehension. Hysterical, numb, afraid, giddy, we tumble through the world. Our hyper-sensitivity gives us an instinctive feeling for all that is happening around us, but our desperate withdrawal plunges us too far within, so that we bypass the inner connection that might enable us to integrate and stabilize our experience. We may rely on others' reflection of us, on sensations, on manic hyper-activity to keep us going, but we have abandoned our own calm center, and so can never really make much sense of the bewildering array of impressions we take through us.

Thus, most insistently of all the planetary aspects, the quintile demands of us that we learn how to enclose and enfold our deeper being, to protect our inner world by detaching ourselves from the surroundings and cultivating an inner life. Once we have diverted the segment of the zodiac enclosed by the quintile towards intensive inner activity, we begin to act freely, for now we can come forth out of our fragrant garden while retaining touch with it all the while. Inimitably ourselves, indomitably original and alive, we are recognized for our own distinctiveness and welcomed for the talents we offer so openly to our fellows. In the turbulent swirl of social affairs, the most consistent and stablizing force will be that of the person who has mastered his quintiles.

Saturn quintile Jupiter people are preoccupied with trying to maintain a delicately poised balance between their own fundamental way of being and that of others. Their charming presence ensures that their own sense of themselves will generally prevail, that others will leave them free to pursue their own destiny. However, Saturnian hyper-conscientiousness normally demands that those with this aspect remain sensitive and alive to the need in others to enjoy such freedom as well. There is a kind, generous, Jupiterian tact and graciousness always on tap here. How much development of this wonderful social capacity will be possible in a given individual's life-pattern is an open question, especially because troubles with oneself can easily take over completely.

When individuals with this aspect are at their best, they are perfectly in tune with the general currents of their time. Alive to and fascinated by myriad facets of life, curious about the way the other person sees things, sparklingly at the center of events in everything they do, there is a prophetic undertone to what they have to say. These are people who can reach and affect others, who draw out the best in anyone responsive to their influence. When they rise to full mobilization of their talents, whether this be in artistic creativity, healing restoration of well-being, or some other appropriate outlet, they radiate a positive, life-instilling quality that attracts considerable acclaim. They seem to have an inside track on what deeply counts, what is most real and essential.

This magic social touch, as strong and resilient and persuasive as it can be at peak expression, can turn sour quite quickly. Although in certain contexts and moods a self-assurance and natural spontaneous ease are very much in evidence, there is a darker side to this picture. When these people start doubting themselves, they will find more and more about themselves that causes them to doubt further, in an accelerating spiral until a dull despondency sets in. Their fine attunement is highly fragile and unsteady. Only when all conditions are supportive do Saturn quintile Jupiter people shine, until they have overcome those things that bother them most about themselves. Among such syndromes may be: When at all weak or depressed, their random impressionability and quick suggestibility causes them to absorb whatever negative cross-currents they encounter and take them to heart; they fall apart when anything about them is called into question because they depend so totally on being seen in a favorable light; they can become blindly willful at times, only to feel remorseful and stupid later; they spend their day subject to every wind that blows through, eminently distractable, seldom putting together the good energies they know they have within them. Generally, they fall into ruts and patterns and expectations and habits that provide continuity and ballast, but that preoccupy them so completely that they never can soar to the heights that are their birthright.

All the faults that seem so humiliating and pathetic to the person inside of Jupiter quintile Saturn are seldom even noticed by others. The extreme self-sensitivity these people harbor seems even less justifiable because everybody else acts as though it's nothing to worry about. Honest critical reflection from friends and family can be a great blessing for them. All these faults that so disturb them are signs of a susceptible, tautly present human being who is hungry for constructive sharing and shocked by greed, callousness, and apathy. If they can begin to sustain an inner discipline, if their easy-going tendency to perpetuate whatever in themselves comes naturally can be tempered by a strengthening and firming up of their reality base, then they will no longer be so malleable to being pulled off-center. Those with Saturn quintile Jupiter must learn to be self-reliant, and to treat the good graces of others as a wonderful gift and assistance, while knowing that they themselves must be the ones to support their own efforts. Their flashes of what they can do when they're "on" should be motivation enough to see them through anything and everything that stands in the way of their being able to radiate cosmic warmth in the least of encounters.

The contrast and conflict between how someone comes across to others and how they feel to themselves is even more accentuated when Saturn quintiles Mars. Here we start to see that blanket perfectionism can be a besetting fault with quintile aspects generally, especially where Saturn is involved. By outward standards, Saturn quintile Mars folks give a sterling accounting of themselves, taking up a role that everyone can benefit from without undue complaint, fluidly rising to occasions of need or stress, proving themselves throughout to be diligent, conscientious, and eminently competent. Yet inside their volcano simmer endless self-doubts and fears and strange notions. Because so few can get close enough to see what's under there, seldom will they get help in dealing with their inner life. They do not invite close scrutiny, insistently maintaining a veneer of normality. Why are they hiding, what is boiling over inside these people?

The neat package of good intentions that Saturn quintile Mars individuals market as themselves is perfectly designed to appease their inner sense of never being able to measure up to what they are capable of or to what others need from them. Saturn requires implicit adherence to the plan one has mapped out for ones life and any falling short Saturn interprets as an intentional and willful betrayal of what is lawful and necessary. Mars, panting to live up to Saturn's standards of behavior, in any Saturn-Mars aspect is out of its depth, trying too hard to accomplish too much at once. Saturn-Mars aspects do not crush or immobilize Mars so much as call into question any Martian efforts, making one press too hard and straight-on in a way that is seldom whole or full or ripe. Saturn-Mars people, sensing this, do everything they can to make up for it, but they cannot in the end fool themselves. In the quintile between these two planets, there is a powerful inner sense of what is possible if the best of Saturn and Mars can be fused. Those with this aspect demand from themselves complete self-abnegation to living the general ideals, to fulfilling the most accepted standards of the community. If they are spiritually inclined, they may further glimpse the possibility of aligning themselves with those formative ideas and ideals that can shape this world in the image of God. They want to be conscious mouthpieces for the Divine Word, giving of their best to the good of the whole, becoming a vessel for the Highest in utter self-immolation. Nothing less satisfies them. And yet how many can live according to this ideal all the time? Even the secular social variation here is extremely difficult to live up to. Nevertheless, the secret aspiration of most of those with Saturn quintile Mars is that their every action be true to the highest and truest or most socially responsible set of standards and ideals.

In order to offset Saturn's stern commands and come to accept their own fallible mortality, those with this aspect will need much hard schooling in life-experience, the only kind of lessons Saturn understands. As they give way a little bit to accommodate what is humanly possible, what had put others off by its stark, severely inaccessible quality begins to blossom in this world. Now no longer striking out in the direction of infinity, the limited but sound abilities of Saturn quintile Mars can find steady expression in a form that rings true, for the inner battles one has survived come across loud and clear in one's quintiles. Others recognize, whether consciously or otherwise, what these people have gone through to be able to do what they do. If they can forgive themselves their imperfections, their world will be happy to second the motion.

It should be clear by now that quintile aspects represent the greatest demands a person can make upon himself or herself, and that all of us must in some degree fall short of their illimitable promise. By being something we can't ever take for granted or feel we've gone as far as we can with, quintiles spur us onward, beyond the familiar and the known. Our quintiles point to a perfect blending of the best of the world around us with the finest that we bear within ourselves. Even a dash of genuine realization at this level proves tremendously stirring. Doing or saying the right thing at the right time, extracting the inner kernel of each experience, artless as a child yet a bit God-like in wisdom, these are characteristic virtues of the quintile stage of life unfoldment. In this aspect, the conscious free individual emerges from the mass to embody all the deeper yearnings which we often feel are unrealistic and must be forgotten. With our quintiles we remember, we see, and we are called to do justice to our vision.

The sextile is the last "major" aspect. All of the issues which have arisen in the other radiating aspects, the trine, conjunction and quintile, culminate here. It should now be apparent that these aspects, which are traditionally considered to be "harmonious" or "flowing" or "easy", seen in effect as affording us a free ride through life, are in reality anything but a boon that we can take for granted. It is in these radiating aspects that we face a stark choice between inner development and dissipation of our forces. When we fall into a dissipated life-pattern, our radiating aspects will rather tend to coat us over with the delusion that everything is going fine than they will in any way rescue us from our blunders. When we move forward into a genuine striving toward self-mastery, our radiating aspects amply reward us with the ability to act rightly in every situation, and to partake consistently of the best of life. But it must be emphasized again that even this wonderful state of affairs is not there for our personal gratification and that we cannot attain to it without first going beyond the inner gnawing desire for self-aggrandizement.

Our sextiles point us toward the final resolution of the drama of the radiating aspects. These are aspects of operative intelligence, in which the scope of our world-view, encompassing the overall patterns and forms that we are able to grasp and express through, determines how far we can go. As we awaken to a whole vision of the world in which we are involved, as we perceive objectively and clearly who we are and what we are intended to do, we find ourselves capable of exquisitely fine self-application to any given task at hand. There is a calm, tranquil, stable, self-contained, life-enhancing quality to the sextile. Because we find here that what we bear within ourselves is perfectly congruent with the need that we encounter in the objective situation before us, we can bring forward in our sextiles a caring, loving, supportive good will that is actively present, and that feels right to all concerned. Interweaving our finest skills with the ins and outs of everyday manifestation, we do what is there to be done the way it is meant to be done.

To the extent to which we fall asleep in our sextiles, we become hopelessly confused and lost. While the wakeful response here is to act in accord with the essential form of reality, determining what is right by keen direct observation, the dreamy counterpart is to live vicariously, absorbing others' impressions and expectations, casting ourselves afloat in rumors and conundrums. We crave desperately in our sextiles for life to go a certain way, the way it's supposed to be. We are hyper-eager to fit in with this pattern, to do each thing right, to make ourselves into a perfect citizen of this world. However, this desire subjects us to everyone's demands, to contextual undercurrents, to the accustomed state of affairs. We may in the bargain sell our soul for superficial social approval, and substitute within our own awareness the way everyone pretends the world is for the way it really is. Then we become lost in our heads, for we sever our cord of direct touch with reality. We become preoccupied with a bundle of cross-currents, always figuring out different angles, preparing for eventualities, obsessed with what-if, what-then, why, how, and each wind that blows through can easily knock us off our course. When we take our cue entirely from outside ourselves, we render ourselves a moral automaton and a worldly functionary, a cog in a wheel that goes through the motions but whose creative individualized spirit is utterly subordinated to mechanical perpetuations of meaningless quasi-adult patterns. Each isolated detail that we are brought up against is neatly stacked next to another just like it, and all of them add up to nothing. We have so forgotten what is essential that we no longer function from our own center at all. We cannot stand still if the world around us is moving, and we cannot make any headway if others are stalled. We are not at all present, for we have succumbed to the enchantment of an easy-going stream of subconscious routine. We are lost in a maze, an intricate webwork of anonymous bits and pieces, and we know no way out, and perhaps no longer even remember that there can be an "out".

Throughout these descriptions, it is important to bear in mind that only the thinnest membrane separates the upper and lower paths, and that these worlds constantly intersect. Those who no longer have any idea what is really going on exist in the same universe with those who know precisely what is happening. Yet the sextile drama reveals clearly why neither world affects the other much. It is in the nature of the positive sextile expression that it engraves itself on the life-situation with such a perfect synchronization of inner and outer reality that it calls no special attention to itself, and needs no particular recognition or confirmation from outside because it knows itself directly through its expression as it happens. It is crucial for the negative sextile expression that if it is to maintain and perpetuate itself in its unconsciousness, it must so thoroughly entangle itself with its surroundings that it comes across as mute and scarcely perceptible against the backdrop of everything else. Thus, both extremes of sextile expression are quiet, implicit, smooth, and neutral. Nobody can tell these two apart unless they can see to their underlying motives and essential nature, and those who can see this are by such perceptiveness obviously themselves in the positive sextile stream. Those who are enmeshed in the negative sextile expression have no way of noticing that anyone else is not. Unless they can stir themselves from their social conditioning and take a good look around them.

How does anyone ever move from the sleepy sextile to the wide-awake one? Anyone who gives of their best to their overall life-situation, even if they exhibit no perspective or spark of originality, by such activity builds up their personal integrity. Very gradually such good intentions can guide them through less and less stereotypical societal patterns. As their world becomes a more alive and fresh place to be, they begin to open up within it. Many in the contemporary scene are emerging over many years from utter conformity incrementally toward some degree of self-realization. The sextile path is throughout an unassuming and gentle one. Even though we can stand back and see a brutal contrast between those who have ventured beyond conventional patterns and those who seem hopelessly mired in the collective sea, there is a slow movement between, and the sextiles lay out a way to grow into new connections, new learning, and greater freedom. If we can persevere in our folly, and are strong enough to stand by our convictions, life itself will point out our errors as we go. However, a passive, acquiescent, weak ego will hold us back indefinitely, and for such among us, the sextile is the instrumentation of their bland willingness to do anything to please, to seem blameless, to be protected from harm.

Saturn sextile Sun people are always monitoring their own behavior, trying to improve their performance. The flaws in their superstructure are often all too apparent to them, and yet they cannot seem to get away from acting in a way that is at times mechanical and absurd. There is a certain subconscious rigid perfectionism that makes it hard for them to do anything spontaneously, naturally, effortlessly. They desperately want to act rightly and to be the best possible version of themselves that they can manage.

Saturn in this aspect presses for tangible results, demands proof that the Sun's dreams for the self are coming true. The Sun, at an opposite pole to Saturn's craving for substance, looks toward positive themes keying on progress and well-being. Those with Saturn sextile Sun find themselves pulled far in the direction of harsh and severe self-discipline and mortifications, and then pulled quite far in the opposing direction of humor, coolness, and a self-reassurance that everything is working out for the best. They almost fall over in one direction and then the other, but an uncanny balance restores them always to operative sanity and good sense. The net they are weaving or maze they are caught in is the question, "How am I doing?" and the answer varies with each passing moment.

Those who pull through this aspect in a wide-awake, eyes open, conscious fashion, will begin to leave behind the worst of their self-doubts and darker moods. They will also feel less and less compelled to "cheer up" and "make the best of things," for they will have a lighter load of inertia to overcome. As Saturn and the Sun collaborate on a life-plan, the feeling dawns that one knows precisely what one is doing. There is often with this aspect a strong subconscious intuitive awareness of an overall plan or series of laws within which each detailed pattern makes sense. When this awareness is cultivated and enhanced through inner development, one begins to see clearly how one is being guided through one's experiences, so that everything that happens in one's life fits into place in terms of the unfolding of one's destiny or karma. The whole picture looms into view, not only of one's own unfoldment, but also of the intricate relationship between who one is intended to be and the world-need. One comes to know and experience vividly a perfect concordance amongst the apparently conflicting details and to indwell the form of destiny, glimpsing its ultimate source. If one can go all the way with this level of experience, imaginative evocative impressions of a greater dimension of life-experience can be brought back to feed a starving world. Even those who stop short of these grand heights demonstrate in this aspect an heroic perseverence in what they know to be right, an undeviating inner clarity and sureness. These are people who have a long way to go, and who are determined to take every step along the way that is necessary to get there. Resilient, audacious, forthright, they endure.

At the other extreme, those who fall back in this aspect feel equally certain that nothing fits together rightly, that their world is inevitably falling asunder and they with it unless they take care and watch out. A strong response to such a state of affairs would be to call the issue, to alert everyone to the forces that are working to undermine the overall welfare. Unfortunately, most of those who succumb to the negative sextile force are too overwhelmed and submerged to act effectively to change matters. They subconsciously feel victimized, exploited, misunderstood, trapped. They blame thir general life situation for doing them in, and proceed to collapse in upon themselves. Eventually, this leads to a pathetic pattern of behavior. Whether they stand aside perversely from society or lose themselves in its midst, they meekly appease the pervasive enemy. They are very afraid, and so they act perfectly innocuous and exaggeratedly normal, trying to disappear. Currying favor with whomever they meet, they adapt themselves to the minutest gestures and habit-patterns of others. They almost seem to memorize the way those around them act so as to be able to duplicate it perfectly. Quintessentially, they flatter, avoid all semblance of conflict, and shrug themselves off completely. Whenever they do trip over themselves despite their strategy, wells of rage, guilt and anxiety threaten to engulf them. All that they repress of their own uniqueness wallows inside as negative emotion, gathering a palpable tension beneath their placid surface.

It should be noted in passing that sextiles are the most paradoxical of aspects, combining elements of the trine and the opposition aspects. Therefore, apparently contradictory tendencies often co-exist in the same person. For example, many with Saturn sextile Sun can come across in some respects heroically courageous, while behaving meekly chameleon-like in other contexts. Nevertheless, the balance falls in one direction or the other. If awareness prevails, the dull conformist tendencies can gradually be resolved. If mediocrity has the upper hand, spurts of dramatic endeavor are doomed to fade to insignificance sooner or later. The deciding factor is: Which side does each individual identify with as himself? It also goes without saying that many fall somewhere in the middle, neither strong and clear nor cowering and lost. The extremes here depicted dramatize the choice that faces everyone with Saturn sextile Sun, whether explicitly or implicitly, obviously or subtly.

Mars sextile Venus is a very strange aspect. On the most basic levels, it's quite simple. Mars-Venus is the planetary function that shows directly, immediately, moment-to-moment how we experience ourselves, and sextiles are aspects of acute attention to each seemingly trivial detail of life as it unfolds. Thus, Mars sextile Venus is the aspect of hyper-conscious attentiveness to the self's experience of itself in the stark frame of each moment. It produces people who cannot but witness exactly what they're doing, how they're doing it, and what results from each action of theirs. However, the first complication is that the Mars-Venus scanning of the situation keys not only on our immediate sensing of ourselves, but also on the relationship this bears to our basic goals and drives, as well as to our surroundings. The criteria by which we judge our performance are long-range viability (are we on-track or off-track, right-on or somehow missing out?) and social interplay (are we doing what we're supposed to do, are we being conscientious, flexible, and effective?). What we want to know is: What exactly is coming forth from us and what is its impact, and how does that impact work into all that we intend and how everybody feels around us?

This is an exceedingly specialized and refined situation. Mars sextile Venus people can be driven almost to distraction by the degree of their attunement to what is happening. A further wrinkle is that in compensation for this tendency, many of those with this aspect try to filter out whole areas of their sense-experience and can do such a good job of this that they become almost entirely absent in many situations to which others are far more attentive and in which greater involvement is experienced by everyone else. Often, Mars sextile Venus folk will try any device they can find to alleviate their self-consciousness, to deaden their responses, to dull their sensibility. Frequent choices are: alcohol, cigarettes, drugs, self-loss in extreme sensation, pronounced eccentricity, and excesses of any kind that lead to satiation and numbness, such as excessive talking, eating, meditating, or immersion in creative expression. Another means of avoiding too great a proliferation of intense experiences is to become highly discriminating about what kinds of things they participate in. In order to be able to choose freely their degree and level of participation, they will do almost anything to keep their world at a comfortable distance.

When this aspect is suffered unconsciously, when those who have it numb themselves successfully and entirely give way to conventional social forms in order to make it easier for them to fit in, matters can grow worse and worse. There are many directions this can take. When Mars sextile Venus feels trapped, confined, forced into a small compass of expression, he or she will compensate in a host of ways. Destructive, aggressive Mars forces that are being partially sublimated in constructive social directions will often be expressed indirectly and deviously in ways that undermine the general situation. An edge of bitter resentment clouds the emotional atmosphere. Laughter at other's expense is one outlet that is acceptable socially. Gossip, sarcasm, meanness, and scapegoating prevail. Venusian needs and desires that are being foregone in favor of ready social acceptability come back in a secondary form. Teasing, petty game-playing, acting supposedly for the good of others in ways that are secretly malicious, and randomly toying with and stretching boundaries of everyones' shared space are typical syndromes here. For us to follow these tendencies further down the line would be morbid at this point. Let's just say that self-destructive behavior such as alcoholism and socially destructive behavior such as compulsive pecking away at others are very common with this aspect. There is so much emotional, sensual energy to suppress and repress with Mars-Venus, and if we do so, it can come back at us very powerfully and often in ways we fail to observe.

The best of the aspect is splendid. If those with this aspect can stay with their own actual experience, they can accomplish a great deal in their world. First of all, they know how to steer clear of messy complications and to do every inch of what they intend to do. Once they set their mind to a given task, they are capable of saturating their being with all that is necessary to carry through. The myriad distractions that beset others can hardly reach them, for they are intimately familiar with these pests and have learned how to get around them. Secondly, what they go through in the way they feel about themselves and their surroundings strikes a resonant chord in many others. Their experiences are so archetypal, so dramatic, so unavoidably what we all go through, although here expressed in the exaggerated style of those who can never really get away from themselves and such energies for a moment. Finally, they have the healing, soothing manner of someone who understands and sympathizes with the most bizarre as well as the most routine of human experiences. They can help people to get through a lot because they are seldom drawn down or tempted into being absorbed in others' personal murk, and yet they seem to know how to help someone pick a way along the edge and out the other side. In all situations, positive Mars sextile Venus folk retain their sang-froid, their calm, steady, "I-know-exactly-what-I'm doing" charm. These are good people to turn to when one needs them. Whenever they can highlight the collective or individual need, and do their part to come up with a solution, they shine forth at their best. In such contexts, they are truly unexcelled.

Venus sextile Mercury breeds a conflict between Venusian self-absorption and Mercurial fascination with others that can never be resolved, but that keeps the world going round. Those with this aspect feel themselves to be divided in their allegiances between their own simple garden of delights and the more exotic varieties of life-experience available to them if they venture forth into the world-at-large. They sentimentally long for their private peace and quiet, yet seem to propel themselves endlessly out into the intricate and complex maze of civilization and of interplay with others. They often become exteriorized into busy miscellaneous interchanges, everyday neccessities, and a thousand other factors that call them out continually. Growing accustomed to never-ending business that is offset by outward pleasures as relief and release, they swallow themselves up in events, cross-currents, bits and pieces of experience. But always there remains within them a love for primal, familiar essentials, for those elements that make life worthwhile.

Whenever they are given a chance to recapture what they have lost, they jump at it. Yet one way or another, it seldom turns out that they can lie back and enjoy solitude and tranquility. Either their paradise is invaded, or they cannot stay there, or they people it with their preoccupations, or something else goes wrong. Their odd mixture of worldly involvement and contemplative detachment compounds on itself no matter what the circumstances, and the truth is that there cannot be any going back to the dream.

As with the other sextiles, this relatively neutral state of affairs can become either a nightmare or a springboard for magnificent accomplishments, depending on the choices, degree of awareness, and inner development of the person involved. Mainly, it takes courage and strength to venture beyond conventional boundaries in our sextiles.

Most Venus sextile Mercury people will fall back into lazy patterns. The start of this is living our life almost entirely for the sake of the way others see us. We identify with the image inside another's mind or the feelings another has about us. We want to be liked, to make sense to others, to get somewhere within the outward maze we find ourselves drawn out into. Characteristically, some who follow the exterior route with this aspect become experts at dramatizing and propagandizing for superficial life-patterns. They become the champions of the status quo, delighting in the pettiest bit of normality, playing up to the most wholesome elements in every situation. Nothing pleases them more than being able to affirm what everyone already agrees on, reinforcing it to the hilt. Those who are weaker still will fall under the spell of suburban-style packaging and the most easily palatable standards and sensibilities, and will fall into a tiny cog in the great wheel. These people are suckers for any societal product that will enhance their respectability and innocuousness. As smoothly as they can, they go along with everything. In the end they become decorative souls on the edges of life, putting up a wonderful appearance but quite out of touch with anything going on inside.

The positive potential here is considerable. There are many stages of possible progression into truly individual expression. The first tentative step forwards lies in acknowledging their Venusian needs and desires, and giving these room to make themselves felt. This means admitting to a more subtle sensibility, a more refined, receptive, and inwardly rich level of experience. Those who take this step develop an unique knack for matching their own inner experience with whatever is going on outside them. They start to be able genuinely to see a bit of themselves in everyone and everything, and a touch of others in them. Where before they compared notes with others always from an egocentric and very outward point of view, now they can see many points of connection with the person or facet of life in front of them, and so they can share of themselves and bring out the best in the other. As they continue awakening along the path of Venus sextile Mercury, they find that nothing they meet is alien to them, that everyone and everything is unique yet intricately related. They build up a fond rapport with many, for they know how to listen attentively, to appreciate special qualities, to cherish the divinity in another. Those who go all the way with Venus sextile Mercury sparkle with joy at the manyness and the oneness, the simple essence and the magnificent reverberations that they feel and know in every direction. Seeing life vividly through their own eyes, they discover endlessly that they can partake of every bit of it and remain entirely themselves in the process.

At the heart of the sextile aspect is a grand challenge: Can we pour out of ourselves to do something as though our life depended on it, as in a dream in which everything is happening despite us or through us, in which all is just going on and we are an intregral part of it? Can we so purify ourselves that we can stand out there, hiding nothing, revealed exactly as we have evolved in our moral stature? Can we find our way to a truly conscious willing in life, to alignment with our inner I? Can we satisfy our merciless social conscience without warping our own inherent nature?

If we cannot, we become immobile and stiff in the expression of our life forces, and lose ourselves in the form of things, at the expense of the inner essence. Negative forces can chip away at us until we scarcely remember who we are at all. We feel that there is no way out, that what must be must be. We scarcely remember why.

The two or more planets that come together in a sextile aspect naturally totally reinforce each other. When the two agree complacently that both are right to see the world from their own egocentric vantage point, they begin to take it for granted that what they so thoroughly agree on is a universal law and must be heeded by one and all. How they see the world hedges them in, and yet they assume that the way they are is the way they have to be, and that it is of course also the way that everyone is. Whatever they agree is real must be strictly adhered to, and anything they cannot readily encompass within their shared framework ceases to exist for them, or else it will call all of their attitudes and biases into question. The two planets give each other no end of trouble on jurisdictional disputes, but they fundamentally take as correct and unquestionable what the other has to say. Thereby, they ensure that their collaboration will be a closed system, an authoritarian structure blocking the way of change, of fresh perspectives.

Each of us knows better. We know that only what we can be pliable enough to receive as it is will ever nourish our growth or even be real to us. We have been told so many times, by our own better judgement and by so many others, that interpreting everything we come into contact with in terms of self-interest, safety, and security, will only do the reverse of what we intend, will call to ourselves exactly what we fear. But are we listening? Do we know what we know? Can we see through the haze of lies? Do we want a world we can live in, or a world we can be dead in? Many questions, and each one must provide his or her own answers.

We now return into the depths of matter and of the unconscious to view one more intensive aspect. Beginning our journey with the square and opposition aspects, we then expanded into the radiating spheres of the trine, conjunction, quintile, and sextile. As we descend at this point into the quincunx or inconjunct aspect of 150 degrees (plus or minus 3 degrees), we glimpse again being thrust in on ourselves and forced to find our way through a thicket of complications if we are ever to master the depths of our being.

The quincunx is an aspect of realignment, reconciliation, inward readjustment and reflection. The primal situation we are faced with in our quincunxes is that of being constantly, unrelentingly bombarded by impressions, sensations, and cross-currents that threaten to submerge us completely. We are here immediately poised within a world in which anything can happen at any time, life rushes at us and through us, everything is wide-open, right-there, up-for-grabs. This feels exhilarating, exhausting, wonderful, nerve-wracking. With the sheer flux of life-experience inundating our senses continually, we must either become adept at handling these energies, or we will become deflated, set back, overwhelmed. The challenge is to be able to respond each time with open, freewheeling enthusiasm and zest for life, to move with the current, to embody the fresh sparkling feeling that all of life lies before us, and that we are capable of anything if we are ready to go. However, as lines of force converge, they also diverge, and so we may be propelled forward, but also may fall captive. The natural tendency wherever too many factors meet is an interaction that is volatile and that sends sparks flying in all directions. To stay on top of so much at once can be quite an attainment.

Usually, the quincunx aspect disorients while sweeping people along, spreads them out, then inundates and sucks them under. This aspect shares with the radiating aspects a propensity for giving up the inner life in favor of a general diffusion, and shares with the intensive aspects a decisive battle to determine one's individual destiny. No other aspect, major or minor, takes us through so many changes, exposes us to such an array of temptations. Most people cannot sustain such a pace without losing control. Inevitably, they become entirely caught up in, even addicted to whatever is pouring through their lives. As one encounters them, they seem to be always in midstream. They feel keenly the need to develop some kind of perspective and inner clarity in order to make their way through what they cannot get away from. Unfortunately, those who cultivate detachment will tend to go too far in the direction of standing aloof and superior to life involvements. It is crucial that they create for themselves a private preserve apart from the press of events to consider and put into order their own sense of what is happening to them, to disentangle themselves from what is coming at them and from what their response is to all that they meet each day. Because all of what goes on around them reverberates inside them endlessly, they need a way to subdue the clamor of events and mental babble if they are ever to find tranquility, balance, the strength to keep going. However, quincunx people remain enveloped within a wraparound environment that never stops sending signals their way, and in their strident efforts to stand back from all this, they are likely to overcompensate by suspending themselves in automatic patterns of mechanically holding off life at a great distance. Anyone in this state of mind inevitably falls back into ancestral patterns of suspicion and negativity. Most of us have been taught from an early age that the world around us is treacherous, strewn with pitfalls, too-much. When we find ourselves time after time awash in stimulus and impressionability, and then move to cut it all off, we are acting defensively, reactively, perhaps even with a strange, refracted, horror-struck sense of not wanting to or being able to touch or move with anything. We then proceed to substitute safe and secure arrangements that will protect us from ever again being compelled to deal with the fundamental difficulties that surround us. We shield our sensitivity, phase out our naive eagerness to participate in the fresh flush of unfolding experience, and make ourselves over into stiff, complacently self-reinforcing stick figures. In our bogus ego set-up, we allow ourselves too much slack and become flabby, lacking any real motivation to come out of ourselves at all. Such self-indulgence imposes a complete stoppage of living, growthful experience. From this point onward, we partake in what is happening, but our heart and soul are not in what we're doing, we are swallowed up in unconscious assumptions. Any crystallization in our quincunxes is highly dangerous, for we create bundles of karma for ourselves by making our own egoism the central focus and tuning out all that we find inconvenient. Sooner or later, what we are suppressing must come forth and be heard.

The quincunx is an aspect of man living in civilization, facing at every step an overwhelming complex of possibilities, among which he must choose his way and then follow it through. Seldom does he feel clear as to all the factors involved in his decisions. Perhaps the only thing he can be sure of is that he will ultimately prevail if he stands strong and dares the fire again and again. Building courage and confidence by each successful encounter, he emerges victorious over his own fears as well as the uncertainties of a world in constant, radical transition. He comes to know in all of his being that every least facet of this life partakes of divinity. He moves toward meeting situations on their own terms, free of egoism, open and objective. Embracing the world-as-it-is, he pours the welcome balm of affirmation onto all that he touches. Knowing that we have somewhere to go, and that that somewhere is worthwhile, his inner resolve can always get things going again. Becoming the focus for the best impulses of people around him, he has the versatility to tackle anything that comes along.

People with Mars quincunx Moon feel pulled in two divergent strategic directions at once. Mars insists on making its own way through life on its own terms. The Moon smooths the path through life by generating a basic level of agreement and rapport in the social sphere. Those with this aspect often have an abrasive, rough Martian thrust at odds with a persuasively silken Lunar mode of participation in the environment. Generally, the Moon prevails most of the time, while Mars simmers, stews, wants out. Periodically Mars pierces through the Lunar crust and defiantly asserts itself in anger, passion, aggression, or intensely personal straightforwardness. Because this impulse takes off on a tangent from the established Lunar reassurances, it seldom lasts very long, and soon we are back to normal.

Mars in this aspect is being disciplined, chastened, forced to repolarize its way of expressing itself. In no way does Mars quincunx Moon leave one free to act as one pleases, to come forward with who one is and what one wants starkly and openly. Anti-social instincts and sharply individualistic tendencies must be rooted out. Every time those with this aspect give themselves up to a regressive mood, sharp consequences follow. Their poison is thrust back at themselves, their fury is unleashed on them in a stronger form than they gave it out. As with all intensive aspects, the issue here is whether the individual involved can recognize that he is the source of his own troubles, whether he can allow himself the perception that what he is getting back is his own negativity and that he will keep receiving it until he stops dishing it out.

Many Mars quincunx Moon folk cannot bear to face this reflection, and so they blame those around them or the world-at-large for everything that happens to them. This leaves them open to becoming the world's most paranoid people, perpetually defending themselves against intrusion or betrayal. Their paranoia draws to itself worse and worse things to be paranoid about. They crawl into a hole of their own creation and view life from a great distance, anxiously and suspiciously. Often they wall themselves off in a pseudo-world of their own where their own egoism can prevail. This keeps them insulated and makes them feel better, but they are no longer encountering life directly in any respect. They are imprisoned in their own fears, fleeing from their own raw vital thrust. From the safety of their own shell, they can rationalize away any enemies that they make and disasters they bring on themselves in off-guard moments. Some become so good at this game that they can make a whole way of life out of avoiding being affected by anything.

Mars in this aspect needs channeling into a work, at best a sacrificial self-giving to the human needs that arise in one's everyday environment. When Mars quincunx Moon forgets itself in its interest in other people, many areas can begin to open up. Free of their own internal pressure to prove themselves, those with this aspect demonstrate a knack for going right to the crux of what is happening in any given situation. If something is missing or wrong, they can help to change it. They can always find the right response within them to meet or complement what comes their way. Often they will be tireless in doing the good, in attending to real needs. Quincunxes challenge us all to grow out of self-imposed conundrums, to leap beyond our own shadow, to get on with what needs doing. Then we can operate from the core of reality, and make way for what wants to unfold. Mars quincunx Moon is the quintessential example of how cramping it can be to get snarled up with ourselves and what a wide-open adventure it is when we channel our emotional energies into what is really standing there in front of us to be met.

The Moon-Sun function is the most significant of all. It points to the heights and the depths of the human being, to the way in which we put together all that we are coming out of (Moon) with all that we are moving towards (Sun). Moon quincunx Sun people seem to be overshadowed by something greater than themselves, but to have a great deal of difficulty yielding themselves to that. Their private, personal point of reference (Moon) is exposed to the light of the higher self within (Sun). But often there is much confusion here between the Solar and Lunar forces. The Moon seems to pull back from and resist the Solar potentiality, and yet simultaneously to feel drawn to and overpowered by the Sun. Vast complications follow from this ambivalence.

Those with this aspect feel themselves to be a problem, an issue. Every chance they get, they will present to others their unresolved sense of themselves, seeking reflection, clarification, renewal. Introverted individuals with Sun quincunx Moon may hold back from giving clear evidence of their dilemma, but despite themselves their disorientation will make itself felt one way or another. Nobody knows what to do with these people. When they raise their identity-question to a more archetypal, universal plane, many will be able to identify with or relate to it. But if they burrow inside themselves and go around and around in ruts, spinning their wheels, asking for help while fundamentally unreachable, they spread their confusion and dismay wherever they go, and undermine others' selfhood to no good end.

Basically, Sun quincunx Moon wants to get out of the self and into the self simultaneously. The quincunx can suspend the self at the edge of itself, holding one at the level of generally agreed upon standards of what a self is supposed to act like, but enacting this none too convincingly. One feels held back from sinking into the deeper elements of experience that have to be worked through if development and growth are to follow. One cannot yet rise into areas which would enable the self to be exalted, by transcendence of petty self-images and stereotypes. There is a relief felt at not being made to bear a heavier weight and at being able to retain a recognizable sense of oneself, but nothing satisfies. The Sun wants to move on and up, the Moon needs to apply itself to something substantial. In between is a twilight realm, neutral and bare and uninviting. Yet one is stuck here until one can make an inner decision either to make way for the greater realities one yearns toward, or to incarnate more fully into one's personal situation.

Many will fluctuate or vacillate between the upper and lower realms. When they descend into the little self, they find themselves flooded with an accumulation of matters to be dealt with. Often they keep busy on this level, very active and energetic and alive. Perhaps they become thoroughly competent in one or two areas of expression, and develop these specialties to a high art. Meanwhile, another part of themselves calls them to a whole other realm. In the inner kingdom, they approach the thrilling realization of each entity coming together with, inter-relating with, and enhancing each other, seeing all of life reflecting upon itself and fulfilling itself endlessly. They may draw hope and faith and inner courage from this vision, but something is still missing or lost, and so they cannot quite unite themselves entirely with what is there within. The ordinary world yanks them back to resume their normal duties.

Resolving the divided allegiance of Moon quincunx Sun is very difficult. The quincunx demands that both realms be heeded and lived into, but there is also an inner necessity to begin to move more in one direction or the other. Those who cannot resolve this dilemma learn to throw themselves off, to make light of the self whenever they are put on the spot. If they can artistically express their razor's edge reality, particularly in periods when an odd edge of uncertainty looms over the whole world, they may be able to evoke the spirit of their age. They can never take anything for granted. Always faced with irreconcilable situations, they have learned to stay cool in adversity, to be at their best when nothing seems to make any sense and more conventional folk lose their heads. The virtue of their continual crisis is that it leads all but the most faint-hearted souls with this aspect to be able to operate without props, reassurances or circumstantial order prevailing. For Moon quincunx Sun, the external indicators of stability are never very convincing anyway.

There are a few with this aspect who will make their way through it by the light of an unquenchable spiritual aspiration and attunement. A mystical fervor liberates them from whatever inside or outside obstacles they must overcome. No longer caught in either their own net or the world's net, they can provide a focal point for higher energies to pour through them. The restless tension of Moon quincunx Sun was so palpable and unavoidable because so much inside craved release and could no longer be held under. Having developed along their path the resiliency and staying power to go their own way regardless of conditions, individuals who have struggled through this aspect are ready for their greater mission. Abounding life forces stream through the quincunx, and now they know how to channel them.

The quincunx aspect pushes us up against a devastating grind of experiences and impressions, a deluge that will never let up unless we act to meet it and turn it back. Finding ourselves hyper-responsive to what is "out there", we must reach back inside to a greater depth in order to tap into our higher capacities and balance out our energies. When the forces of the upper man overcome the lower forces in our world and in ourselves, when the natural diffusion of events is met by an inner strengthening and concentration, our greed at last gives way and we are free. Quincunxes provoke us to reclaim the true worth of what we bear within ourselves so that we can check the destructive forces in our world. Each quincunx represents an emergency, an urgent demand to take control. And when we respond, we are simultaneously released from the forces within us that cause us to be over-materialized, dense, tight. We can now improvise, be spontaneous, come back to life full force. In this state, we come to realize that the cynical assumption that the inner man must always be at war with the outer world is the greatest deception of all. We find that world and self cross and interchange, that outer and inner experiences merge. And an ancient truth comes forward to be heeded once again: "When man doth know himself, his self becomes the world. When man doth know the world, the world becomes his self."

In the end we arrive at the septile aspect, the most complex, involved, multi-faceted aspect of all. Neigher freely radiating (conjunctions, trines, sextiles, quintiles) nor thoroughly intensive (squares, oppositions, quincunxes), the septile, which divides the circle in seven segments of 51 degrees 26 minutes (plus or minus 2 degrees orb), cannot readily be categorized. The inner predicaments we are plunged into here are as starkly irrevocable and deeply engulfing as in any intensive aspect; the soaring cosmic potentialities we can move toward here will match the most glorious radiating aspect. This is where extremes of destruction and creation propel us through forces and counter-forces, chaos and flux, rumblings from distant pasts and glimmerings of far futures, and direct reflections of our innermost depths in all that happens to us. We are capable of absolutely anything in our septiles and pressed into battle, at one time or another, with virtually everything in the world around us.

Primarily, septiles are the aspect through which we are intended to learn our most crucial life-lessons. The timing of our septiles is such that at key junctures in our lives we are faced with the sum-total of every bottomless fear, every act of compassion, and every element of too-muchness that we carry around deep inside of us, now coming at us seemingly from outside, to see what we will make of it. Unless we can stand up to our own accumulations, we will be shattered by their impact. Ripe karma calls us to liquidate old causes continually, or else we are fated to perpetuate outmoded patterns helplessly and mutely. Most importantly, we must break through to an inward serenity of the spirit, we must here find the entrance to the spiritual worlds, or we will have little choice but to seek a lesser outlet, to flee into an illusory world, there to close in on ourselves and succumb to a numb inertia.

The two planets that meet in a septile aspect have long struggled against one another within our ancient past, and in this life they are forced to be welded tightly together, either gradually to form a unified and ordered whole, or to erupt and fragment into a remote isolation from each other, plunging us downward into self-alienation. Lest this seem an unduly harsh ultimatum, it should be pointed out that in general only when the shock of profound sorrow carries us to the brink of existence, only when we are touched by the shadow of death, only when we are thrust into the most impossible predicaments, when everything is dramatically at-stake and on-the-edge, do we ever burst free from self-consciousness, are we ever likely to accept the world selflessly and purely. Our selfish and furtive search for spurious fulfillment dies hard. Each septile in our charts signifies such an imperative toward final reckonings that shake us to our very core.

In our septiles we are magnificently self-obsessed, carried along by super-human currents, discovering ourselves endlessly, encompassed by all that surrounds us, trying to navigate through into the Infinite Beyond. Within the dynamic from conjunction to opposition and back to conjunction again, the last seventh as well as the first seventh of every planetary cycle is permeated by the septile challenge. These are times of decision, of precipitation, of culmination, in which perfect stillness and total motion interweave, when we are utterly free and in the same breath desperately fated, trapped, and lost. The septile times fill us with keen expectancy, as inner seething forces of inevitability project us through the eye of the needle. If we resolve our septiles, we come at last to a far shore, where we find ourselves truly, lastingly at one with spirit purposes. We join the invisible fellowship of all those who have been able to achieve the same catharsis, who have extinguished their separate preoccupations. In these intimate soul-depths, we know the essence of other beings and the inner nature of reality. We are in communion with the core of all Being, and thus in penetrating into the hidden depths of anything, we are now capable of bringing about a state of calmness and rest. When we turn our attention back upon ourselves, we can observe and reflect upon the self in a spirit of selfless self-love and self-preservation, in which with a profoundly open mind we mediate our own range of infinite possibilities. At the gates of true Initiation, we are free to choose how far in we will go. When we later return to the common stream of humanity, the real needs that cry out throughout the human family sing to us in subtle, secret inner voices. Our inner revelations have cast everything in a whole different perspective. From this point onward, only what is essential to human evolutionary purposes can reach through to us, and we sternly remorselessly exclude whatever is irrelevant to our quintessential mission.

Jupiter septile Mercury epitomizes the proliferation of possibilities within the septile aspect. The Jupiter-Mercury function is the most exteriorizing combination of any of the twenty-one formed by the seven classical planets of astrology. Jupiter always aspires to pour forth out of the self into life as a whole. Mercury restlessly craves constant sense-experience, encountering, living through, and getting to know the world around. Together, Jupiter and Mercury enthusiastically seek out every variety of shared experience in the social sphere, jumping full force into the complex civilization of our times. Their dominating motivation is to get the most out of whatever is happening and then to move on, looking always toward exciting, stimulating contacts with intelligent, alive people.

With the septile, the actual experiences often turn out to be disappointing and disillusioning. Whenever Jupiter septile Mercury loses itself in all that is happening in every direction, the overall situation fails to reflect the self back to itself in the way that is desired and needed. Those with this aspect frequently feel let down by others, misunderstood or by-passed or ignored. They may then react by sitting back passively, martyred to their loss, and draw to themselves thereby more and more of what seems so uncalled for and unfair. There is a tremendous impulse in this aspect to stream outward, to immolate oneself in life-events. But seldom does a fullness seem to result, seldom does it seem worth the effort.

Many extreme personality quirks become activated here to compensate and keep everything going while inwardly withdrawing or sulking. A few possibilities: They become tremulously hyper-sensitive to everything that might possibly go against them, turning defensive and even thoroughly paranoid and strange; they turn off their hurt reactions and numbly put themselves on automatic pilot, stiffly going through the motions of carrying on while inwardly far removed, resentful, and sad; they act as alive and enthusiastic as ever, but their body and mind start rebelling in unpredictable and devastating ways;

154

they press ever further outward, denying any personal needs for relief or release from their manic rounds, and eventually go much too far, rebound on themselves and hit bottom. One way or another, the need to keep going on with the show battles with a growing edge of desperation and confusion that pulls the self out of the situation, toward a pause for inner reflection, or, if the pain has gotten overwhelming enough, toward a need to deny and destroy, to do anything necessary to end all the suffering.

What is it about these people that invites such continual disappointment and frustration? Everything they do seems calculated to provoke a response. They manipulate every situation to go a certain way, scarcely noticing themselves doing this. Seldom is the other person free to be themselves, to act naturally. Instead, Jupiter septile Mercury forces everyone into definite positions in relation to themselves. This aspect easily can become a mad whirl of multiplex mirrorings, in which every concept, assumption, belief or notion that is going around inside one's conscious or subconscious mind metamorphoses and then comes back at the self as though from the outside and from others. Whatever is bothering Jupiter septile Mercury, whatever remains unresolved inside, becomes grist for their mill, and they fill their world with these issues and fragmentations. Because this happens so subtly, everyone usually fails to see that it is coming from the person with this aspect, expecially the one with the aspect.

Thus, with our septiles we permeate the surrounding atmosphere with whatever we happen to be going through, and then have it reflected to us largely through outward momentums that may have no apparent connection with all that is churning inside. But they have everything to do with us. We are here setting up our world to be an arena for acting out our most tortuous inner conflicts. And one of the main reasons we fail to see what is really happening is that it is a pattern we have inherited from our own past, perhaps powerfully reinforced by our early upbringing, and it is therefore so much a part of us that we identify with it entirely from far inside, and thus seldom recognize it when it confronts us from the outside in every direction. This is precisely the fundamental struggle we must go through in our septiles. We are called to awaken to who we are in the midst of all that we no longer want to be, to overthrow old patterns of fatality by taking our destiny in our own hands and by taking complete responsibility for whatever happens to us. To the extent to which we do this, the sting of negativity goes out of our world and we see again with fresh, open, glad eyes. If we back off from our own reflected image in each jarred fragment of our experience, we continue to be tormented by our own subconscious, tyrannized by residues, memories, and predispositions.

For those with Venus septile Moon, subjective emotional reaction-patterns can present quite a problem. Both Venus and the Moon try to draw to themselves that which is desired or needed, to magnetize whatever they appreciate or long for. Venus straightforwardly loves and busies itself setting the stage for all good things to take place. The Moon secretly absorbs anything in the vicinity that is possible food for growth or emotional sustenance. Together, they reach out and do everything in their power to get what they want.

Women often seem particularly susceptible to the engulfing tides of this aspect. When they feel an emotional pull within them, it tends to be urgent, all-absorbing in such a way that everything they meet either reminds them of it or becomes a facet of the pull or desire. Similarly, whatever their response is to a given situation, they burrow inside that response and become ever more and more consumed within it. Everything that happens to them seems tremendously significant. They cloak their emotions in archetypal images, cosmic vasts, sweeping generalizations. Jumping to abrupt conclusions at the slightest whiff of trouble or hope, running off to infinity with whatever tugs at their heartstrings, they rationalize at every step along the way, seemingly able to convince themselves of absolutely anything they feel a need to imagine or assume. The palpable strength and total conviction they display often prevails over less dramatic and dynamic feelings in others. Everything about them seems to say that they know, that there can be no mistake, that whatever they are picking up on is the heart of the real.

Men with Venus septile Moon are also usually quite emotional and subjective in their reactions, but their minds often get in the way. Like the more masculine-minded women with this aspect, these men excessively employ their minds to keep control over situations, to confirm and elaborate their impulsive responses, and to make whatever they feel seem eminently plausible, clear, and sane. Their instinctive aversion to alien energies and whole-hearted embrace of whatever is close to their heart are quite marked. Although they may attempt in their calmer moments to intellectualize their experience into dry abstractions, most of the time they bounce off of vibrations in their surroundings, take almost everything personally, and stick with what is real for them adamantly and blindly.

All those with this aspect would benefit tremendously from intensive disciplines that place lower emotions into a broader perspective. It is vital that they find some way to overcome themselves, to learn how to moderate gut-reactions and to correct them in the light of a greater reality. The problem meanwhile is that their emotional predispositions come from far back in time and feel like they've been with these people forever. Naturally, they have grown thoroughly attached to their own long-cultivated and characteristic way of experiencing the direct impact of sense-impressions and phenomena. And they seldom see what their subjectivity does to them as well as those around them. Simply put, it cuts off self and others from any ability to be in calm touch with what is really going on. A thick shell of personal convictions walls out the light of truth and supplants it with a mirror world in which all that Venus septile Moon perceives is its own reflection, refracted and distorted. Utterly caught up in the self, often fantasizing that that self is a direct reflection of greater Self, deluding the self in so many ways, the person with this aspect is trapped and isolated until they break through into all-that-is. The one essential step towards doing this is to stop reinforcing every least notion going around inside, to begin to silence the myriad busy inner voices in order to tune in to the quietude that resides deeper within. This will not be easy. Most with this aspect have become so far removed from their wholeness that they will have to battle through a total conflict of wills within the self. Facing their own suppressed fears, emotional blocks and radical insecurity, they will undoubtedly go through phases of their lives in which they feel convinced that it is not worth it, that others are trying to do them in, that the world is against them. But it is worth it, and these bouts of gloom are merely the reverberations of their own negative emotions thrown back on them. If they go through all of their sensations, habit syndromes, and fundamental emotional-sets, they will eventually come to be the person they had always pretended to be. Vibrantly in touch with the life all around, open to a greater level of experience, ready to be there for others and to give sacrificially of the self, they have become a truly whole, integrated human being. The joy and delight of this attainment is boundless.

Septiles demand of us that we put all of ourselves on the line, that we expose ourselves to renewing, transforming ways of perceiving and of being. We can avoid this necessity, put it off, escape from it into nebulous other-worldly infinities, but ultimately, sooner or later, we will be brought face-to-face with all that is unregenerate within ourselves in the given area of life-unfoldment. If we are not ready to deal with this directly, there is another way of working through much of our compulsive wrong-headedness. We can give of ourselves utterly to those in extreme need or to situations that are relentlessly demanding and urgent in a fashion that reproduces outwardly a similar condition to our own internal ongoing melodrama. This effort can relieve us of our bleak isolation, supplanting it with a productive mode of existence that vicariously works off a great many misspent pasts.

Alternately, many who have not yet developed the strength and selflessness in themselves to go even this far, find one last way out. Feeling weak and scared, they crave desperately some kind of anchorage or exterior frame of reference on which they can pin their hopes. Perhaps they seek out a person or situation, group or overall idea that they hope will see them through their travail by being all there for them while they go through their changes. If what they have chosen stands still and strong and is able to be attentive and sympathetic, supportive and firm, they may be able to grow under its protection, remaining safe and secure through great changes. The one great pitfall here is that one can only draw to oneself that which is reflective of who one already is. Therefore, this strategy cannot really help unless a certain purity is already there within the septile person. In such an instance, they will use the encompassing framework as an outpicturing and reinforcement of their own untapped inner strength and reserves.

Septiles thrust us into a world where everything is happening at once, and all of it is meaningful both for our own further development and everyone's future. Discoveries and revelations abound, but yawning chasms of self-annihilation and dark nights of the soul are also there to tempt and test us. The best and the worst are thrown together, swirling about us entangled and all-of-a-piece. Because in our septiles we become whatever we feel drawn to, diffusion and dispersal always threaten to take us over and carry us very far from the goal. But nowhere is there a greater strength of individuality, a more absolute will, a more tremendous stature and inner fortitude than in the septile repertoire. Septile people are potentially powerhouses, self-sufficient and unique, charged with their own destiny. They are ready for their greatest of tasks, to utterly transform themselves, if they can open to the spirit sources that are there to aid them. Their world can seem all treachery or all grandeur and glory, depending on whether they view it through the narrow slits of self-interest or open to the broad expanses of the inner realms of being. Now in this last aspect, the statement can freely, boldly be made: Their world is exactly what they make it. However, the little self lacks the forces to take on this resounding challenge. Only if septile people step aside and allow the gods to pour through and seep into every weary corner of themselves can the new life dawn. Whoever too long resists this command is also guided, without knowing it, but by darker powers. And the difference is that only the true gods give us back ourselves when they have done their part, enhanced and far more truly who we really are.

Only the most dynamic and dramatic planetary aspects have been chosen for this discussion. These have been gone into thoroughly and directly, but a great many factors have been neglected in the process. We could have discussed waxing and waning aspects, applying and separating, allowable orbs, aspects to outer planets or asteroids, larger aspect patterns such as grand trines and t-crosses, and so many other facets that enter into assessing the likely expression of a particular aspect in a given astrological chart.

Nor has there been much discussion as to how these analyses were arrived at, what system the author uses to understand the workings of the planetary aspects as a whole. Many possible applications of these insights on the aspects to various areas of astrology have been left open. Thus, concerning how we can better work with progressions and transits, chart comparisons, the prenatal chart, constellations, or heliocentric astrology in terms of the planetary aspects that are centrally important in these as well as other areas, nothing has been suggested in these directions.

Leaving for the indefinite future any further writings in the area of planetary aspects on my part, we are left with the skeletal materials here presented, in themselves covering the area in a more detailed and in depth way than almost anywhere else in the known astrological literature. What we do have here is a delineation of astrological forces at work that keys on the human drama, the subtler motivations and the cosmic themes being lived through in each of the eight important aspects. The concern has been primarily to forge an astrology that can be effective in counseling real people and in understanding oneself from the inside. How we conceive of the human being and his or her make-up is very much in question in the last twenty years of the twentieth century. If we really believe we can be depicted in simplistic formulas of social scientists or social astrologers, we will do everything in our power to make ourselves over into fitting such sterile molds. If we can make the leap into being able to imagine a being of stature, depth, and with many subtle, refined qualities, and then see that archetype in every person we meet, our world will form itself accordingly in a challenging alive direction.

No longer can we pretend that there is one way to be that is fortunate and blessed, and an opposite way that is afflicted and perverse, just as simple as that. The "good" aspects do not promise or afford a more constructive life than "bad" ones do. The radiating aspects are quite distinct from the intensive ones. But the difference is not one that lets us off the hook, so that we can put out an effort in certain areas of our lives, but coast or ease along in others. Rather, whatever we do, and whether we plunge thoroughly into the depths of material existence (intensive aspects) or soar to the heights of a greater reality (radiating aspects), we are called upon to move forward, to grow, to evolve into something more. Each of us uniquely interweaves intensive involvement with radiating expansion. The ingredients are the same for all.

We emerge from this journey with two culminating insights. One is that unless we put our very best energy and awareness into looking again at what kind of being we are and can come to be, we will fall prey to the widespread propaganda insisting that we are far less than we really are. For astrologers, this effort requires calling into question the assumptions of a pervasively materialistic psychology. The other insight is that none of us can go back to a simpler time in which we were either smiled upon or frowned on by the gods. For us today, our relation to the Greater Beings is an individual matter, it is up to us to decide. Any astrological chart, using whatever system of calculation and interpretation, can only point out the forces we have to work with. What we will do with our potential, our challenges, and our internal obstacles, remains to be seen.

THE ASTEROIDS AS CONTEMPORARY SIGNPOSTS
by William Lonsdale

A jumble of errant rocks, cast here and there, makes up the asteroid belt of our Solar System. They are airless, tiny, seemingly insignificant. Yet does not our modern life feel in ways like a life on one of these rocks, bombarded by forces and objects from every direction, exposed to the elements, bare and stark and rocky? Atomized fragments viewed against the cosmic vastness, small colonies of insubstantiality, these asteroids speak to us of our condition, mirror our fate. And they call us beyond to something they point toward, but cannot denote.

The four large asteroids (that have come to represent the whole system) were all discovered during the first eight years of the nineteenth century. Whatever they mean to us now, they share a historical seed-time. Yet the modern asteroidal drama has been slow to unfold. Only towards the late nineteenth century did the multiple facets of a new time begin to surface and to crystallize in many places at once. Only from the mid twentieth century has the world caught the contagion of consumer goods, progressive promises, super machines, and a different breed of human creature. When we turn back from the late twentieth century to the first stirring and quickenings of a turbulence we find ourselves enveloped by, and are drawn to the early 1800s, we encounter an agitation, a gotta-get-on-with-it that has since become the bottom line of our existence.

Outwardly, the 1800s awaken the furnace of industry burning hot, manual labor in factories, the external chimera of progress—fumes and action and big money, and also challenge and bold innovation. England is the first place the fever catches on. Soon America will fall in with it, then Germany, the rest of Europe, and eventually parts of Asia, Australia, South America, Africa—by 1982 all but the jungles, deserts, and arid plains. It is coming there also. A new scenario emerges on the planet: long hours of hard labor; dark gray, sooty, overcrowded cities; an inferno of perpetual human endeavor without nature or God for solace. These forms seemed already taken for granted from the beginning and allowed to spread with little opposition, as if they were centuries old at birth. Why? They had behind them momentum, capital, fierce energy. The time had come seemingly for life to fragment, to seek its darker depths; for separate egos to clash and compete, to cooperate and perhaps even love. So the asteroids loomed into view, a natural correspondence to what was taking over below on Earth. But other currents were stirring also.

Napoleon had betrayed the French Revolution while extending its temporal conquests. Segments of society that had before ruled supreme were now driven into the background, while others that had been powerless rushed to seize the trident and consolidate the new secular throne. In America the revolution of a quarter century earlier was now bearing its young fruit: a new kind of nation, gradually extending its borders, stabilizing and girding for a central role in later stages of the modern drama. On the world scene at large the dark seeds were being sown, and an expansive dynamism sprouted everywhere, a dynamism that would end by shattering all previous patterns, all coherent structures. Where before an individual could be sustained by ritual, by continuity, by commonly recognized and carefully maintained connections with other individuals, now a vortex was forming, and we would eventually be sucked into it—out of the last

161

remnants of our shared participation into a world where we would be on our own.

These were symptoms of a deeper labor and a far more turbulent transformation. The feminist revolution began in the early years of the nineteenth century with the births of Dorothea Dix, Margaret Fuller, and Elizabeth Cody Stanton. Today's liberationists look back to these women as innovators who had the courage and initiative to call attention to the oppression of women and to their dawning consciousness. The feminine element is particularly central to our story. When the four main asteroids were named after pivotal Greek and Roman mythological goddesses, they became the first significant cosmic bodies in our Western solar system since the Moon and Venus to reveal the feminine aspect. While pivotal male gods were assigned to the major planets discovered in modern times, most of the new asteroids continued to be named after goddesses. Overtly this smacks of typical male superiority—giving only "ordinary" planetoids to goddesses. Yet something else is working here. The asteroids serve as foci for the feminine dimensions of experience; hidden elements of underlying significance combine to bring the feminine to prominence as the central missing ingredient of our lives in the waning years of the twentieth century. These elements are then embodied in the astrological meanings of the asteroid belt as a whole (and the four main asteroids in particular).

Uranus, Neptune, and Pluto—each in its own way—struggle to break through former bounds of self and world and to arrive at a true universal basis for existence. Vesta, Juno, Ceres, and Pallas deal with the personal process each of us must move through in wearing away outmoded forms and allegiances, in coming to an integrated wholeness far different from the tribal unity of premodern times. The feminine half of contemporary life is less tumultuous, less boastful, more pervasive and radically thorough. The feminine in both women and men receives into itself the dynamics of concrete situations and fosters the human element in all activity.

Beside the revolution and ferment, the turn of the nineteenth century was marked by the romantic "movement" in art and literature. Two central romantic writers embody the new world springing up around them. In England the undertow almost snapped the mind of Samuel Taylor Coleridge. He developed an opium habit he could not shake and retreated more and more within himself. His writings are mostly fragmentary. But Coleridge saw what was coming, lived within it, and said enough about it to provide us with a crucial piece of the puzzle. He unveiled the law of polarity—that any likeness moves in relation to two poles, sameness and difference. Everywhere in nature opposing forces form a unity prior to their duality, a power, a dynamic, a living quality—not an abstract principle. The opposing forces are generative of each other, they exist by virtue of each other. They cannot be divided because each seemingly unique quality or character is also present in the other. From an asteroidal point of view, modern life is a battleground between a deep hidden polarity of powerful vying seed-forms and a random and meaningless surface plunging toward entropy.

The other key figure was Goethe, the creator of the *Faust* myth in its most significant and dreadful form. Goethe worked most of his life on his *Faust,* from 1770 to 1831. But while he wrote, the world around him as well as he himself enacted the myth he was revealing. Goethe touched the soul's plight in a modern world. He saw that the strong, ambitious, "great" individuals of our times are tantalized by demonic forces to "go for it," to do what they will and sacrifice all for the satisfaction of results. He perceived how inevitable such a challenge must seem, how inviting and hard to shun or deny. He made it clear that we cannot but fall, we must descend in fact to the depths of our situation if we are ever later to rise into a living understanding of everyone's predicament and to bring the force of our innermost being to bear upon the situation we face as a sentient creation. Coleridge and Goethe approached life and experience from within, so both were torn from the common world of the 1700s to a meeting with the monster and his radical unknown proposition. If we synthesize the visions of Coleridge and Goethe from here, we see that we shall go through whatever we must go through, that any given extreme partakes of its opposite and is not merely a barren temptation, that life springs anew in the oddest places, that we can take no world for granted. Where there is movement and flux, old categories are not adequate. Readiness is all.

Now we come to the heart of our drama. Let us try to imagine a celebration in the heavens, a vast extended ritual or cult across the skies. The spirit of prophecy is all-pervasive. It is the end of the eighteenth, the beginning of the nineteenth century down on Earth. In the worlds of the spirit are gathered the beings of those who will be incarnating on Earth during the late nineteenth and the twentieth centuries. The occasion is a commemoration of many past struggles and joys, but also a collective looking forward to a radically new time with its own peril and hope. Leading the procession is a great being of light who is to guide the modern age toward a cosmopolitan freedom of will, a spirit of embracing life as a whole. After the party is over, an epic unfolds over time, and many different individuals in diverse spheres of life strive to meet the call of crisis on earth, to rally themselves and others to do what is required.

Inherent in the earthly drama is the same force that confronted Faust. Humans no longer live in the heavens. The very bodies we come into are so dense and hard that it is difficult to bring our essence through them. Our intellects are so sharply-honed and powerful that we cannot see clearly or feel deeply much of the time. Our environment is full of poisons; even the food we eat is more and more dead, not fit for inner growth. Our schooling is oppressive and damaging. The media inundate us with insidious conditioning. Families cannot hold together or give us what we need. Where our heart cries out for love, we meet the hard edge of sexual obsession. Where our mind craves to learn, we are taught that who we are cannot be. Where our will seeks challenge and encounter, we are met with thwarting and resistance from every side. The foundations of our own being seem shaky and threatened by myriad outer earthquakes. The bomb hangs over our heads, ready to explode all our dreams in an instant.

In all this and through this, there rings deep inside many of us a knowing that the worst will pass, that we are being tested, that life is good, and that I AM. What was clear once in the heavens still shines in the summit of our being as we walk this earth. It demands to be brought down and lived, even down into all the miniscule encounters of daily life. Our depths are asleep and growling, while in the heights we enjoy abundance and ease. Yet here let us heed Coleridge and not lunge with our minds into the abyss between outward appearance and inner reality. Ultimately, each of us is whole and can bring the light we bear right down into our very cells. No division is final. We can find access to all that we are, as well as abundant resources in others' being and the world around us. And we can give of ourselves fully so that others will find themselves less alone, will be strengthened by the presence of a fellow worker at their side. To receive or to give we must penetrate the shell of this world, break through the husk of the asteroids; we must come to ourselves in the thick of the noise and the pollution.

II

It comes down to simple matters. Each of the main asteroids speaks of one of the four elemental directions from which the winds of change are blowing.

With Vesta, the first asteroid out from Mars toward Jupiter, we stand at a crossroads—holding to a hidden source of strength and receptivity, a sustaining inwardness, while outwardly maintaining a calm and neutral stance. Individuals with Vesta prominent in their charts feel keenly the disparity between what they bear within themselves and what their daily reality demands of them. They want to meet the external situation correctly, but something inside will not let go and pulls them back into an existence at the core of self. Their life enacts itself between these two poles.

The Roman goddess Vesta (related to the Greek goddess Hestia) was considered the silent, reflective and invisible core of Roman life. Her face was not seen; she did not reside in statues but in the rounded architecture of earth temples. She was revered in the home as the cornerstone of daily life. A special class of women were in her exclusive service from age six. These vestal virgins were the only ones entrusted to tend her flame. Everyone knew without saying that this flame was the life of the people, the focal point of social existence; wonder and awe and mystery dwelled therein, never far from the unknown known. Direct from heaven into the bowels of the earth, the vestal sacrificial flame struck an unbroken and unbreakable continuity of inner and outer life, of domicile and cosmos. The main meal began and ended with invocations of Vesta; some of the finest food was set aside for her. If the spinster goddess protected the well-being of the social organism all would survive the secret peril.

Seldom does Vesta figure in myths, for she was the underlying constant, not one to engage in war or frivolity. The elder sister of Jupiter, she dedicated her life to those essentials that might otherwise be neglected. The other gods and goddesses went off, but she remained behind, to take care, to greet them on their return with hospitable cheer. They might ignore her, but she was the glue of cosmic exchange. Vesta provokes little passionate excitement, yet nothing could go on without her.

For the modern individual, the asteroid named after Vesta raises a spirit that is strange, remote, hard to get at. Particularly in our time this force does not come forth and play its own active role in keeping the wheels rolling. She is that one who looks on at all the commotion with reserve. Of course, nobody is immune to the exacting demands of our contemporary existence, least of all the person who feels Vesta tugging back inside. By Coleridge's law of polarity, wherever there is a pulling away from something, a counter-pull toward that very thing will assert itself. Put simply, what we try to get away from will not let us alone. The more urgently we try to withdraw or avoid, the more insistent is the thing we fear or resist. In this case, we find that it is precisely the Vesta-influenced individual who is besieged by the everyday world, especially those facets of that world which seem most hard to bear. The gift of Vesta is that as we cease struggling to get away, the insistence of the shadow lessens in kind. A subtle tug-of-war goes on, and the world-as-it-is demands its due.

A peaceful moment, a meditative discipline, a rural tranquillity, these are characteristic instances of the Vesta experience. They are essential if life is to have any depth of meaning, if the weight of daily demands is to be borne with equanimity. What is needed is a dwelling within, a grounding in the abiding presence of inner life. One of the distortions of modern conditioning and mass education is the assumption that such a calm is somehow a luxury reserved either for the privileged or for lucky or gifted or simple people. Even when we know better than this, we subconsciously let this notion dictate how we spend time and energy and how much we believe in. A breath of solitude amidst clamor is qualitatively priceless. The forms it can take are infinite. The essential experience is vital in each person's unfoldment. Vesta shows up in every chart in modern times. And for some of us, this becomes more than an interval or underlying harmonic. For the Vesta-inspired individual, the ripe fostering of body and soul is the alpha and omega, the very stuff of life itself.

Why body as well as soul? The Vesta mysteries take root in the bodily organism. The analogies of womb and heart and body with a living temple are self-evident. The rounded Vesta temple embodies how we stand under the heavens as earth-based creatures, alive and free, in harmony with our surroundings, integrally a part of the evolutionary pattern. In order to live this truly, we need to observe the rhythms of our body, to tend to its needs, to keep its flame burning steadily. Because of the recent fads of health consciousness and recreation, we are all "aware" we need to exercise, eat well, and pay attention to our physical condition to prevent disease before it begins. Vesta tells us that we are more than mere mechanisms to be kept functioning at peak capacity or animals to be appeased continually. We are each rather a spark of God, a living flame that neeeds to be brought into every facet of life, so that our native vibrance comes through. That is to say, we are children of the universe, gifted with superbly designed physical vehicles so that we can perform our work and experience ourselves fully, but also so that we can blaze the light within through our cells and into the world around. With Vesta this becomes a modest venture. It involves simply being alive to the sphere of physical forces and responding to them wholeheartedly, feeling good in our bodies and radiating without egoism, doing what we do each day consciously, affirmatively, with a vital presence and enthusiasm, especially at the times of unavoidable routines.

A healthy physical existence flowers with openness to other people. After we overcome the late twentieth century crisis, we will begin a world in which brotherhood and sisterhood are as vital as the air we breathe. Even at this point, in order to get through the crisis, some of us will need to bear the seed of this quality. Vesta stirs a deep longing to touch another, to provide a basis for the other to grow and be filled with blessings. In being open to Vesta, we begin to make a place inside ourselves for others. The feminine aspect of soul spreads it wings to embrace, to be-at-one-with. We are first given this by the intimate love of our mother, but the spiritual dimension of our experience involves a giving birth to ourselves through the healing presence of God. Intense love relations can be a workshop for being opened and seen in a total way and for being the one who opens and sees what is living in the other. Just being ready and available for daily encounters and their surprise elements is another dimension of Vesta unfolding. For most of us, this full flowering can seem very far away much of the time. We often feel we must preserve our own domain against invasion, to make sure nothing alien poisons what we are trying to build inside or outside. Keeping to ourselves comes instinctively at the Vesta stage. It is crucial to know where to set our boundaries, to discriminate concerning unwelcome sides of life. But let us now turn to the harshest and most troublesome stage of the four, the one that can make us or break us.

Vesta blows in as a gentle wind from the west. Juno blows in powerful and hot from the south. She confronts us with what is critically wrong inside ourselves and in the continuum of our environment. Juno-influenced individuals can never get away from themselves or from their problems for a moment. At the Juno stage each facet of existence is ironically juxtaposed to every other, everything bounces off and conflicts with or is at odd angles to everything else. This is an all-consuming situation, demanding mobilization, threatening dissolution.

The Roman goddess Juno (better known in the mythology of her Greek cousin Hera) was highly revered as the queen of the heavens, the wife of Jupiter, the supreme female principle in ancient mythology. Her privileges and prerogatives were emphatically clear. Nothing was to stand in her way. In drastic contrast to Vesta, she appeared in countless stories, an ever-present figure to be reckoned with. She was mainly featured maintaining and defending her position at all costs. Frequently her husband indulged himself in frivolous escapades with attractive goddesses, Earth women, and every variety of female, and almost as frequently Juno took her revenge by afterwards punishing the women for their indiscretion and incursion on her territory. It apparently mattered little to her whether her husband had raped the woman or been invited; some eternal damnation was in store for the one who had dared to rival Juno. Eventually she tired of this and left Jupiter, only to be followed and won back again, perhaps on her own terms now. Even when Juno was not busy ravaging Jupiter's lovers, she is revealed in the myths as irritable, reactionary, clinging to her high office, ill-disposed to anyone in her way. She complains, argues, attacks, is bitter and resentful. Not a sympathetic figure.

What are we to make of Juno? For here we have pictured an aspect of the negative feminine, the martyred-to-duty never-appreciated-enough endurer of the worst. What really distressed Juno in the myths was the way Jupiter treated her, the general mess she found herself in, and her own chronic insecurity in the midst of it all. The general tone of Juno is beleaguered earnestness. Destructive influences abound, and nothing is being done to make it all better. "A solution must be found," says Juno.

As she walks through her cluttered and frantic world, Juno must meet up with irrational elements by the score. Children are screaming and tugging at her. Her husband has his own business to attend to and little time for her. The phone rings constantly, bringing mostly surface arrangements or unwelcome disruptions. There is so much for her to do, not enough time to do it. Whenever she is looking for a break a particularly huge pile of demands threatens to submerge her completely.

Or, she works hard at the welfare office so she can help those poor people. Two of her friends have been laid off, her pay is cut, her caseload doubled in the last six months. The air conditioner works intermittently. Her boss will not let her alone. She really wants to do some good, but under the circumstances finds herself becoming a routine functionary, rubber-stamping peoples' demands to be taken care of materially so that they can get through the month. (And, she says to herself, even that is no longer possible with the economy the way it is). But she desperately needs the job.

One can find Juno everywhere in modern life. These bleak common patterns are multiplying and intensifying throughout our culture, and we are busy exporting our bourgeois materialism to the world. The beat grows more frenetic all the time. What can Juno point to through all this? Where can we go with this mess?

We have gotten ourselves into the material miasma for a good reason. We are trying to build inside ourselves an indestructible energy to move through the worst fragmentation of our being and to bear a regenerative impulse into areas where there seems to be an impossible impasse. In effect, we have created for ourselves a scenario depicting clearly what death forces do when allowed to run rampant, unchecked by forces of new life, forces that could triumph over every inch of death and decay that we have sown. But we cannot break through to them, we cannot unite ourselves with these potent energies until we put behind us the insensate self-obsession that made us prisoner in the first place. When we react with fury or scorn, appeasement or mockery, we do so because we are made of the same stuff as what is coming at us. Projections of our illness permeate our own surroundings. The evolved Juno-inspired individual can be the finest person for getting through these impossible situations again and again because she can own every difficulty within herself and seldom stands back in judgement or pretense. She knows what she is up against because she experiences it as herself, as her own self-ambition, her desire to perpetuate herself and ensure her welfare.

The process involved in healing the Juno bind is painful. We are called on at this point to observe where we are triggered, what we react to most compulsively, angrily, and fearfully. Forgiving ourselves, being patient with the tenacity of the habit patterns is basic. The harshest obstacle we may have to face is a creeping and insidious self-loathing that has taken us over unconsciously.

The positive expression of Juno can be beautiful. It starts with forthright determination, the will to meet our life-situation with gusto. As we rise to each occasion, the inner side of the Juno genius begins to emerge. The Juno-influenced individual has broadened her horizons wide enough to admit the light of truth. She understands what she can do and she does it without strings attached. Juno is nimble on her feet, ready for action. She can sense what will happen when she acts a given way and she therefore learns to respond to a situation wisely. She grows through her mistakes, is willing to acknowledge them, to correct her course and change accordingly. Life is making her more of who she is each day. She invites this process ever to expand and grow fuller. Juno has found her rightful position and no longer need cling to upholding one factor against another. For her now each phase becomes part of it, indescribably worth it, to be worked with and furthered. What else is there to do?

Ceres is the main asteroid of the whole belt. By Bode's Law, a full planet should be orbiting the Sun very close to where Ceres actually moves between Mars and Jupiter, and Ceres certainly represents the general theme of the asteroids. It is the largest, the least eccentric in orbit, rotates the slowest, and was the first to be discovered.

What Ceres brings to us is the issue of caring for one's fellow human beings in a world that seems increasingly chaotic and strange. This fresh wind blowing out of the east calls us to a broader social consciousness. If we are to meet her challenge, we must transform ourselves beyond any trace of personal egotism or bias, and become a vessel for a greater light.

The Roman goddess Ceres (better known in the Greek related form of Demeter) tended the grain each year so that food could grow abundantly on the earth. She was a figure of light and warmth, radiating goodness steadily, serenely, effortlessly. Under her guidance, life was full and rich. However, Ceres is mainly represented to us in the myth of Demeter and Persephone: Demeter (Ceres) is busy about her duties when her daughter cries out from afar; Demeter drops what she is doing to rush to Persephone. When she comes to where she left her daughter, the girl has vanished. Eventually Demeter finds that Hades (Pluto), god of the underworld, has taken Pesephone to his kingdom of the deep. She knows that her brother Zeus (Jupiter) consented in this and so will no longer take her place among the gods and goddesses.

Demeter now walks the earth, searching and wishing for her daughter hopelessly, grieving and neglecting all her tasks. The earth is drying up and starvation looms for man. For a while, Demeter cares for a human child and tries to grant it immortality by placing it among the fiery coals each night, but the mother one night discovers this and takes her child back from the veiled goddess. Eventually, Zeus is forced to relent, sending Hermes (Mercury) to the land of shades to bring Persephone back to her mother. This he does, but at the last moment, Hades persuades the maiden to eat of the pomegranate tree. Mother and daughter are joyously reunited, but Persephone has eaten of the world below and must henceforth spend a portion of each year as queen of the shadow-realm; she can return to Demeter only during the bright spring and summer.

Ceres the asteroid corresponds to a mythology of remembrance and loss, of fond attachment and its inevitable sundering. The cosmic wisdom cannot be brought intact into our physical existence. In order to come to it afresh, first we must surrender it, leave it behind, die to it, and then later we will have earned a portion of this wisdom as our earthly treasure, as an integral part of our manifest life. Yet as we leave behind the worlds we have known, and with them the sustaining grace of the spirit, we fear becoming lost in this world and we harken back to a dim recollection of our origins. The Ceres-inspired person often clings to images of what-has-been, to traditions and fond memories. So easily these backward gazes can be colored by what we wish to remember, and can hinder our flexibility in meeting what is still to come, diminishing our strength and enthusiasm in the new. A lingering sense that one is somehow different from others, better in some indefinable way, superior in endowment, can creep into the Ceres individual and lead to the last triumphant stand of colossal egoism. Often masked or mute, such an underlying assumption need not be direct or outwardly dramatic to undefmine the fabric of social relations.

Accompanying this remembered glory and part of the attempt to reconstitute it somehow in the present is a fierce possessiveness toward one's own personal world. It is as though these familiar and common ties were about to be ripped away forever, and for one last extended moment they must be savored and clutched. It is difficult to let go at this stage, to walk away, to move on from old patterns and fond allegiances. In compensation for this, Ceres may choose a life of perpetual motion and change, with little depth of involvement. Perhaps these patterns will alternate with each other, so that in certain spheres Ceres avoids entanglement while in others she embraces elements of sentiment and intimacy. Whatever the combination in an individual case, the polaric trends of trying to hold onto the past and to what seems a part of oneself and of steering clear of nets of emotional involvement are the parameters of the orbit of Ceres.

At this stage of the journey through the asteroids, the collective implications of these tendencies loom as pivotal. The issues of Ceres are the issues we are all faced with at critical junctures of past and future. In the myth, Demeter or Ceres cannot be given back her daughter until she has gone through an inner realignment. When she wanders the earth, veiled in her goddess nature, seeming to be an ordinary person, as we all wander incognito, her condition changes, her heart goes out to some of the ordinary people she encounters. Only after she has humbled herself, pouring forth to them without the reverential acknowledgement of her goddess stature in return, can she be present and ready for the reunion with Persephone, with the part of herself that has become frozen down below. Yet even then, she cannot stay together with that part of herself, but must periodically give it over into the deeps for inner renewal. Purification must always go further. The eternal uncertainty Ceres must face is a mirror of our collective exile.

We find ourselves cut off from a past we want to perpetuate or honor or lean on. Ahead of us lies a dark unknown in which nothing we have brought with us out of past experience and lessons seems to hold or apply. Even though our fear and dread are palpable and pervasive, even though the tension of walking along this edge is agonizing, hard to bear, we must sustain it beyond the breaking point of our images of normality and commonsense, and accept whatever comes our way. We will then stand before the dawn to come, shaken, trembling, uncertain of anything anymore, with our surface defense of self-sureness wiped away. In this condition we find deeper wells within ourselves, we give without martyred masochistic absorption.

Each one of us, each stream or group or faction, has become convinced of her own point of view, the centrality of her own contribution or program. If we are thus ideologically or culturally bound to precedent and position, we cannot unite ourselves with the humanity of the future. The inevitable consequence of the world remaining cut up into myriad special interests and power blocks is that we will not come into our planetary destiny ever, at all.

One piece of caution must be added here: we cannot possibly legislate or force everybody to become enlightened and see things our way. That is the old politics of coercion. If we are to evolve further, we must awaken from within to the obsolescence of our habits and strict forms; we must begin to think globally, without being manipulated from outside or above. This cannot come cheaply or easily. An agony of collective grief and mourning is inevitable before the folly of our tower of babel sinks in. Meanwhile, Ceres calls us onward, tugging at our roots, encouraging our moments of truth.

The lifegiving fertility of Ceres is extraordinary. We are presented with the possibility of coming afresh into source comfort and strength, so that we can stand for a truth that cannot be effaced. At their best, Ceres-inspired individuals work selflessly and tirelessly, available to needs that arise in spontaneous willingness. Even for such people, however, the underworld must be entered time and again. No matter how good it looks or feels, the Ceres ability to surrender itself and pour forth must be tempered by experiences that are humbling, perhaps undermining, that call everything into question. Eventually, the Ceres person comes to welcome these dark journeys as intervals when one approaches the core of life once again. The polaric change circulating through this age of the asteroids will not let up.

Pallas, the one that moves closest to Jupiter, the final asteroid, is a cold and bracing wind from the north. The ultimate asteroidal issues shine forth boldly, powerfully. There is within each of us an exquisite sensitivity and susceptibility. Our challenge is to metamorphose this vulnerability into a courage and presence of mind, a generosity that can meet the issues our sensitivity exposes us to. At this stage, we have little time to fool around, for critical choices press upon us and there is no turning back at all.

The Greek goddess Pallas Athena (related to the Roman goddess Minerva) was a superlative feminine force. She it was who appeared to those in need and brought wisdom and strength. The Odysseus in Homer's *Odyssey* was aided by Pallas Athena at crucial junctures. She came particularly to orchestrate collective situations and oversee great decisions in which heroic restraint was required. We find her in the myths appearing on the progressive side in each dispute, often opposed to her brother Ares (Mars) and spurring everyone toward an enlightened course.

Pallas Athena sprang full-blown from the head of Zeus, her father, and was in many ways his female counterpart. She was renowned for keeping her wits, for acting quickly and providentially, for being true to what was most essential in every situation. Grey-eyed, clear, and brave, she was the embodiment of the native genius of Athens, the center of culture and learning named after her. One senses that without her, the foolish impulsiveness of other gods and goddesses might have prevailed far more often and perhaps even overturned the divine order.

For our time, Pallas is indeed a wonder. Behind her stands that great being who gathered the souls in the cosmic cult of the late 1700s and early 1800s, known some places as Vidar and more commonly as the Archangel Michael. Built into this mythos is a living truth beyond any we have encountered thus far. The inspiration of Pallas Athena borne by the asteroid called Pallas charges us through our susceptibility to this world with the task of redeeming what we can and making way for what is to unfold in the future. This goddess must act only in response to human initiative, so she stands silently by and awaits our awakening. Her call is urgent and extreme. Whatever traces remain of separative egoism are to be obliterated and from their ashes an enduring compassionate love will be able to emerge. Yet only a finely and thoroughly developed selfhood can be sacrificed in freedom. In essence, this is the stage of complete self-overcoming, of finishing what Juno began and Ceres furthered. The greatest inner battles must be fought at this point, with the outcome far from certain.

What we are up against is quite formidable. Here we are no longer putting behind us syndromes, tendencies, habit patterns, but rather the very self in its primal need to center life around its own inner experience. Whatever weakness stops us now becomes highlighted, exposed mercilessly, unavoidable. Any karmic tendencies to bail out, to jump to extremes or excess, to spare the self under duress are ruthlessly driven home to us by circumstances, by other people, and by the hidden machinations of our own deeper being. It is all too easy with Pallas at issue to project our struggles onto the world prematurely. We experience ourselves as passive victims of everything-but-ourselves, pathetically cast into overwhelming outer difficulties, forced to endure without reason or justice what is grossly wrong. Becoming ensnared in this delusion, we retract upon ourselves, fatalistically convinced we are doomed to be misunderstood, misused, and forsaken. An inner abyss of frightful nothingness looms before us.

Even short of such a breakdown, a lesser misery of intense self-thwarting can occur. When we bear the weight of Pallas, we invariably feel inadequate to the task, crippled, small, stunned at what our destiny seems to demand. If we attempt to carry this load ourselves, we are in for trouble. Individuals at this stage are fired by a deep-felt self-righteousness, perhaps even messianic. They feel it is up to them to stand against the conspiracy of corruption and untruth everywhere, to shine a candle in the dark. Yet when it comes down to it, their only resource is their own instinctive feeling for what counts, drawn out of experience and a buried memory of many pasts. This is not good enough. A personal tinge is cast over their every utterance or act. We have uncovered a prevalent contemporary trend, the quixotic lone individual self-appointed to force her way through every barrier of resistance by the battering ram of a voice that must be heard, regardless of consequences.

Such byways are endless at the Pallas stage. The embattled hyper-conscientious voice of the collective conscience engaged in thankless infinities of dedication has many off-shoots—the pure innocent soul of goodness trampled on by others' crude insensitivity, the simple childlike champion of everyone's right to live as they will. The underlying disease is the addiction to self-confirmation, the need to be right, to be gratified or enveloped by euphoric feelings. The fulfillment of Pallas can come only when one accepts the world utterly as it is, stands free of self-consciousness, and uncovers the purity of heart and crystalline clarity that can pass one through the eye of the needle and liberate ages of frustration and fear.

In Pallas' fruition, we feel an abundance of life forces and of warmth, a surplus to be given away. Whatever needs doing, we are firmly in place to do, more than our part, more than seems possible. Most characteristic of all is an uncanny knack for perceiving what life is asking and responding accordingly. We feel drawn to whatever furthers the divine world order, held away from whatever disrupts this. In command of ourselves, venturesome and courageous, we now stand as the living truth of what the self-appointed savior could only mock and caricature. The difference is that our source is not in ourselves but in God and in the overall good in the deepest and truest sense. An agent of wholeness, serene and ready, we have been bombarded from all sides, but we have weathered the worst of the asteroid belt, and we are awake to what is yet to unfold, beyond the trauma of fragmentation.

III

I would now like to place the asteroid interpretations I have given so far within the context of present-day practical astrology. Virgo is, I believe, exoterically connected with the asteroids. That is, there is sufficient affinity between what the sign of Virgo is about and what the asteroid belt is about that Virgo can be seen as "ruled" by the asteroids, as well as by Mercury, its generally accepted ruler. I should add however that on a deeper level each asteroid seems to have a sub-rulership over the esoteric aspect of a particular astrological sign. Thus, Vesta is doubly Virgoan, being connected inwardly as well as outwardly with Virgo. Juno connects with Aquarius. Ceres connects with Cancer. Pallas connects with Scorpio.*

The asteroids are to be used in individual birth charts; each is equivalent to a planet and to be interpreted accordingly. Despite their small size and fragmentary nature as parts of a larger entity or body, they are best understood as full-fledged members of the cosmic community. For purposes of any astrological practical work, they should be viewed as such, at least provisionally.

This might be the place to point out that this article makes no pretense of being definitive. It is a progress report of eight and a half years of intensive research placing the asteroids in every chart I interpret. But it will take a lot more time and work than that to determine what these asteroids truly are.

Finally, one brief note on sequence of the asteroids. I place Pallas after Ceres, not before as most do. This is, first, because it orbits at times closest to Jupiter, secondly because of Pallas' mythological affinity with her father Jupiter, but mainly because this asteroid seems to me to carry the weight of the final phase of the asteroid journey.

Now we can ground the asteroid interpretations in everyday outward experience. Just as Virgo seems condemned to work through awkward predicaments, to find itself perpetually on edge, caught between varying realities and perspectives, so the asteroids can be seen as the ill-fitting garment of what our everyday reality puts us through. Basically, we are teetering between spheres or life-worlds, each of which is experienced as unstable and unreliable. Each life-world is relativized by its relationship to each of the others. Even our own identity comes into question as we try to "get somewhere" through the maze of social experiences and meanings. We are thrown back upon ourselves, but are none too sure of what we might find inside.

Within this overall sphere, Vesta is the stage of holding to our individual rights, our autonomy, whatever "freedom" we can make our own. The permanent identity-crisis of modern times is sharply depicted here in its beginnings. We grapple to make sure there is a place for what we bring and for who we are as personal entities. We do not want to be squeezed out.

It is sufficient for the Vesta-influenced individual to feel that she is held in high esteem by those she respects or feels close to. Flattery or outward show embarrasses her, but heart-felt appreciation keeps her going. If she has to force it out of

*See *Rhythms of Life: The Signs of the Zodiac in the Late Twentieth Century* (North Atlantic Books, 1983).

someone, it does her little good. She longs to be known and valued for who she is inside. Generally she will substitute something else for what is missing, hoping all the while that what she really wants and needs will be granted her at some point. The surrogate qualifications she favors are just the kind of cues astrologers generally look for. She may opt for financial security, for beautiful things, for a cozy home. She often feels drawn to symbols of well-being, prize possessions or keepsakes, trophies or charms. She may rather seek mental paraphernalia such as reassuring phrases or positive attitudes.

An accent on quality defines her activities, surroundings, and basic approach to life. Vesta thrives on small confirmations, subtle cues, special corners of delight. Much of this comes unconsciously or is taken for granted, but it plays a powerful role inside. For the Vesta person a stark reality can be devastating. The principle of polarity reminds us, though, that this does not mean she will never choose starkness. Astrologers get caught in either/or reasoning, forgetting that life is constant process and change and that infinite interlocking worlds can be inhabited by one person at different times and in different ways. A Vesta person may well consign herself to stark bare simplicity for a while, if only to dramatize her inner state to herself.

The environment of Vesta is very often an expression of lack or deprivation. Lonely estranged wandering, an uneasy sense of never being at home anywhere, an edgy restless feeling invade Vesta's private universe. Anything can happen in a world that is up for grabs. That is precisely what disturbs Vesta and what rescues her from petty egoism. Nothing is so binding as idiosyncratic materialism or fussy attachments. The wind that roars through Vesta's world may liberate her to seek her treasures in heaven.

With Juno the ability of the self to adjust to changing conditions, to fit into place, to be seen as acceptable, competent, earthworthy is called into question. We reflect upon ourselves searchingly, question and doubt and evaluate whatever we do, wonder whether we can somehow "hold it together."

The life-world of the Juno-influenced person can easily seem to her cluttered, cramped, abrasive. She wants to get out of herself, to make something work, to attain clearly-set goals. She thrives on fertile busyness, constructive hardship. Not likely to lie about idle or content, the Juno person can never get enough of the stuff of life. She must be learning, moving, building, striving, having an evident impact. The satisfaction of a job well-done is a bellyful for Juno.

When not out on some personal crusade or cleaning up after everybody else, Juno is generally busy scheming new ways to get into trouble. Tackling the greatest difficulties in her chosen sphere of activity, she puts her whole body into the operation. As with Vesta and Ceres, the key is in the mind. Juno does what she does because she has recognized that it is there to do and needs doing.

There are a considerable number of Juno people who turn this sort of activity in upon themselves. Scouring inner rooms, sweating out personal conflicts, struggling to overcome oneself is a central Juno preoccupation. The more introspective or introverted carriers of the Juno impulse can devote their lives primarily to these battles. Even for them, however, it is the finished product that counts. Juno's true goal, often hidden from herself, is to drive into being a deeper aspect of incarnation so that what she is here for can better take place.

Little comes easy where Juno is concerned. The physical body may not cooperate. The work situation may not be right. Other people may get in the way. Integrating the various spheres of one's life meaningfully can be the hardest task of all. Juggling segments of reality, commitments, spheres of interest is often a Juno nightmare. At the same time, this is where some of the greatest rewards lie. The Juno-influenced individual desperately wants to see herself as able to cope with whatever arises, as flexible, multi-faceted, supple. If she can somehow reconcile the various levels of her concern and involvement, she is as happy as Juno ever gets.

The most troublesome aspect of manifest existence from Juno's standpoint is determining whether she is right, whether she is worth anything, whether she can use her performance as fuel to counter her negative self-image. The handicap of not believing in oneself takes a lot to overcome. Juno may have to work harder than anyone else, have more to prove to rationalize or justify her existence. She compensates by cultivating an air of innocuous blankness, or by working too hard to win everyone over to her side. Juno folks often carry themselves around as a problem, a puzzle that cannot seem to get worked out. Naturally, all these ploys, strategems, and defenses leave others baffled, over-impressed, or annoyed. It can be as hard for them to know what to make of the Juno person as it is for herself. She is indeed her own worst enemy, a perpetual issue or obstacle to herself. The only way out for her is through.

The Ceres dilemma can be seen as the all-too-familiar mainstream reality of our times. There is nothing out there to be sure of, to rely on, to organize one's life around. The government is unsound, business often short-sighted and rapacious, the professions and institutions mostly malignant. Lies and persuasion and propaganda flood us with what we do not need. In such a world any personal life is built on sand, perhaps even quicksand.

Under the circumstances, we are turned back inside to our own personal experience as an axis of life. But from the Ceres point of view, this is extremely disheartening. The Ceres in us needs and must have a larger frame to be part of, to work within. For most people, this means an outward worldly form.

Primarily there is the family. Ceres needs to belong, to be surrounded by kin and friends, to sink her roots into the earth. Characteristically, the Ceres-influenced individual will want to put time and energy into family affairs, or a close circle of friends or peers. She feels nourished by longstanding ties, wants to steep her life in good times, remembered occasions. In Part II, we considered this a Ceres hang-up, a throwback. However, in this section we are acknowledging the basic reality-orientation of each stage and depicting its struggles and issues. More than any of the other asteroids, Ceres tends to seek out what is ultimately not going to see her through.

Ceres wants to express who she is in her work, to bring her unique gifts forward and show the world what she is made of. Ideally, she will choose or find a job specially suited to her particular capacities, and stick with it, growing ever stronger and more accomplished as she grows accustomed to the situation. On her own, she is incomplete, adrift, anonymous. Her life-needs center around a warm and inviting or challenging context. Living where you want to live and doing what you do best now seem luxuries of the past. Ceres will have to provide these herself. Once she has visible work to do or a family of individuals to pour herself into, her influence spreads and others share the wealth. This is quintessentially fulfilling for her, but sometimes it seems she is more intent on modelling the way it should be than on living all that this involves. The ideal of generative institutions and social forms can overwhelm concrete realities. Additionally, what she builds may well have to be torn down by those who come after. But if even for a while Ceres can convince herself that she has found her form or forms, everything does indeed fall into place around that neatly and miraculously. For a while.

Pallas is radical even in its worldly manifestation. It stands for the aspect of modern life that most see as its greatest treachery, a few as its dangerous opportunity. Our identity itself is wide-open, highly transitory, summoned to perpetual regeneration. Nothing that we are stays put. We have already seen the uncertain personal life of Vesta, the oppressive social milieu of Juno, and the crumbling civilization of Ceres; here we have the abyss of the modern world itself. From Pallas' point of view, we are not a given, a firm basis, an underlying constant. The self is not safely contained, a finished fact, a backbone of simple being. Every inch of our life is up for renewal.

The strongly Pallas-influenced person feels like the perennial outsider, knowing herself (if at all) as somehow other. She may go to great lengths to fulfill social rituals, to seem to be like everyone else, or she may revel in her non-conformity, affecting eccentric or idiosyncratic character traits. Whichever way she plays it, Pallas stands outside looking in at common affairs. A seed of tomorrow, a stirring of long ago are alive inside her.

What does she fill her life with, what facets of existence is she likely to seek out? Given the resonance of an extra dimension of meaning and intensity working through her, she will often dive into the core of whatever promises her release and renewal, a way to be that matches her sensibility in some fashion. More than that of any other asteroid, the outer form of Pallas varies tremendously. In fact, outer form is not the key to Pallas. I see the first three asteroids as mind-centered and Pallas as heart-centered. This means that what feels right is everything for Pallas, what feels right and not so much what is outwardly steady or firm or judged appropriate. The Pallas person guides herself by sensitive antennae of possibility as others depend on recognizably solid properties. Pallas knows somehow what she is after, what makes sense for her. This will make little sense to those around her, for they cannot get inside her aspect.

For those with Pallas prominent in their charts, whatever they do is a means to an end, a way *through* rather than *into*. This is not to say Ms. Pallas can simply do as she pleases. Far from it. She is karmically propelled into each phase. A force from behind takes hold of her and guides her steps. In ordinary terms, fate-like happenings fill her life. Strange coincidences, convergences and divergences that seem beyond her conscious control mark key turning points in her life. When fundamentally conservative people have Pallas powerfully in their chart and being, it can mean quite a ride.

Under this influence many hitch their star to another person who can tell them who to be and make it all seem simple. Others lose themselves completely in something substantive and ongoing. A few retreat to basics and hold frantically.

For most of these folks, a fear of the open-endedness of their own nature drives them to get away from ever having to be alone. Sooner or later, that is just what they need to do. Neither hyper-activity nor self-forgetfulness will hold back the flood indefinitely.

For those who go with Pallas, what frightens others begins a fascinating, if unpredictable journey. Even for those who cannot embrace the radical uncertainty of the Pallas adventure, the simple act of allowing themselves to admit that they inhabit many different inner rooms is a giant step forward. Suspended between worlds, receiving messages from all sides, Pallas open to itself carries a potent force of being.

IV

The Voyager and Pioneer space probes have focused mankind's attention on the outer Solar System. After photographing the systems of Jupiter and Saturn, the far distant realms of Uranus and Neptune loom next into view for the late 1980s. But for now (1982) the spotlight is on Jupiter, Saturn, and their moons. A mother lode of new information has flooded us, crystallizing the collective image of these magnificent planets and systems. What we come away with is the sense that out there beyond Mars and the asteroid belt lies the realm of exploration, discovery, and adventure. In various ways, the terran planets, Mars, Venus, and Mercury have been astronomically disappointing. But Jupiter and Saturn are huge, complex, and startling. They and their moons hold many keys to our past and our future.

What has this to do with astrology? Everything. As the collective perception of what is out there changes, so does the range of ways in which we must respond to the archetypal potency of the spheres of the planets. Jupiter and Saturn now come closer; they stand before us as twin sentinels of this our solar system. The timing of this assignation could not be more apt.

It is my conviction that the asteroids function as an astrological gateway to Jupiter, Saturn, and beyond. They provide stages of gradual unfoldment from the personal focus of the planets that cluster around the Earth and Sun, especially Mars, to the metapersonal journey of the greater planets beginning with Jupiter. In fact, they can be seen as minor initiations to wean us from the egocentricity of Mars and prepare us for the open territory and potential of Jupiter and Saturn. Briefly, the story goes as follows.

The personal "planets" (Sun, Moon, Mercury, Venus, Earth, Mars, in general, and Mars in particular) embody a challenge to come to ourselves and fulfill our individual impulse. Mars takes this challenge to the limit. In Mars we find ourselves spurred relentlessly forward, stripped of concern with any intrusive considerations that would impede our capacity to act effectively, directly, and with passion. We want to get where we are going and do not want anyone or anything to stop us or slow us down. In its primal extreme, Mars is the point at which our contemporary civilization is identified and lost. To make it through a tough world the Mars-oriented person must perceive himself as a separate physical entity occupying a limited portion of space. He drives hard to win in competition, to make his mark. The realms of technological science and mechanism, the military, big business and organized sports provide him free rein. He knows himself by pushing others away and placing his impulses foremost.

Contrastingly, Jupiter and Saturn usher us into a realm that can no longer be navigated by the light of primal personal drive. They share a dimension of experience that keys on a participatory dynamic. This can no longer be the original participation natural to primitive or ancient conditions. Since the discovery of the asteroids and outer planets, the thrust of the two planets that stand between these newly revealed segments is to prepare the ground for the major initiations of Uranus, Neptune, and Pluto (as well as any planets beyond Pluto). This means that Jupiter and Saturn are concerned with final participation, a potential new direction for humanity today. This direction is the offspring of the polarity between original participation in the cosmos and a modern separative awareness that no longer acknowledges our intricate involvement in the universal workings. We started out knowing intuitively and naively that we were children of God, inhabiting a star among myriad stars, bound up with all that we see and feel. Then we fell into the delusion that we are the product of chance afloat on an arbitrary body in empty space, able perhaps still to observe and enjoy nature and to conceive of a God, but by our very make-up incapable of genuinely being interpenetrative with nature, God, or cosmos. Now we are beginning to remember that we are indeed wedded by destiny to the whole of existence, and contain within ourselves in some form every facet of what we meet outside. Nothing is truly alien. But this final participation is founded on our individual freedom, on the awakening to ourselves that has been possible in the modern age. Only when we were convinced that we had cut ourselves off from the heavens and the gods and one another could we recognize our nakedness and clothe ourselves in light. Each of us is responsible for and responsive to the whole of life. The dynamic force that will make it possible to survive the current planetary consciousness is now nurtured by individuals who can renounce the egocentricity of the nineteenth and twentieth centuries and emerge into being free.

Jupiter can restore us to an openness to what is forming toward the future. Fertilizing seeds are being sown in many different places, an organism of consciousness begins to be woven. A warm regard for each particular possibility characterizes the true Jupiterian.

Saturn can be a focal point for bridging our many pasts into this new world that is forming. Saturnian forces of cosmic and karmic memory keep us aware of the ancient wisdom and its immortal source potency. This is metamorphosed when combined with Jupiter's forward gaze. Then, instead of being the dark feared influence it has seemed in astrology, Saturn becomes the unveiled path each of us must walk because it is in us to do so, because any other way would not be true to our origins, our heritage, all that we have ever been through.

The asteroids come forward in this light as far more than the errant miscellaneous rocks they seem. It is a long way from Mars to Jupiter and Saturn. There is much agony and learning to go through if we are to repolarize genuinely and lastingly. Through the asteroids, how we think about and view what is happening is more decisive that what happens out there. Vesta, Juno, and Ceres represent three stages of realization, each more encompassing and demanding than the previous one, as we move toward Jupiter. With Pallas, the awakening permeates our being and becomes alive in our heart. In Pallas we are flooded by impressions of an intricacy and subtlety that call forth a deep receptivity to take them in and bring them further along. Pallas is a fulfillment of a key aspect of the feminine side of our nature.

The counseling of astrologers can be reinvigorated by bringing the asteroids into the chart. Their sign, house, aspects, degree, and overall significance show how each individual is called to help form the world that we all need, and how each encounters tremendous struggles along the way. The house of life becomes roomier and more inhabitable with the asteroids within it.

Welcome to the Virgoan little things that add up. Make yourself at home.

Set where the upper streams of Simois flow
Was the Palladium, high 'mid rock and wood;
And Hector was in Ilium, far below,
And fought, and saw it not—but there it stood!

It stood, and sun and moonshine rain'd their light
On the pure columns of its glen-built hall.
Backward and forward roll'd the waves of fight
Round Troy—but while this stood, Troy could not fall.

So, in its lovely moonlight, lives the soul.
Mountains surround it, and sweet virgin air;
Cold plashing, past it, crystal waters roll;
We visit it by moments, ah, too rare!

We shall renew the battle in the plain
To-morrow;—red with blood will Xanthus be;
Hector and Ajax will be there again,
Helen will come upon the wall to see.

Then we shall rust in shade, or shine in strife,
And fluctuate 'twixt blind hopes and blind despairs,
And fancy that we put forth all our life,
And never know how with the soul it fares.

Still doth the soul, from its lone fastness high,
Upon our life a ruling effluence send.
And when it fails, fight as we will, we die;
And while it lasts, we cannot wholly end.

Matthew Arnold, *Palladium*